This We Believe
in Action

Implementing Successful Middle Level Schools

Association for Middle Level Education
Westerville, Ohio

Association for Middle Level Education

4151 Executive Parkway, Suite 300, Westerville, Ohio 43081
tel: 800.528.6672 fax: 614.895.4750 www.amle.org

Library of Congress Cataloging-in-Publication Data

This we believe in action : implementing successful middle level schools.

   p. cm.

ISBN 978-1-56090-244-7

   1. Middle school education--United States. 2. School improvement programs--United States. I. Association for Middle Level Education.

LB1623.5.T45 2012

373.12--dc22

            2011032155

Contents

Foreword

ooooooooooooooooooooooooooooooooooooooooooooooo

The 2010 *This We Believe: Keys to Educating Young Adolescents* sets forth a vision identifying essential characteristics of a school that is appropriate for young adolescents. Now, *This We Believe in Action: Implementing Successful Middle Level Schools* shows what each of the 16 characteristics looks like in the classroom. In addition, videos that accompany the book illustrate in dramatic fashion examples of each of the 16 characteristics in *This We Believe* (2010). The authors deserve thanks for producing a resource relevant to the challenges middle level education faces in an age of accountability and school reform.

After a preface and a foundational chapter, chapters 1–16 correspond in order to the characteristics outlined in *This We Believe*. The concluding chapter draws generalizations from efforts to implement the middle school concept over the last three decades while it challenges educators to renew their commitment to young adolescents.

The Association for Middle Level Education (AMLE) would like to especially thank students, parents, teachers, and administrators from the eight schools featured in the videos that accompany this book (found at www.amle.org/TWBinAction). Being identified as models for everyone else is a large task, but one that these schools handle well.

> » Central Middle School, Kansas City, Missouri
> » Chapel Hill Middle School, Douglasville, Georgia
> » Jefferson Middle School, Champaign, Illinois
> » Maranacook Community Middle School, Readfield, Maine
> » Scuola Vita Nuova, Kansas City, Missouri
> » Thurgood Marshall Middle School, Chicago, Illinois
> » Warsaw Middle School, Pittsfield, Maine
> » William Thomas Middle School, American Falls, Idaho

Many thanks to Tom Erb, former editor of *Middle School Journal*, for his excellent work in editing *This We Believe in Action* (1995), which is the foundation for this revised work. Thanks also to Mary Henton, who managed the original video project. Eric Johnson of Educational Video Publishing in Yellow Springs, Ohio, directed the technical aspects of producing the videos. His skill in capturing both students and educators engaged in their ongoing—and unrehearsed—activities is very evident. Linda Hopping and Chris Toy each provided insights and critical feedback to guide the revision, and Cheri Howman rendered the manuscript consistent with her proofing skills. John Lounsbury added perspective and wisdom to this revision through his editing. Carla Weiland deserves special recognition, for she managed all phases of the development of this major document, communicated with the authors, and was the overall editor.

The *This We Believe in Action* book and videos will be useful to schools, parent groups, community organizations, and others who seek to implement successful middle schools.

William D. Waidelich, Ed.D.
Executive Director
Association for Middle Level Education

Preface

ϾϾϾ

Educators, patrons, and policymakers continue the search for the best way to educate young adolescents. In the first decade of the 21st century, the federally-mandated No Child Left Behind (NCLB) initiative entered the scene and narrowed the focus of the curriculum to reading, writing, and basic math, relegating core subjects such as social studies and science, not to mention electives and exploratory classes, to insignificant, or even nonexistent, roles in the curriculum. At the same time, many urban districts have confirmed that large middle schools, ones that have not implemented the middle school concept, are failing to provide a quality education to their young adolescents. Adding fuel to the debate about effective middle schools, these districts are often deciding to move their sixth, seventh, and eighth graders from separate middle grades schools into K–8 settings in an attempt to solve an educational problem by administrative action—and perhaps save money as well. The popular press is full of rhetoric focusing on one aspect of middle grades schooling or another, primarily on student achievement as determined by standardized tests. Achievements of our students are continuously compared negatively to those of students in other countries, and teaching 21st century skills—an aim of AMLE (formerly NMSA) since its inception— are recurring media and political stories. Research shows that at least in high poverty environments, it is possible to identify in the middle grades up to half, and sometimes even more, eventual high school dropouts. (Balfanz, 2009).

Proven practices

In *This We Believe in Action*, 27 of the foremost authorities on the education of young adolescents describe those policies, programs, and practices that have shown themselves to be effective in developing the talents, skills, knowledge, and character of young adolescents. *This We Believe in Action* does not focus on just one or two aspects of education, but rather on the

elements and educational objectives that make up a complete educational program
for youngsters who are coming of age.

AMLE leads

Leading the fight to improve the education of young adolescents in North America and
throughout the world has been AMLE. For 30 years it has provided the research and
publication of a consensus view of essential elements of middle school education through its
editions of *This We Believe*.

The Carnegie Council on Adolescent Development, which counted among its members
representatives from the fields of medicine, academia, public school education, state and
national government, and the private sector, issued a report, *Turning Points: Preparing American
Youth for the 21st Century*. Decrying the fact that middle grades schools had been virtually
ignored in the discussions of educational reform in the decade of the 80s, the task force found
"a volatile mismatch …between the organization and curriculum of middle grades schools and
the intellectual, emotional, and interpersonal needs of young adolescents" (p. 8).

Unlike standards documents issued by various groups in the '90s or the No Child Left Behind
legislation, which focuses on a narrow curricular spectrum, *Turning Points 2000* (Carnegie
Corporation) and *This We Believe in Action* examine the entire school experience of young
adolescents and provide thought-provoking guidance for those not satisfied with the state of
education for young adolescents.

Allies of AMLE over the years have helped in the battle to provide young adolescents the
education suited to their developmental needs. The National Association of Secondary
School Principals (NASSP) published *Breaking Ranks in the Middle* in 2006. In addition, the
National Forum's Comprehensive School Reform project, its Schools To Watch criteria, and
its Vision Statement are valuable guides to whole-school reform for middle grades education.
These organizations and their publications "speak with one voice" to provide a vision, a
conceptualization of schooling, descriptions of practice, and evidences of success to guide those
who desire to improve the education of young adolescents. By so doing, these publications,
alone among the mass of reports and mandates, will help educators sort out the conflicting
recommendations in order to create a total-school program that is concurrently academically
sound, developmentally responsive, and socially equitable.

How To Use This Resource

∞∞∞∞∞∞∞∞∞∞∞∞∞∞∞∞∞∞∞∞∞∞∞∞∞∞∞∞∞∞∞∞∞∞∞∞∞

This We Believe: Educating Young Adolescents identifies 16 characteristics that work in concert to create successful middle level schools. Grouped into three categories, five of the characteristics are facets of Curriculum, Instruction, and Assessment; five describe facets of Leadership and Organization; and six detail Culture and Community of such schools. This classification helps us understand the interconnectedness of all 16 characteristics, recognizing the influence each has on every other. In the dynamic atmosphere of successful schools, curriculum, leadership, and culture work together; change one and every other aspect of a school is also changed.

Videos

The videos, found at www.amle.org/TWBinAction, are also organized according to the 16 characteristics described in *This We Believe: Keys to Educating Young Adolescents*. The richness of each characteristic is illustrated through five or six video clips, each showing a cultural characteristic or middle grades practice in one of the schools. Every video clip weaves scenes, interviews, and narrative to highlight how that school implements practices to exploit its strengths and best meet its students' needs. Because schools are tapestries of culture and practices, some video clips appear in more than one place online.

We encourage you to carefully consider the complexity of each characteristic as described in *This We Believe* as you watch each video clip. Be prepared to look at each cultural characteristic or each practice from your own vantage and experience as well as from the different contexts of the schools presented in the videos. While no short video clip can fully demonstrate the richness with which a school implements middle school practices and nurtures a healthy culture, it is our hope that each clip will unveil new perspectives to assist you in your work.

The videos and book are complementary and interdependent. The eight schools that have been filmed are different from those referenced by any chapter authors. Pictures and quotes from the videos are placed in appropriate places with identifying information to assist the reader in reviewing the related video clip(s). Our goal is to offer many examples, in the hopes that you will find yourself and your students in these pages and images, and consider new possibilities.

There is no one right way to use this book and videos. Use them in whatever way best fits your needs or interests. You may want to just explore the text and videos at first to get a feel for the materials, to view several video segments, or to see how pictures and quotes from the videos relate to the text. You may want to choose a starting point based on

» Personal interest or known collective interest of the staff
» Priorities, highlighted in the school improvement plan
» Reaffirming and building on known strengths.

Following are some general suggestions for how to use *This We Believe in Action* for professional development:

» Staff members read a particular chapter prior to a meeting and together view and discuss one or more video segments on that characteristic. Over the course of future meetings, faculty reviews other segments

» Use one or two video segments and then follow up by reading the appropriate chapter before gathering for discussion, either at the next meeting or in teams.

» Small teams meet for preliminary discussion around a specific characteristic, then view the video segments as a larger staff.

» Study the opening chapter on middle grades reform and the concluding chapter on lessons learned; both warrant study and discussion, individually and by teams or faculty.

» To further enrich learning, use complementary material from *This We Believe: Keys to Educating Young Adolescents*. For example, staff members come to a session having read a chapter from This We Believe in Action. Staff views video segments as a group, then follows up by examining the corresponding material from *This We Believe: Keys to Educating Young Adolescents*, with subsequent discussion.

Readers should quickly recognize that *This We Believe in Action* is not just another good book worth reading; it is rather a unique and rich resource like no other, a very functional tool that can assist in implementing more fully the research-supported middle school concept. Exploit its manifold possibilities—for the sake of our young.

16 Characteristics

Curriculum, Instruction, and Assessment

Educators value young adolescents and are prepared to teach them. *Value Young Adolescents*

Students and teachers are engaged in active, purposeful learning. *Active Learning*

Curriculum is challenging, exploratory, integrative, and relevant. *Challenging Curriculum*

Educators use multiple learning and teaching approaches. *Multiple Learning Approaches*

Varied and ongoing assessments advance learning as well as measure it. *Varied Assessments*

Leadership and Organization

A shared vision developed by all stakeholders guides every decision. *Shared Vision*

Leaders are committed to and knowledgeable about this age group, educational research, and best practices. *Committed Leaders*

Leaders demonstrate courage and collaboration. *Courageous & Collaborative Leaders*

Ongoing professional development reflects best educational practices. *Professional Development*

Organizational structures foster purposeful learning and meaningful relationships. *Organizational Structures*

Culture and Community

The school environment is inviting, safe, inclusive, and supportive of all. *School Environment*

Every student's academic and personal development is guided by an adult advocate. *Adult Advocate*

Comprehensive guidance and support services meet the needs of young adolescents. *Guidance Services*

Health and wellness are supported in curricula, school-wide programs, and related policies. *Health & Wellness*

The school actively involves families in the education of their children. *Family Involvement*

The school includes community and business partners. *Community & Business*

Essential Attributes

An education for young adolescents must be

Developmentally Responsive
using the nature of young adolescents as the foundation on which all decisions are made.

Challenging
recognizing that every student can learn and everyone is held to high expectations.

Empowering
providing all students with the knowledge and skills they need to take control of their lives.

Equitable
advocating for every student's right to learn and providing challenging and relevant learning opportunities.

Association for Middle Level Education

Successful Schools
for
Young Adolescents

Introduction: Enacting Comprehensive Middle Grades Reform

One of the most powerful lessons of the past decade is how necessary it is to implement multiple elements of middle grades reform and maintain those elements over time to realize positive outcomes for students. A learning environment is very complex, and young adolescents' academic success is highly dependent upon physical, intellectual, moral, psychological, and social-emotional factors— all inexorably intertwined. Flexible structures and a shared vision are important, but without a challenging curriculum, varied learning approaches, and programs for health and wellness, among other essential components, the middle grades school will likely function with diminished capacity and fail to achieve its tremendous potential.

> Without a challenging curriculum, varied learning approaches, and programs for health and wellness, the middle grades school will function with diminished capacity.

Designing programs

Over the last 30 years, research from National Middle School Association (2010), Carnegie Council on Adolescent Development (1989), National Association of Secondary School Principals (1985, 2006), and National Forum to Accelerate Middle-Grades Reform (1998, 1994-2003a, 1994-2003b) along with *Turning Points 2000: Educating Young Adolescents in the 21st Century* (Jackson and Davis, 2000) has formed bedrock of knowledge about how young adolescents learn best. This knowledge and understanding can then be applied in designing programs and practices that will make it possible for young adolescents to meet the following broad goals for middle level education.

The Association for Middle Level Education asserts that to become a fully functioning, self-actualized person, each young adolescent should

» Become actively aware of the larger world, asking significant and relevant questions about that world and wrestling with big ideas and questions for which there may not be one right answer.

» Be able to think rationally and critically and express thoughts clearly.

» Read deeply to independently gather, assess, and interpret information from a variety of sources and read avidly for enjoyment and lifelong learning.

» Use digital tools to explore, communicate, and collaborate with the world and learn from the rich and varied resources available.

» Be a good steward of the earth and its resources and a wise and intelligent consumer of the wide array of goods and services available.

» Understand and use the major concepts, skills, and tools of inquiry in the areas of health, physical education, language arts, world languages, mathematics, natural and physical sciences, and the social sciences.

» Explore music, art, and careers, and recognize their importance to personal growth and learning.

» Develop his or her strengths, particular skills, talents, or interests and have an emerging understanding of his or her potential contributions to society and to personal fulfillment.

» Recognize, articulate, and make responsible, ethical decisions concerning his or her own health and wellness needs.

» Respect and value the diverse ways people look, speak, think, and act within the immediate community and around the world.

» Develop the interpersonal and social skills needed to learn, work, and play with others harmoniously and confidently.

» Assume responsibility for his or her own actions and be cognizant of and ready to accept obligations for the welfare of others.

» Understand local, national, and global civic responsibilities and demonstrate active citizenship through participation in endeavors that serve and benefit those larger communities.

Achieving the goals An education for young adolescents must be developmentally responsive, challenging, empowering, and equitable. These four attributes can be made evident and operative through the 16 characteristics displayed on page xii. Each of these characteristics is described in a separate chapter that follows. The characteristics are grouped in three categories: 1. Curriculum, Instruction, and Assessment; 2. Leadership and Organization; and 3. Culture and Community. Although these categories seem distinct, they are, in reality, very interdependent and all characteristics need to be implemented in concert.

Planned vs. Experienced Curriculum

Curriculum for many is the set of pre-determined content with related standards or goals for student performance. Most standards statements are limited to a narrow view of curriculum, which might be called the "planned" curriculum. However, what educational leaders and standards writers prescribe as the curriculum is not what teachers actually teach nor what individual students ultimately learn. The taught or "enacted" curriculum is influenced by several factors. If the goal is to ensure success for every student, we must be concerned about this "experienced" curriculum.

Curriculums are planned for different groups based on assumptions about the commonality of the needs and interests of each group. The crux of the middle school curriculum problem is this reality: The middle school curriculum is a common, general education program, but it is offered to students who are distinguished by the degree they differ form one another. "The stubborn facts of individual differences show up in maturity, general ability, readiness to learn, and in preferred ways to learn…. The degree that students vary one from another reaches its peak during the middle level years as young adolescents, each in his or her own time and rate, mature physically, socially, emotionally, intellectually, and morally. No scheme of school organization or federal mandate for uniform achievement can wash away human variability" (Lounsbury, 2004, p. xv). The experienced curriculum thus becomes an individualized curriculum.

It is easy to see why the social and academic aspects that are interwoven in a learning community cannot be reduced to setting standards and assessing with tests. The academic aspects include engaging students in problem solving, using multiple sources of information, and using technology effectively. The social aspects include such things as understanding how to respect and rely on others, how to listen, share, and be constructive partners and team members. The standards promulgated by the separate disciplinary associations—useful as they are—and the assessments produced by the several states—politically necessary as they are—provide only fragmented frameworks for reform. Neither provides specifics on how to construct learning environments that truly lead to the growth and development of every student.

Fully Implementing Reform

Regardless of where a school may find itself, the explanations and descriptions in *This We Believe in Action* can help a faculty take the next steps toward a fuller implementation of a successful and truly developmentally responsive middle school. We know from research done on middle grades reform in the past decade (Anfara & Lipka, 2003; Backes, Ralston, & Ingwalson, 1999; Brown, Roney, & Anfara, 2003; Davis & Thompson, 2004; Erb & Stevenson, 1999a, 1999b; Felner, Jackson, Kasak, Mulhall, Brand, & Flowers, 1997; Flowers, Mertens, & Mulhall, 1999, 2000, 2003; Mertens & Flowers, 2003; Picucci, Brownson, Kahlert, & Sobel, 2004; Stevenson & Erb, 1998) that implementing more elements for longer periods of time does, with certainty, lead to improved student outcomes in all three major goal areas—academic, behavioral, and attitudinal. Yet most schools that are trying to systematically improve have focused only on one of the three areas.

It is difficult for schools to maintain their momentum for improvement as they get closer to the heart of schooling —what happens in individual classrooms. Some schools change structures but go no further. Without improvements in curriculum and classroom practice, the goal of ensuring success for every student will remain out of reach.

This We Believe in Action provides a fleshed-out vision of middle grades reform. Keep in mind as you delve into this resource, that while it is important to understand the dimensions of each characteristic of reform, it is also important to realize that these characteristics are not just additive; they are interactive. As has already been emphasized, when these characteristics are implemented over a substantial period of time, you will be able to demonstrate to your school board, patrons, and politicians that your students are achieving at higher levels than previously were recorded.

References

Anfara, V. A., Jr., & Lipka, R. P. (2003). Relating the middle school concept to student achievement. *Middle School Journal, 35*(1), 24–32.

Backes, J., Ralston, A., & Ingwalson, G. (1999). Middle level reform: The impact on student achievement. *Research in Middle Level Education Quarterly, 22*(3), 43–57.

Brown, K. M., Roney, K., & Anfara, V. A., Jr. (2003). Organizational health directly influences student performance at the middle level. *Middle School Journal, 34*(5), 5–15.

Carnegie Council on Adolescent Development. (1989). *Turning points: Preparing American youth for the 21st century.* New York: The Carnegie Corporation.

Davis, D. M., & Thompson, S. C. (2004). Creating high-performing middle schools in segregated settings: 50 years after Brown. *Middle School Journal, 36*(2), 4–12.

Erb, T. O., & Stevenson, C. (1999a). What difference does teaming make? *Middle School Journal, 30*(3), 47–50.

Erb, T. O., & Stevenson, C. (1999b). Fostering growth inducing environments for student success. *Middle School Journal, 30*(4), 63–67.

Felner, R. D., Jackson, A. W., Kasak, D., Mulhall, P., Brand, S., & Flowers, N. (1997). The impact of school reform for the middle years: A longitudinal study of a network engaged in Turning Points-based comprehensive school transformation. *Phi Delta Kappan, 78*, 528–532, 541–550.

Flowers, N., Mertens, S. B., & Mulhall, P. F. (1999). The impact of teaming: Five research-based outcomes. *Middle School Journal, 31*(2), 57–60.

Flowers, N., Mertens, S. B., & Mulhall, P. F. (2000). What makes interdisciplinary teams effective? *Middle School Journal, 31*(4), 53–56.

Flowers, H., Mertens, S. B., & Mulhall, P. F. (2003). Lessons learned from more than a decade of middle grades research. *Middle School Journal, 35*(2), 55–59.

Jackson, A. W., & Davis, G. A. (2000). *Turning points 2000: Educating adolescents in the 21st century.* New York & Westerville, OH: Teachers College Press & National Middle School Association.

Lounsbury, J. (2004). Introduction: Policymakers, please think on these "things." In S. Thompson (Ed.), *Reforming middle level education: Considerations for policymakers* (p. xv). Greenwich, CT & Westerville, OH: Information Age & National Middle School Association.

Mertens, S. B., & Flowers, N. (2003). Middle school practices improve student achievement in high poverty schools. *Middle School Journal, 35*(1), 33–45.

National Association of Secondary School Principals (n.d. [1985]). *An agenda for excellence at the middle level.* Reston, VA: Author.

National Association of Secondary School Principals. (2006). *Breaking ranks in the middle: Strategies for leading middle level reform.* Reston, VA: Author.

National Forum to Accelerate Middle-Grades Reform. (1998). *Vision Statement.* Retrieved July 23, 2005, from http://www.mgforum.org/about/vision.asp

National Forum to Accelerate Middle-Grades Reform. (1994–2003a). *Criteria for Schools to Watch.* Retrieved July 23, 2005 from http:// www.mgforum.org/Improvingschools/STW/STWcriteria.asp

National Forum to Accelerate Middle-Grades Reform. (1994–2003b). *Comprehensive School Reform Models.* Retrieved July 23, 2005, from http://www.mgforum.org/Improvingschools/CSR/csr_intro.htm

National Middle School Association. (2010). *This we believe: Keys to educating young adolescents.* Westerville, OH: Author.

1

Value Young Adolescents

Educators value young adolescents and are prepared to teach them.

C. Kenneth McEwin & Thomas S. Dickinson

The most successful middle level teachers value teaching young adolescents and interact with them in other ways to maximize their learning and support their healthy development. They make conscious choices to teach young adolescents. One of the most important qualities middle level teachers bring to their classrooms is their commitment to the young adolescents they teach. Without this commitment there is little substantive progress for either party, and teaching and learning is reduced to a lifeless and mechanical act, the consequences of which fall most heavily on the young adolescents, their families, and ultimately the nation. Teachers, administrators, and other middle level educators who are committed to working with young adolescents, however, breathe life and opportunity into their teaching and into the future of the youth with whom they work.

The Duality of Commitment

"Educators who value working with this age group" (National Middle School Association, 2010, p. 15) are characterized by two equally important aspects of their commitment:

1. The provision of significant academic learning experiences for young adolescent students, learning experiences that are characterized by rigorous content and high expectations for all learners.

2. The provision of developmentally appropriate classrooms, schools, programs, and activities for all young adolescent students within the learning community.

The presence of significant learning experiences (rigorous content and high expectations) within a developmentally appropriate, safe, and supportive school context is an identifiable characteristic of developmentally responsive middle level schools. And while *This We Believe: Keys to Educating Young Adolescents* (NMSA, 2010) is a policy document that establishes broad goals for the profession, these twin aspects of commitment are attainable, regardless of the specific characteristics of individual school communities, or the grade configuration of buildings.

This duality of commitment (significant academic learning and developmentally appropriate context) has numerous implications for the roles of middle level teachers. Teachers of young adolescents committed to the students they teach perform at least five specific but overlapping roles: (a) student advocate, (b) role model, (c) supporter of diversity, (d) collaborator, and (e) lifelong learner. As well, the duality of commitment has implications for the professional preparation of middle level teachers and for their continuing professional development that focuses on acquiring, refining, and extending their knowledge, dispositions, and skills to perform their many roles successfully.

The role of advocate

Being a student advocate is a complex, but essential, responsibility of middle level educators.. This advocacy has two fundamental audiences—a readily recognizable external audience (e.g., parents, colleagues, administrators, and the wider community) and a less-well acknowledged internal audience made up of the young adolescents themselves. The role of student advocate revolves around the dual aspects of commitment: advocating for developmentally appropriate programs and practices within classrooms and schools and advocating for learning experiences that are "rich" (Arnold, 1993) in all their curricular and instructional aspects.

Committed middle level educators use their positions to help educate family members and others about the developmental realities of early adolescence while discrediting some of the negative myths that are frequently associated with the age group.

To advocate for young adolescents to external audiences calls for depth of knowledge about "the developmental uniqueness of young adolescents"

(NMSA, 2010, p. 15). Committed middle level educators use their positions to help educate family members and others about the developmental realities of early adolescence while discrediting some of the negative and degrading myths that unfortunately are still frequently associated with the age group.

Middle level teachers who are committed to working with young adolescents advocate for realistic assessments of where individuals are and where they are going. These teachers value teaching the age group as their students increase their knowledge, learn new skills, chart new avenues of growth, and confront the challenges and promises of life.

Role model

Teaching under relentless scrutiny is a fact of life for middle level teachers. Acting as a positive role model for youth during such examinations brings with it moral obligations.

Being an appropriate role model takes several complementary avenues at the middle level. The most visible is to model behaviors for young adolescent students.

The second aspect of being a role model for young adolescents involves modeling relationships. Young adolescents learn how to affiliate with others by observing both peers and adults. The ways teachers cooperate with colleagues, their appreciation of differences, and their dispositions towards others speak volumes, often more powerfully than the planned curriculum. And the way they interact

Meeting in weekly study groups, teachers model lifelong learning and cooperation.

— Video, Scuola Vita Nuova, "Book Studies"

with students is equally powerful, especially as they build relationships and handle the inevitable behavior problems.

The third aspect of modeling for young adolescents involves a relatively newly emphasized phase of teacher responsibility—modeling healthy development. In an age when risk factors abound for youth, the approach that teachers take to their own health, wellness, and safety has acquired increased significance.

Supporter of diversity

Teachers who value working with young adolescents are marked by their dedication and respect for the diversity inherent in middle level classrooms. This implies both the traditional definitions of diversity (e.g., age, race, ethnicity, gender) and other facets such as developmental differences, learning styles, and exceptionalities. By being supporters of diversity, committed middle level teachers embrace rather than overlook the needs, interests, and special abilities of all of their students.

Collaborator

Being a committed middle level teacher means that professionally one has connections with members of an interdisciplinary team, other teams, and to other teachers throughout the building, as well as to administrators and support staff. Being a successful middle level teacher is a role that is characterized by a series of nested relationships.

Within individual classrooms there are innumerable connections existing. These connections are about the young adolescents the team has in common, the intersections that characterize the team's curriculum, and the instructional practices that support and sustain student learning. Collaborating with colleagues calls for cooperation for student purposes—high achievement for all. But collaboration goes beyond the team because middle level teachers who value working with their students have an obligation to be part of programs at the grade and school level, whether or not these programs involve advisories, intramurals, exploratories, clubs, or other aspects of the middle level learning environment.

Lifelong learner

A committed middle level teacher is a model of lifelong learning. This learning is widespread and continuous: new teaching materials and teaching techniques, new and emerging technologies that have impact in the classroom, new subject matter knowledge, and an awareness of on-going events and developments in the culture and community. As the knowledge explosion continues, committed middle level teachers read, experiment, travel, and study. Their learning stance takes them

> Lifelong learners know that moving beyond their own immediate comfort zones as learners is important for themselves and their students.

to seminars, formal coursework, travel, focused training and apprenticeships, adventures in individual study, and other learning opportunities—and the students are well aware that their teachers are lifelong learners.

Lifelong learners know that moving beyond their own immediate comfort zones as learners is important for themselves and their students. They also know that one does not just learn "things "but also develops an appreciation of the what and how behind the learning. They develop an understanding of how truly difficult some aspects of learning are and what it means to try and fail as well as to try and succeed.

Specialized Middle Level Teacher Preparation

Making conscious decisions to teach at the middle level and being dedicated to teaching young adolescents are very important beginning points for those entering the profession. It seems logical that these dedicated professionals would begin their careers well-equipped with the specialized knowledge, skills, and dispositions needed to be successful in the challenging and rewarding world of teaching young adolescents. However, far too many prospective teachers who make decisions to teach young adolescents find that specialized professional preparation programs that focus on teaching 10- to 15-year-olds are unavailable in their states. Further, they frequently learn that if they wish to have a career in middle level education, they must major in elementary education or in a content area in secondary education. Those who are not discouraged and select one of these options typically spend the vast majority of their professional preparation learning

All teachers at William Thomas Middle School receive instruction and coaching in reading and writing across the curriculum.

— Video, William Thomas MS, "School-Wide Literacy"

about teaching young children or focusing on teaching a subject in senior high schools. Upon completion of these programs, they are awarded licensure to teach in the elementary and middle grades (K-8) or the middle and senior high school grades (6-12) after receiving little or no specialized professional preparation for teaching young adolescents.

The fact that these preparation programs can be completed and licensure awarded without candidates' receiving specific preparation for teaching young adolescents or completing middle level field experiences serves as an example of the malpractice in which many teacher preparation programs and licensure agencies or professional practice boards are currently engaged. They are not promoting and protecting the rights of young adolescents by guaranteeing that middle level teachers have demonstrated the specialized knowledge, skills, and dispositions needed to teach effectively. In many states, the message from teacher preparation institutions, licensure agencies and boards, and even the profession itself seems to be, "Anyone with any kind of professional teacher preparation can teach at the middle level. There is no specialization needed." As has been the case historically, the education and welfare of young adolescents and their teachers have been largely ignored and forgotten in the name of politics and administrative convenience (McEwin, Dickinson, & Smith, 2003; 2004; NMSA, 2006).

One major result of the unfortunate situation just discussed is that many middle level teachers and other educators work intensely in well-intentioned ways that damage rather than enhance the quality of learning opportunities provided for young adolescents. This lack of match between intentions and appropriate behaviors rarely results from malice or a lack of caring, but rather is virtually always the result of a lack of knowledge that should have been a crucial part of professional preparation programs that focused directly and exclusively on teaching young adolescents.

Consensus on the need for specialized programs

There is a growing consensus regarding the importance of and need for specialized middle level teacher preparation. Advocacy for comprehensive, specialized middle level courses, field experiences, and other program components that are considered essential for effective middle level teacher preparation is increasingly emerging from teacher educators, foundations, professional organizations, and other sources. There is also increasing support from middle level teachers for comprehensive, specialized middle level teacher preparation (Arth, Lounsbury, McEwin, & Swaim, 1995; Jackson & Davis, 2000; Jackson, Andrews, Holland, & Pardini, 2004; McEwin, Dickinson, Erb, & Scales, 1995; McEwin, Dickinson, & Hamilton, 2000; McEwin, Dickinson, & Smith, 2003, 2004; National Forum to Accelerate

> There is a growing consensus regarding the importance of and need for specialized middle level teacher preparation.

Middle-Grades Reform, 2004; NMSA, 2006). Additionally, founders and other prominent middle level education leaders strongly support the importance of specialized middle level teacher preparation. After interviewing 18 founders and other prominent middle school leaders, Smith and McEwin (2011) found that "Without exception, participants in this study are advocates of specialized middle level teacher preparation. They see it as critical to the success of young adolescent students. . . . In addition, when middle level teachers are knowledgeable about young adolescents and the programs needed to serve them, they are better positioned to lead innovative efforts on behalf of the students" (p. 375).

Essential program components

A solid consensus about the essential programmatic components that should be included in specialized middle level teacher preparation has also emerged (Cooney, 2000; Jackson & Davis, 2000; Ference & McDowell, 2005; McEwin, Dickinson, & Anfara, 2005; McEwin, Dickinson, & Smith, 2003, 2004; National Forum to Accelerate to Middle-Grades Reform, 2004; National Middle School Association, 2006.). Furthermore, middle level teacher preparation standards, written by National Middle School Association and approved by the National Council for Accreditation of Teacher Education (NCATE), that reflect these essential components are widely used throughout the nation (NMSA, n.d.).

The following components represent those that are unique to the middle level program and do not include other elements that are essential to all teacher preparation programs (e.g., diversity, instructional technology). These particular components are:

(a) a comprehensive study of young adolescent development, middle level philosophy and organization, and middle level curriculum;

(b) an intensive focus on planning, teaching, and assessment using developmentally and culturally responsive practices;

(c) early and continuing field experiences in a variety of good middle level settings;

(d) study and practice in the collaborative role of middle level teachers in working with colleagues, families, and community members;

(e) content preparation in two broad teaching fields; and,

(f) a collaborative teacher preparation partnership between faculty at middle level schools and university-based middle level teacher educators.

Looking to the future

In large measure, the future success of young adolescents depends greatly upon the dedication and hard work of teachers and other educators who choose to teach them and serve them in other important ways. Deliberate career choices and dedicated work alone are not sufficient to guarantee that all young adolescents will have opportunities to achieve their full potential. Teachers and other educators in every state need access to professional preparation programs that provide them with the specialized knowledge, skills, and dispositions needed to be highly accomplished in their practice.

Agreeing that the specialized professional preparation of middle level educators is an important idea is not sufficient. Courageous steps need to be taken by middle level educators, professional associations, accreditation agencies, and other stakeholders to develop and support specialized middle level professional preparation programs and the middle level licensure that support and sustain

> Teachers and other educators need access to preparation programs that provide them with the specialized knowledge, skills, and dispositions needed to be highly accomplished in their practice.

them. Only when action is taken to significantly improve the professional preparation of all who teach and work with young adolescents will middle level schooling universally provide the high quality educational opportunities needed to assure successful futures for our nation's youth.

References

Arnold, J. (1993). A curriculum to empower young adolescents. *Midpoints Occasional Paper 4*(1). Columbus, OH: National Middle School Association.

Arth, A. A., Lounsbury, J. H., McEwin, C. K., & Swaim, J. H. (1995). *Portraits of excellence.* Columbus, OH: National Middle School Association and Reston, VA: National Association of Secondary School Principals.

Cooney, S. (2000). *A middle grades message: A well-qualified teacher in every classroom matters.* Atlanta, GA: Southern Regional Education Board.

Ference, R., & McDowell, J (2005). Essential elements of specialized middle level teacher preparation programs. *Middle School Journal, 36*(3), 4-10.

Jackson, A. W., Andrews, P. G., Holland, H., & Pardini, P. (2004). *Making the most of middle school: A field guide for parents and others.* New York, NY: Teachers College Press.

Jackson, A. W., & Davis, G. (2000). *Turning points 2000: Educating adolescents in the 21st century.* New York, NY: Teachers College Press and Westerville, OH: National Middle School Association.

McEwin, C. K., Dickinson, T. S., & Anfara, V. A. 2005). The professional preparation of middle level teachers and principals. In V. A. Anfara, G. Andrews, & S. Mertens (Eds.), *The encyclopedia of middle grades education* (pp. 59-67). Greenwich, CT: Information Age Publishing and Westerville, OH: National Middle School Association.

McEwin, C. K., Dickinson, T. S., Erb, T. O., & Scales, P. C. (1995). *A vision of excellence: Organizing principles for middle grades teacher preparation.* Columbus, OH: National Middle School Education.

McEwin, C. K., Dickinson, T. S., & Hamilton, H. (2000). National board certified teachers' views regarding specialized middle level teacher preparation. *The Clearing House, 73*(4), 211-213.

McEwin, C. K., Dickinson, T. S., & Smith, T. W. (2003). Middle level teacher preparation: Status, progress, and challenges. In P. G. Andrews and V. A. Anfara (Eds.), *Leaders for a movement: Professional preparation and development of middle level teachers and administrators* (pp. 3-26). Greenwich, CT: Information Age Publishing.

McEwin, C. K., Dickinson, T. S., & Smith, T. W. (2004). The role of teacher preparation, licensure, and retention in creating high performing middle schools. In S. Thompson (Ed.), *Creating high performing middle Schools: A focus on policy issues* (pp. 109-129). Greenwich, CT: Information Age Publishing.

National Forum to Accelerate Middle-Grades Reform. (2004). *Teacher preparation, licensure, and recruitment.* Retrieved from http://www.mgforum.org/Portals/0/MGFdocs/TeacherPrep.pdf

National Middle School Association (2006). *National Middle School Association's Position Statement on Professional Preparation of Middle Level Teachers.* Retrieved from http://www.mgforum.org/Portals/0/MGFdocs/TeacherPrep.pdf

National Middle School Association (2010). *This we believe: Keys to educating young adolescents.* Westerville, OH: Author.

National Middle School Association (n.d.). *National Middle School Association- National Council for Accreditation of Teacher Education-Approved Middle Level Teacher Preparation Standards.* Retrieved from http://www.nmsa.org/ProfessionalPreparation/NMSAStandards/tabid/374/Default.aspx

Smith, T. W., & McEwin, C. K. (Eds.). (2011). *The legacy of middle school leaders: In their own words.* Charlotte, NC: Information Age.

2

Active Learning
Students and teachers are engaged in active, purposeful learning.

Gert Nesin

∞∞∞

Middle school educators regularly affirm the desirability of active learning, but many limit the definition to the physical, hands-on activity of the learners. Although physical activity certainly should be considered an important aspect of learning, active learning entails much more. According to *This We Believe: Keys to Educating Young Adolescents* (National Middle School Association, 2010), being developmentally responsive involves teachers and students collaborating in "hands-joined" activities, ones that teachers and students work together in developing (p. 16). Active learning engages the intellect and the social and moral sensibilities of the learners. Active learning thrives in a classroom community built on trust and democratic participation. Active learning, as discussed in this chapter, not only affects students, but also the teacher's role, curriculum, and assessment.

Building a Community for Active Learning

Active learning requires participants to take risks intellectually, socially, and emotionally. Willingness to take risks depends on the safety net built in the classroom through providing a safe and supportive classroom environment (Charney, 2002; Knowles & Brown, 2000; National Research Council [NRC], 2000). This is especially critical for young adolescents who are regularly concerned about peer acceptance and belonging to a group (NMSA,

2010). A community for active learning means that students recognize, respect, and value the diversity that each participant brings to the learning. Every young person learns at different rates and in various ways. An effective classroom community values the richness of that variety, thus making each member feel safe and willing to take risks to learn.

To be engaged in the learning environment, students must, in collaboration with teachers, build the classroom environment around clear and common expectations for their learning and their interactions with others. Expectations guide learning and social behavior. Infringements of the guidelines offer opportunities for personal and community growth rather than just punishments for noncompliance. Missteps also enrich and guide academic growth. According to the NRC (2000), "Learning seems to be enhanced by social norms that . . . allow students (and teachers) the freedom to make mistakes in order to learn" (p. 145). Thoughtful consideration of the development and growth of the classroom community involves students and teachers joined in taking responsibility for growth and interactions, setting the stage for learning that is active intellectually, socially, morally, and physically.

Active Cognitive Learning

Young adolescents are at a unique place in their intellectual and cognitive development. With a newfound awareness of their surroundings, they show intense curiosity about the world and how it works. They begin to think abstractly and see shades of gray rather than only black and white. As they develop an awareness of their own strengths and challenges, they compare themselves to others and often lose confidence in their own abilities to learn and achieve.

> Young adolescents begin to think abstractly and see shades of gray rather than only black and white.

With active learning strategies, young people can develop self-awareness and a sense of self-efficacy as well as a deeper understanding of content and the world beyond the classroom.

Cognitive science informs active teaching and learning strategies. Although a relatively new field of study, it is based on sound research from cognitive psychology, social psychology, and neuroscience. Cognitive scientists define worthwhile education as

> Helping students develop the intellectual tools and learning strategies needed to acquire the knowledge that allows people to think productively about history,

science and technology, social phenomena, mathematics, and arts. Fundamental understanding about subjects, including how to frame and ask meaningful questions . . . contributes to individuals' more basic understanding of principles of learning that can assist them in becoming self-sustaining, lifelong learners. (NRC, 2000, p. 5)

Such an active approach to learning can assist students in understanding themselves and their worlds now and throughout their lives. Essential components of active learning, according to cognitive science, are a view of intelligence as incrementally gained, concept learning based on existing knowledge, learning transfer, and metacognition.

Beliefs About Intelligence

Beliefs about intelligence influence active learning (Deci, Vallerand, Pelletier, & Ryan, 1991; Dweck, 2000; Maehr & Anderman, 1993; NRC, 2000). On the one hand, students may believe intelligence to be a fixed entity that one possesses in a set quantity. While being adept at and willing to tackle easy tasks, this view of intelligence causes learners to balk at challenges to avoid making mistakes. They believe lack of immediate success provides proof of limited intelligence. These students shy away from active learning because it may confirm their fears of limited abilities.

In contrast, intelligence can be viewed as incremental, flexible and expanding, depending on the effort applied. Students who have this view of intelligence expect to make mistakes and approach new situations and challenges with enthusiasm and a belief that they can learn. Most learners do not believe strictly in one or the other view of intelligence, but rather fall somewhere on the continuum between them. The challenge

> The challenge for educators is to teach students in a way that encourages them toward the incremental view of intelligence and more active participation in their learning.

for educators is to teach students in a way that encourages them toward the incremental view of intelligence and more active participation in their learning. Rather than having students focus on being smart or accomplishing a task quickly or correctly the first time, teachers should recognize that effort and perseverance are associated with a more incremental view of learning. As has been said, it is not a matter of how smart one is but rather, how one is smart.

Young adolescents, who are beginning to intellectually identify themselves, can benefit tremendously from an incremental view of intelligence. Instead of seeing themselves as individuals locked in a box determined by fixed intelligence, they instead recognize the expanded possibilities open to them through effort and perseverance. Students realize they can impact their learning and their futures—that through active participation and with support, they can shape who they are and who they will become.

Building Advanced Concepts

In *How People Learn: Brain, Mind, Experience, and School*, the NRC (2000) described how learners develop sophisticated understanding. Students bring existing knowledge, concepts, and misconceptions with them into a learning situation. Simple concepts are a hallmark of beginning learning, and the goal for educators is to help learners achieve expert understanding. Experts find key information and patterns based on a deep understanding of fundamental concepts and apply the concepts to new situations.

The teaching team at Scuola Vita Nuova adjusts the schedule so that every student can participate in the musical production during the school day.

— "Theater Production"

Building expert understanding requires extended time to question misconceptions, work with resources to explore meanings, and develop patterns and concepts based on this exploration. In developing concepts, teachers guide students in making observations, asking pertinent questions, identifying other resources, and using effective methods to answer the questions. In short, teachers guide students in actively building understanding rather than telling them what they should understand.

Some teachers assume that middle school students are ready for extended lectures when new material is presented. Students continually complain about lectures being overused, unengaging, and simply boring; and cognitive science supports such perceptions. A lecture or oral presentation can be an effective teaching tool in small doses, but only after students have developed a readiness and been given time to question misconceptions, investigate patterns, and build concepts based on personal interaction with events and ideas. In this way, lecture becomes part of an active learning process rather than a passive absorption of new information.

Experts understand and can apply their content and disciplines because they have developed deep and lasting concepts rather than just possessing a collection of facts (NRC, 2000). New facts and understandings are built into the schema of the existing concepts, allowing for further understanding, retrieval, and application. Facts are like sets of earrings. If they are thrown together in a pile, they are difficult to find, not easy to examine when making a selection, and likely to get lost. Concepts are like an earring tree; the earrings (facts) can be attached to the tree in an order that is logical to the owner and easily retrieved as needed. Other earrings can be added to the tree, and the earrings may even need to be re-ordered on occasion to incorporate new types.

Incorporating previous experiences with new ones to develop increasingly sophisticated concepts requires active cognitive learning. The learner must be engaged in the process for it to happen. Facts are necessary; they are the stuff of which concepts are built. On their own, however, they do not build themselves into understanding. Young adolescents crave interaction with facts and ideas so that they can build concepts to help make order out of their expanding reality.

Learning transfer

Young adolescents often ask the question, "When will I ever use this?" They express frustration about the lack of transfer of learning to the real world. The ultimate goal of learning should be application in other contexts and situations, particularly beyond the classroom. According to the NRC (2000), learning transfer is a "dynamic process that requires learners to actively choose and evaluate strategies, consider resources, and receive feedback" (p. 66). This differs from the more passive view of learning in which teachers present students with some initial information and then immediately ask them to solve several problems obviously connected to the new information. Learning for transfer gives students significant

Producing a musical provides students and teachers with active learning opportunities as they work together learning roles, sewing costumes, and building sets.

— Video, Scuola Vita Nuova, "Theater Production"

responsibility in the process of collecting, evaluating, and analyzing information to build concepts and understanding. Not only do students learn the content, but they also better understand the process of learning. (Spencer, 2010).

Motivation and multiple contexts also contribute to transfer of learning (NRC, 2000). Motivation can be increased through meaningful curriculum that is applicable to the outside world. Multiple contexts refers to using new learning to solve a variety of related but unique problems. However, what is usually requested is for students to learn an algebraic concept and apply it to similar algebra problems. Even if they do several problems in algebra class that vary slightly from the original, students will likely not be able to transfer that concept to anything else in algebra and almost surely not outside of the class. If, on the other hand, the same concept is used to solve very different algebra problems, problems related to other subjects, and especially problems existing in the real world, the students practice transfer and will be able to use the concept in the future.

Metacognition

Throughout the process of learning, metacognition defines the last fundamental cognitive aspect of active learning. According to the NRC (2000), metacognition includes

> Knowledge about learning, knowledge of their own learning strengths and weaknesses, and the demands of the learning task at hand. Metacognition also includes self-regulation—the ability to orchestrate one's learning: to plan, monitor success, and correct errors when appropriate. (p. 97)

Young adolescents become increasingly capable of self-regulation and reflection, making them active participants in their learning. These skills, however, do not happen automatically. As with any other new skills, metacognition must be taught, practiced, and developed. To be learned well, metacognition should be repeatedly incorporated into learning activities. Students should regularly think and talk about group and individual learning goals, progress toward goals, and further their plans to reach the goals. In this way, they actively orchestrate their own learning.

> Young adolescents become increasingly capable of self-regulation and reflection, making them active participants in their learning.

Active learning calls for cognitive engagement, which requires teaching students to assume responsibility for helping to plan and assess their learning. Students must also adopt an incremental view of intelligence, realizing that effort coupled with support increases learning. Thoughtful participation leads to learning transfer, which is a major goal and one especially important to young adolescents.

Active Social, Moral, and Physical Learning

In addition to cognitive activity, young adolescents crave social, moral, and physical involvement. Socially and morally, they begin to be concerned about others, often the downtrodden. They want to make a difference in the world. They are concerned about inconsistencies they notice in others and in society, and they need to participate in peer interactions and discussions of social and moral issues.(NMSA, 2010). Active learning in this context means being involved in the world outside of the classroom, in a way that improves society and addresses injustices.

Service learning offers one way to engage young adolescents in their communities and beyond (Fertman, White, & White, 1996; Jackson & Davis, 2000; Schine, 1997). In this model, service in the community becomes embedded in the curriculum. Through their classroom learning, students discover and investigate a problem in their community, state, country, or even the world. Students, in collaboration with teachers and community representatives, then devise and carry out a plan to address that problem. Not only does this kind of learning actively engage young adolescents' social and moral sensibilities, it also increases motivation for learning because it is connected to something that matters.

French teacher Ty Bryant leads students in a game of academic "Simon Says" to engage them and sharpen their command of the language.

— Chapel Hill MS

Collaborating with peers in learning also engages young adolescents socially. Throughout the strategies previously described, interaction with peers must be a prime consideration. In many learning situations these interactions offer an opportunity to further develop learning, to foster respect for each other, and to provide a chance to socialize around some common purpose. Students may not necessarily conduct interactions in an appropriate or productive way—especially with peers not considered friends—but with explicit teaching, needed skills, too, can be learned.

Although active learning encompasses much more, physical activity remains an important consideration. Young people need to move to release energy, engage all of their senses, and give their growing bodies an opportunity to stretch. Hands-on learning continues to be as important for middle school students as it was for them in elementary school. Experiments, manipulatives, and group challenges are examples of some of the ways to engage young adolescents physically.

Implications for Curriculum, Assessment, and the Teacher's Role

Active learning is inseparable from curriculum and assessment. To create a learning environment in which students want to become engaged requires a meaningful curriculum. For young adolescents, meaningful curriculum directly relates to their interests and concerns in the context of the world in and out of school. Curriculum must be important to them now, not just for some vague future use in academics or even in life. Curriculum that young people perceive as important and relevant will likely engage them in meaningful learning.

> The teacher's role becomes primarily collaborative rather than predominantly directive.

Assessment plays a key role in active learning as well. However, common grading practices often disengage learners from active participation. If based on some average or percentage of correct answers, it reinforces the fixed view of intelligence. Averaging also punishes students for making mistakes, even if those mistakes are later understood and corrected. Further, traditional grades discourage students from taking intellectual risks and challenges because anything other than immediate success negatively affects the final grade. The more difficulty students face in learning quickly, the more likely these practices will disengage them from learning.

Assessment, if focused on learning concepts and goals, can encourage active learning and offer feedback. If students clearly understand the goals, they can make individual and group plans to meet those goals. Teachers and peers provide frequent and specific feedback on progress toward the goals, which in turn leads to further development and adjustment to the plans for meeting goals. Mistakes become part of the feedback, and plans for further learning become not only essential, but also valued. Metacognition, an incremental view of intelligence and concepts—all components of active learning—are embedded in this view of assessment.

To create the active learning described in this chapter, the teacher's role becomes primarily collaborative rather than predominantly directive. Instead of telling students what and how to learn, providing resources, and assessing student learning, the teacher facilitates students in making those decisions. The teacher remains the educational expert and assures that student decisions move them toward stated ends, but the teacher's goal becomes teaching students how to monitor and control their own learning. For students to become active in their learning, teachers have to surrender some control, which is difficult for many teachers to do.

Contrasting Passive and Active Learning: An Example

In this chapter, active learning is described in the context of cognitive, social, moral, and physical development of young adolescents and the implications it carries for curriculum, assessment, and teachers. Two examples of classroom learning follow; one illustrates predominantly passive learning and the other active learning. The example of predominantly passive learning does not represent the extreme of passive learning, but one that might typically occur in any middle school. The second represents how a similar situation, with moderate changes, becomes active learning.

Example #1: Predominantly passive learning

A team of middle school teachers looks at the curriculum and determines that a unit on drug abuse and addiction will meet standards and likely appeal to their group of students. They plan lectures and activities to teach students about addiction, environments, and choices concerning substance use. The teachers review resources in and out of school and select what they believe are the best and most interesting. During the next few weeks, students move through the activities that teachers plan, construct posters on some facet of the unit, take notes on mini-lectures, and engage in some teacher-directed discussions.

Example #2: Active learning

A group of young adolescents and their teacher collaboratively pose the questions "Why do only certain people become addicted to drugs and alcohol?" and "What are the chances that I will become addicted to some substance?" The students, with the teacher as facilitator, discuss possible ways to answer the questions and develop a list that includes researching the genetics of addiction, investigating family histories, reading about environmental factors that increase addictive behaviors, conducting a confidential survey among their peers, and interviewing addicts, counselors, and doctors.

They search for resources that best answer their questions leads to some Internet resources that are reliable and valid while others are biased, incomplete, or just plain incorrect. They find that some primary sources interview well, but others do not seem to help them understand. They discover that a lecture from the teacher or a guest speaker at just the right time can be informative and interesting. As they progress through their list of activities, they collaborate with their teacher to determine what they have learned about their questions and what they still have to learn. They develop a few additional activities to address weaknesses in their understanding. When they finally develop some possible answers to the original question, they go back to their human sources for feedback on their answers. Finally, they develop a plan to present to the school board about how to effectively teach their peers about substance abuse.

Buy-in to learning increases significantly when students such as Maggie are partners with their teachers in designing curriculum.

— Video, Maranacook Community MS,
"Curriculum Development"

In the first example, students may well have been engaged in learning about substance abuse because it is a topic of high interest. They may gather similar information as the second group of students and may even build similar concepts. They have not, however, actively participated in their own learning to any significant degree.

The second group consciously became motivated because the questions belonged to the students. They found and evaluated their own resources and sought feedback to assess their progress toward their goal of answering the questions. They collaborated with each other and engaged with their communities to develop a solution for substance abuse among their peers. In short, they became active participants, taking increasing responsibility for every aspect of their learning. The teachers in the second example allowed the learning to be more

Find videos at www.amle.org/TWBinAction

active for students by collaborating with the students rather than controlling and directing the learning themselves.

Young adolescents are not only capable of active learning, but they learn best when they are allowed to take responsibility for significant decisions in their educational lives. They have important questions and concerns; they are ready to engage. Educators have only to share the reins.

References

Charney, R. (2002). *Teaching children to care: Classroom management for ethical and academic growth, K-8* (Rev. ed.). Greenfield, MA: National Foundation for Children.

Deci, E., Vallerand, R., Pelletier, L., & Ryan, R. (1991). Motivation and education: The self-determination perspective. *Educational Psychologist, 26*(3 & 4), 325-346.

Dweck, C. (2000). Self-theories: *Their role in motivation, personality, and development.* Florence, KY: Psychology Press.

Fertman, C., White, G., & White, L. (1996). *Service learning in the middle school: Building a culture of service.* Columbus, OH: National Middle School Association.

Jackson, A. W., & Davis, G. (2000). *Turning points 2000: Educating adolescents in the 21st century.* New York: Teachers College Press and Westerville, OH: National Middle School Association.

Knowles, T., & Brown, D. (2007). *What every middle school teacher should know.* Portsmouth, NH: Heinemann.

Maehr, M., & Anderman, E . (1993). Reinventing schools for early adolescents: Emphasizing task goals. *The Elementary School Journal, 93*, 593-620.

National Middle School Association. (2010). *This we believe: Keys to educating young adolescents.* Westerville, OH: Author.

National Research Council. (2000). *How people learn: Brain, mind, experience, and school.* Washington, DC: National Academy Press.

Schine, J. (1997). Service learning and young adolescents: A good fit. In J. L. Irvin (Ed.), *What current research says to the middle level practitioner* (pp. 257-263). Columbus, OH: National Middle School Association.

Spencer, J. (2010). *Teaming rocks! Collaborate in powerful ways to ensure student success.* Westeville, OH: National Middle School Association.

3

Challenging Curriculum
Curriculum is challenging, exploratory, integrative, and relevant.

Chris Stevenson & Penny A. Bishop

∞∞∞

One sunny, early fall afternoon, Chris left his office a bit early to catch the second half of a University of Vermont soccer game on campus. As he climbed into the sparsely filled grandstand, he noticed a row of seven or eight young adolescent girls and boys chattering among themselves while watching the game. Not one to pass up such a good opportunity for a "double feature," he took a seat behind the middle of their row. This was an irresistible opportunity to unobtrusively check out a sample of adolescent culture while at the same time, enjoy some soccer.

The kids' talk was wide-ranging, jumping quickly from topic to topic. Sometimes they seemed to agree, but more often it was as if the conversation was a competition for the most profound observations. Distinctions between fact and opinion blurred. Unable to detect any coherent theme from the center of the row, Chris eased his way to one end where Joe was attempting to explain soccer rules to Amy, who presented herself as earnestly attentive. An apparent novice to the sport, she struggled to understand and to reassure him that his tutorial made sense. Try as he might, however, Joe's explanations of the offside rule in particular did not clear up Amy's confusion. Although she tried mightily, it was apparent that she was just not getting it. Joe finally concluded his lesson with the reassurance that, "it makes a lot more sense when you're doing it."

We think Joe is onto something fundamentally important to our quest for middle level curriculum and pedagogy. Especially among young adolescents, "it makes a lot more sense when you're doing it." Joe understands that when one is 11, 12, or 13 years old, enduring useful knowledge is associated with firsthand engagement of the subject matter. While this truth is widely espoused among middle level educators, it is all too infrequently a primary focus affecting adults' curricular decisions.

From the earliest beginnings of the middle school concept, the most steadfast rationale in approaching curriculum decisions has been a dogged emphasis on educational methods that complement "the distinctive nature of young adolescents" (NMSA, 2010, p.13).

> Authentic learning leaves unmistakable tracks in learners' talk with each other and with adults.

Somehow, however, our search for the composition of that curriculum inevitably has seemed reduced to discussions, debates, and proposals about "disciplines vs. interdisciplinary" or "subject specific vs. integrated" dualities. Interesting and often entertaining, but irresolvable arguments have too easily diverted us from our espoused goal of creating successful matches between our kids and their studies. The issue is not whether life is inherently discipline-based or interdisciplinary, because it is both. We submit that Joe would have us seek and find our direction by examining more closely the interactions between the subject matter (e.g., soccer rules) and the learner's derivation of meaning (e.g., his and Amy's separate understandings). Authentic learning leaves unmistakable tracks in learners' talk with each other and with adults. Consider some examples of students whose engagement in learning is self-evident. Who could dispute that the curriculum in these examples was challenging, exploratory, integrative, and relevant to them?

Kids Genuinely Engaged in Curriculum

Snapshot I

Brian and Amelia, eighth graders at a charter middle school in the Pacific Northwest, returned from their winter break filled with questions about the recent devastating tsunami in Asia. Questions and commentary about the tragedy rang through the halls while students jostled one another as they tried to fit bulky backpacks into their lockers. Informally debating the recent events on their way to class, Amelia argued, "I think it was an earthquake," while

Brian asserted, "No, I heard it was a tidal wave." Their friend Etienne overheard them as he scooted through the doorway at the last minute and interjected, "I heard more than 100,000 people died. My mom said that's bigger than our city."

Although their first-year science teacher, Ms. Joyner, had spent most of her break carefully planning their next unit on forensic science, she recognized the teachable moment inherent in her students' discussion. She decided that morning, therefore, to postpone the forensic science unit and turn to the study of tsunamis, capitalizing on her students' obvious and intense interest. She began class by inviting students to share what they already knew about tsunamis and this recent event. As they spoke, she listed their thoughts on the white board at the front of the room. Their prior knowledge was based primarily on images from network news coverage and fell into three broad categories: scientific perspectives on how tsunamis are formed; a geographical knowledge of the region in Asia where the tsunami occurred; and widely ranging thoughts on the degree of the devastation, including the number of deaths and damaged or destroyed villages.

With assistance from their teachers, students develop curriculum which helps them answer questions about their world and themselves.

— Video, Maranacook Community MS, "Sled Project," "Curriculum Development," "Ice Fishing"

Next Ms. Joyner encouraged students to pose questions in pairs about the natural disaster. Students turned to a partner and began to list on notepaper the questions that had emerged for them as well as ones provoked by the initial class discussion. She then asked them to share their questions aloud, while she made notes on the white board for all to see. The questions included, what is the difference between a tidal wave and a tsunami? How does a tsunami begin? Can anything stop it? Has it ever happened before? How many cities and villages were hit? How many people died? Could the same thing happen here? What will happen to the children who have no parents? What can I do to help?

In integrated curriculum, we each come up with ideas we want to learn about. We put them all on a poster and narrow it down to the top 10 ideas and vote. It is much more fun to learn about stuff you want to learn about rather than what you are give.

— Maggie, Maranacook Community MS, "Curriculum Development"

The students' questions formed the foundation for what turned out to be a three-week unit on tsunamis, the force and physics of water, soil salinity, and geography. Students helped construct a wave pool with materials donated from a local plastics plant, and then they used the apparatus to reconstruct and analyze the force of water. As is often characteristic of young adolescents, they felt a call to action. Brian and Amelia decided to host a community-wide pancake breakfast to raise money to donate to tsunami relief, and they quickly earned the support of their peers. Ms. Joyner helped the class to think about and identify various jobs that would be necessary to sponsor such an event. They formed committees to handle the project: Public Awareness, Donations, Food Prep, Serving, and Clean-up. The team's teachers devoted their usual advisory time each day to planning the event. The Donations Committee solicited donations of ingredients from local grocery stores while students on the Public Awareness Committee busily prepared posters, advertising copy, and letters to the editors of surrounding newspapers urging citizens to donate generously.

When the designated Saturday morning arrived, the school's cafeteria was taken over by the Food Prep, Serving, and Clean-up teams, who enthusiastically rolled up their sleeves as they greeted and served their neighbors. The fundraiser was very successful, and they donated their proceeds to an established relief organization aimed at helping surviving children of the tsunami.

Ms. Joyner felt a lot of satisfaction in such a successful curriculum project that grew out of her students' concerns and questions. In observing their deep engagement in the subject matter, she knew without a doubt that the project was a great educational success. Students gained a new sense of personal efficacy as they learned about what was timely and relevant, and they gave to their global community from their local community in the purest spirit of "think globally, act locally."

Snapshot II

Meg and Sara, seventh graders on the Harmony Team, attended an urban middle school. They had recently become best friends, prompted in part by a shared traumatic experience: legal separations and impending divorce by both sets of parents. One part of the curriculum provided by Harmony was comprised of independent studies called "Orbital Studies" that can be carried out by individuals or combinations of students who have a shared interest (Stevenson, 2002, pp. 162, 202). Meg openly wanted to know more about what divorce meant for her and her family, and although Sara tended to keep her feelings more private, she agreed with Meg that exploring divorce and its effects on everyone in their two families was highly relevant and worthy as a focus for an orbital study. One of their teachers, Mrs. Redmond, was eager to support them, in part because she had been divorced for three years and was the custodial parent for her two children in elementary school.

Mrs. Redmond helped them get started by inviting them to compile three lists: things they already knew about separation and divorce; questions they wanted to answer; and issues and questions they wanted to discuss with their parents. She also helped them identify possible resources for their investigations: court-related children's service providers, attorneys who specialized in family matters, judges, and published materials about divorce for children their age, of which they found very few. The girls were especially interested in learning about the experiences and opinions of other students whose families had split. Even before they finished creating a web of resources and expanding their lists of questions and issues— Harmony requirements for Orbital Studies—their investigation was well under way. Every couple of days they met with Mrs. Redmond to show her their progress, ask questions, and get her advice.

> The volume students eventually produced evolved as a blend of personal stories, mostly from other adolescents, with information learned from people and community agencies dealing with divorce.

After less than two weeks, they decided on a culminating product: they decided to write a book for kids their ages about separation and divorce. Because they had found almost nothing written by kids for kids, Mrs. Redmond helped them see that they could address a literary niche. The material for the book would come from print and human resources readily available in their school and community, but the approach and voice would be uniquely theirs.

The volume they eventually produced, Kids Helping Kids with Divorce, evolved as a blend of personal stories, mostly from other adolescents, with information learned from people and community agencies dealing with divorce. Conceptualizing and producing a volume of such magnitude not only was a giant stride for Meg and Sara, it also showed them a constructive way to deal with painful personal issues. Even during a time of their own intense personal struggle, the girls' parents trusted Mrs. Redmond and the other Harmony teachers to help the girls with both their scholarly and personal needs over the several weeks of their investigation. Interest in their study by other adolescents and parents triggered the formation of a "Divorce Group" taught by the school's counselors and made up of students across the school who shared personal experience with separation and divorce. Meg and Sara's book became required reading. Everyone benefited from this experience of creating an authentic opportunity for firsthand inquiry and learning about an issue that matters to growing numbers of young adolescents. Meg and Sara learned about a difficult issue in their lives, and their study helped other kids going through the same difficult time. Mrs. Redmond and her colleagues also gained both personally and as teachers from the girls' work.

Snapshot III

Casey was a sixth grader on an interdisciplinary team in a New England middle school. Afternoons on his team were dedicated to the integrated study of science and social studies called Life Studies. Students signed up for Life Studies groups based on their interests and the state's approved standards that linked to their personal and academic goals for the month. In February Casey's Life Studies group focused on inventing new technology. The students were to select technology that is commonly used today, research the historical evolution of that technology, and speculate about how it might evolve 20 years from now.

Knowledge is content put into action.

— Video, Maranacook Community MS, "Curriculum Development"

Because Casey loved working with computers, he became quite excited about this task. He contributed eagerly to the class, brainstorming various technologies on which they might focus. He was, by self-admission, stubborn at times and, as a result, often found collaboration on projects a challenge. He was greatly relieved when his teacher, Mr. Edwards, told students they could choose their own partners. Casey teamed up with his good friend, Jared, and they excitedly moved to a computer to begin to capture their ideas.

Casey and Jared began talking about a friend who suffers from diabetes. They were interested in the fact that her "state of the art" insulin pump had already broken five times. They did not understand why it should break with so many filters on it to ensure that it was reliable. Mr. Edwards circulated around the room and crouched by the computer to listen to the boys' conversation. He encouraged them to pursue this important question and guided them to

Find videos at www.amle.org/TWBinAction

several diabetes websites to learn more about the disease and various insulin pumps on the market.

The two boys spent three weeks learning about diabetes, the role of insulin in the body, and current biomedical technology. Their work culminated in the design of an implanted insulin pump that would be inserted into the body with multiple filters to automatically monitor a person's insulin levels. Mr. Edwards introduced them to new software that assisted them with multidimensional graphics and with which they were able to construct their new technology on the computer, finally uploading it to their own webpage. Casey and Jared felt a sense of competence and accomplishment in designing a tool that could respond to real needs in the world, as well as to the needs of someone they know and care about. Mr. Edwards especially enjoyed his role as a facilitator in the boys' work as he watched two capable and motivated students find real-world relevance in their learning.

Characteristics of Effective Curriculum

What do the students in the middle schools framed by these snapshots have in common? Certainly they exhibit palpable engagement with curriculum that is challenging, exploratory, integrative, and relevant. None of these studies would have taken place without the support, encouragement, and guidance of savvy, learning-oriented teachers who perceptively and wisely guided their students' learning. In each case, students enjoyed rich and substantive learning because they first felt confident enough in relationships with their teachers to be able to express their ideas, interests, and questions.

When students find teachers indifferent to their ideas, then such ideas do not get expressed. These youngsters also benefitted from teachers who not only were open to the possibility of authentic student choice but who understood and valued the power of learning driven by strong personal interests. Showing eager learners how to plan and proceed, staying in touch with them as they progress, and helping them wrap up their study is the proverbial "piece of cake." It gives meaning to teaching in ways that transcend the usual.

Challenging

The teacher's role in moving beyond mere coverage of content to curriculum that "addresses substantive issues and skills, is geared to (students') levels of understanding, and increasingly enables them to assume control of their own learning" (NMSA, 2010, p. 18) is critical. The previous snapshots illustrate learning that is grounded in rigorous concepts and skills and that teaches developing young people how to take greater personal responsibility for their own learning.

Mrs. Redmond, for example, began by working closely with Meg and Sara to help them identify questions and locate resources. She gradually transitioned into more of an advisory role, interjecting advice or questions when needed, but allowing Meg and Sara to direct their work and learning in accord with their own inclinations. Similarly, Mr. Edwards skillfully guided Casey and Jared toward resources for their study and taught them to use new software. At the same time, he ensured that they addressed their substantive questions and controlled their project. Casey and Jared's project also represents the opportunity for challenging curriculum to reduce the gap between students' in-school and out-of-school technology lives. Such work can capitalize on young adolescents' affinity for technology and deepen their acquisition of 21st century skills. In all cases, the concepts under study were challenging for young adolescents, and the tasks were achievable.

Exploratory

National Middle School Association (2010) urges middle level educators to consider exploration as "an attitude and approach, not a classification of content" (p. 20). For too long the term "exploratory" has referred to unified arts or other classes thought to be outside the realm of the "core" academic areas such areas such as technology education and family and consumer science. We argue that all curricula for middle grades students must involve exploration. Surely, no teacher or parent can deny that young adolescents are by nature inquisitive. A rich middle level program capitalizes on that intellectual curiosity by opening up young people's potential for future career interests and recreational pursuits. It enables students to investigate beyond their immediate realm, regardless of gender, social class, ethnicity, or life circumstances, and to consider limitless possibilities. As they empowered their students to become authors, scientists, human service advocates, and inventors, Mrs. Redmond, Ms. Joyner, and Mr. Edwards created activities

> For too long the term "exploratory" has referred to unified arts or other classes thought to be outside the realm of the "core" academic areas such areas such as technology education or family and consumer science.

that broadened students' views of the world, themselves, and their futures. These teachers embody exploration as an attitude and approach, regardless of their specific subject matter specializations.

Integrative

Often defying arbitrary subject boundaries, integrative curriculum "helps students make sense of their lives and the world around them" (NMSA, 2010, p. 21). In each of the three snapshots, students were deeply immersed in grasping concepts that by nature crossed the lines of subject-specific disciplines. In the study of a tsunami tragedy, for example, Brian, Amelia, and their peers acquired and applied map reading and other geography skills to contrast world regions affected by the natural disaster. They used scientific methods to design and conduct their own investigation of the connections between the earth's crustal plates and the force of water. And they honed persuasive writing skills as they carefully composed and revised their letters to

When students gather plant and animal specimens from the school pond and study the ground water system, they learn science in the context of their region's ecology.

— Video, Jefferson MS, "Prairie Curriculum"

the community, ever aware of the authentic audience. In each case, students made ongoing and meaningful decisions about their learning, critiquing and modifying their approaches along the way. Without Ms. Joyner's willingness to ground curriculum in students' questions, or her ability to see the possibilities beyond her own academic discipline, the students' investigation would have been limited to a relatively conventional science class. Instead, their eyes were opened to the rich and inherently interdisciplinary world in which they live.

Relevant

"Curriculum is relevant when it allows students to pursue answers to questions they have about themselves, content, and the world" (NMSA, 2010, p. 22). Unquestionably, the Asian tsunami, divorce, and diabetes were content of momentous personal relevance to these students. Based on their own questions, excellent curriculum and meaningful learning emerged from their earnest desire to understand new concepts and world events. Helping others is a common theme evident through each of the snapshots: designing an implanted insulin pump to help a friend, composing a book to help kids get through divorce, raising money to help victims of a natural disaster thousands of miles away.

In each case, students found personal relevance in following their own lines of inquiry to understand the world around them. Their increasing needs for relevance were addressed by service learning initiatives, heightening their personal involvement in academic and civic life (Allen, 2003; Chiaravalloti, 2009). It is encouraging to see more and more service learning opportunities in middle schools. These snapshots meld service into academic learning, drawing together the best of both worlds. Young adolescents long to make a real and felt difference, and they love to be recognized for their intelligence and budding expertise.

> Young adolescents long to make a real and felt difference in the world, and they love to be recognized for their intelligence and budding expertise

Curriculum and Student Engagement

Savvy middle level teachers know from experience that the quickest way to find out how learning happens for young adolescents is simply to ask them. We do not refer here to occasional conversational inquiries, although such occasions may produce valuable insights. What we recommend is a foundational assessment that invites students on a regular schedule to reflect on current and recent experiences and identify factors that have been effective in helping them learn. Such inquiries require young people to become reflective and analytical about their progress as learners. Students learn about their strengths and their continuing learning needs, and these data inform their planning of subsequent studies.

Similarly, teachers improve their own practice by creating a formal time to listen to students reflect on what works and what does not. For too long, educators have underestimated or neglected entirely the knowledge to be gained from engaging students in self-assessment and formal documentation of their strengths and needs as learners. As Cook-Sather (2002) asserted, "We as educators . . . must seriously question the assumption that we know more than the young people of today about how they learn or what they need to learn in preparation for the decades ahead" (p. 3).

In order to understand how middle school students learn, and to help them come to know themselves well as learners, we have found the concept of *engagement* to be a helpful one.

Because we know that engaged students learn more (Valentine & Collins, 2011), inviting students to consider times of engagement and times of disengagement in learning can reveal powerful insights for learners and teachers alike. For example, interviews with middle schoolers from six schools (Bishop & Pflaum, 2005a, 2005b) revealed the critical role of relevance in curriculum just mentioned. When asked to describe any time in her schooling when she felt deeply engaged in her learning, eighth grader Amelia was eager to talk about her literature group's

> Students who are invited into a reflective dialogue about learning enhance their ability to set demanding yet achievable personal and academic goals for themselves.

recent discussion of Kafka's *Metamorphosis*. She described that this was the first time she had learned about the concept of alienation. Amelia explained, "I didn't know it was such a big issue and then I came into the course and then I realized that it was, like, pretty important. . . . Most everybody is alienated, so just, like, think how *you're* alienated" (2005a, p. 36). For Amelia, finding relevance in a topic such as alienation engaged her deeply. Knowing that relevance can help engage her, therefore, increases her learning, Amelia can consider how to find relevance when designing her own learning. Her teacher can build on this knowledge to ensure Amelia makes connections between her studies and her life.

Other students find they are most successful when working at their own individual pace. One fifth grader, Nad, explained that he loved sustained silent reading because, "I like going at my own pace. . . . Some kids in my group, they don't read with any expression. And they read really slowly, even though I understand that they can't read as well but . . . I really, I like to just, I really like to read alone" (Bishop & Pflaum, 2005a, p. 9). He contrasted that with a math class in which he was unsuccessful and disengaged, confiding that, "I don't usually get it in my head the first time he explains it" (p. 10). With these insights, Nad discovered the importance an individualized pace plays in his learning, and he can consider that when planning future work. His teacher gains important information that Nad might otherwise not offer, given the class-wide novels and whole-group math instruction that are the norm in his class.

We do not think there is a recipe to follow for engaging middle school students in challenging, exploratory, integrative, and relevant curriculum. On the contrary, young adolescents are constantly changing and are by nature a developmentally diverse group. Rather, students who are invited into a reflective dialogue about learning enhance their ability to set demanding yet achievable personal and academic goals for themselves. They are equipped with growing self-knowledge. Amelia and Nad are two of many examples of youngsters involved in reflecting on their learning needs and on the curriculum in relation to these needs. Such opportunities enhance students' sense of personal efficacy; they enable teachers to reflect on their teaching and the inherent match or mismatch between their approaches and the youngsters in their classrooms.

Curriculum and Adolescent Development

Looking comprehensively at young adolescents' healthy and enthusiastic learning would cause one to consider the curriculum in relation to the learner himself or herself. What should be the primary purpose of curriculum at the middle level? *This We Believe* posits that middle level curriculum must be "challenging, exploratory, integrative, and relevant" (2010, p. 17). It is fair to rejoin, "To whom?" Might sincere adults use such descriptors to justify any curriculum content or program or guide for any age students? If our focus is truly on young adolescent learners, then we will emphasize their challenging and being challenged by their schoolwork, *their* successfully integrating new learning into their continuously modified existing knowledge, and *their* exploring the ideas and questions that interest them.

Hamburg (1993) stated well the primary purpose and nature of middle level curriculum:

> What are the requirements for healthy adolescent development? In my view, it is essential that we help young adolescents to acquire constructive knowledge and skills, inquiring habits of mind, dependable human relationships, reliable basis for learning respect, a sense of belonging in a valued group, and a way of being useful to their communities. (p. 467)

Given the range of developmental diversity among children during these years, it does not seem feasible for any single curriculum plan conceived by adults in isolation from a particular group of students and administered to all students at the same time to possibly accommodate everyone. Fortunately, such a single plan is not our only option. One of the great benefits of working with these students is their readiness to make responsible choices as to what they will study and learn. The more choices they are able to make, the more seriously they are inclined to trust the choices adults are also making for them. Perhaps the

> Perhaps the greatest challenge to educators is to summon the courage to form partnerships with students by which they share curriculum planning.

greatest challenge to educators is to summon the courage to form partnerships with students by which they share curriculum planning. Beane's (1993, 2005) works compel teachers to enter into just such coalitions, and student-maintained records of their work in portfolios enables teachers to more fully understand the extent to which curriculum is actually cultivating competence and responsibility as well as testimonials of affiliation, awareness, and ethical perceptions of themselves.

Middle level educators should focus on the ways students are growing and changing during these transition years between childhood and late adolescence. We know with certainty that they undergo distinctive changes from the ways of their earlier childhood.

We also know that there is a great deal of variability among them; differentness is the norm in early adolescence. Individuals change according to idiosyncratic schedules, and they also develop uniquely in terms of intelligence, disposition, attitudes and tastes, interests, work habits, and aspirations. It seems to us that the abundance of possibilities for children during this brief period of human life invites curriculum initiatives that complement individual differences and transcend established curriculum paradigms. This perspective does not demean those curricula; rather, it ensures that our focus on the growth and development of individual children is preserved. For this brief period of schooling, our abiding concern should be the effectiveness with which our children learn both how to learn and the disposition that they can learn successfully.

Curriculum and Personal Efficacy

What if our primary purpose in planning curriculum is to ensure the healthy development of young adolescent learners? What are their predominant needs as learners and citizens? Three decades of interviews with young adolescent students and countless collaborations with middle level teachers point to some developmental needs that can be satisfied through curriculum designs that preserve learner efficacy as the focal point. Students who demonstrate personal efficacy in school and in their relationships with peers and adults exhibit some essential traits: competency, responsibility, affiliation, awareness, and ethical perception of self.

Competence

Young adolescents care a great deal about being competent. Those few who have become alienated from their inner nature as learners are victims of bankrupt schooling. Successful students identify themselves by the things they do well, and they relish opportunities to do those things. Whether it is running, or spelling, or shooting baskets, or solving equations, a powerful need for personal expertise perseveres. It does not follow that individuals have to be the very best at their particular competency, that no one else is equally as good as they are. But it does seem to matter that one be somewhat set apart from others by this expertise. The very best of circumstances is when classmates and significant others, especially older adolescents and adults, also acknowledge one's competence. Good curriculum from students' perspectives assures that they grow steadily in competencies that they acknowledge as useful and worthwhile. When youngsters are failing to grow in competence in their own eyes and in the perceptions of others, a fundamental developmental need is being denied.

Responsibility

A second attribute of young adolescent learners who seem to be thriving is their perception of themselves as accountable and responsible in ways that approximate adulthood. They know they are not yet ready for a more fully independent adult role, but they value taking greater responsibility for themselves and being recognized for evidence of greater maturity. Initiative, dependability, and resourcefulness are qualities they value in themselves and each other. They care about being at ease with planning and organizing learning, working either alone or with selected peers. They prefer to think of themselves as good choosers and fair judges, and their personally constructed academic portfolios exude personal accountability and self-awareness. Curriculum that matches well with these qualities cultivates the very self-reliance we know to be essential to successful learners and strong individuals.

Affiliation

As longtime teachers of young adolescents and as observers of others who teach them well, we have noted that the best curriculum takes on something of a life of its own. There is a palpable "curriculum transcendence" through which students derive remarkable degrees of engagement and energy. Observe students preparing a drama production or doing a project together: they give lots of energy to such work, and, in turn, they are energized. Such experiences become benchmarks of future learning, and students articulate intense feelings of affiliation with those learning events. Sometimes the significance of the experience comes from the value of the compelling working relationships with peers or with teachers in the school; oftentimes significant relationships are created while working with other adults in the community. At its very best, after all, learning is an energy loop: one invests energy in a process that, in turn, energizes that same individual. Whatever curriculum unit middle level teachers may choose to teach, if there is no evidence of student passion and ownership, enduring learning is not likely to occur.

Awareness

No one likes to be taken for a fool, especially young adolescents. Perhaps because of the intensity of the identity formation process, these youngsters are especially sensitive about how they are perceived and treated. Note their language, humor, dress, and interactions with peer groups as evidence of their need to be regarded by others as "with it." Being involved, savvy, and "tuned in" are paramount. Believing that "I know what's going on," affirms a sense of worth. Insights about one's abilities and strengths give rise to reflections and theories about how things are and how things should be done. We have found young adolescents to be especially responsive to inquiries about the dynamics of peer relationships, their school, and the community (Stevenson, 2002; Bishop, Allen-Malley & Brinegar, 2007). Curriculum that serves these students well provides a climate and context in which they recognize the relevance of their studies and have ample opportunities to demonstrate their knowledge to others, especially parents, older adolescents, and community people.

> Young adolescents are especially responsive to inquiries designed to explain their perceptions about the dynamics of peer relationships, their school, and the community.

Ethical perception of self

Perhaps the most reassuring indicator of sound education and human development is evidence of our children's natural inclination toward moral ideals. It is crucial for them to regard themselves as good people of high moral standing. Their growing interest in existential questions, concern about injustices, and readiness for activism in worthy causes signals the youngster's need to believe in himself or herself as a good person, an individual of worth who is making a difference in the world. Advocacy for animals, stewardship of the environment, and compassion for the needy and disadvantaged are natural causes they are eager to support as a matter of principle. As they grow in knowledge of the exigencies of political and economic systems, they come to recognize both the promise and vulnerabilities of democracy. A growing sophistication about how things work in a morally conscious and responsible community portends active citizenship that brings vitality to the school today and the larger community tomorrow. Any curriculum design that does not provide opportunities and support for students to do "right things" alongside the significant adults in their lives is sadly incomplete. Kids understand the value of being good through doing good.

A Caveat for the Bold

Pressures on all teachers to adhere to prescribed curriculum are greater today than they have ever been. Under the illusion of "accountability," school system policies vastly over emphasize testing that covers specific prescribed content, and the media extends this tragic illusion of "quality of education" by reporting test scores and comparing schools' performance as an indication of "excellence." As a result, teachers find it harder and harder to make time for more authentic means of assessment and evaluation. Further, most middle level teachers are licensed to teach only one or two subject matter areas, and this very designation can discourage them from teaching beyond their subject areas. Federal injunctions contained in the No Child Left Behind Act easily intimidate many administrators and teachers from deviating from assumed deductive, prescriptive teaching, and textbook-centered modes of instruction that have long proved inadequate and inappropriate to the experienced observer of young adolescents' learning and healthy development.

We should not be surprised at these developments, given the extent to which politicians who have no experience with the actualities of children's learning and development issue mandates about the content of curriculum and methods of evaluation. The general public remains amazingly gullible in accepting this falsification of high standards of education. Even more disappointing, most of these high-stakes tests do not assess the knowledge and skills our children will need to be active and productive citizens in the 21st century.

The good news is that there remain numbers of middle level teachers like Ms. Joyner, Mrs. Redmond, and Mr. Edwards who grasp early adolescence and who also have strength of professional conviction to trust both their understanding and their students to pursue curriculum that is challenging, exploratory, integrative, and relevant. We know there are numerous other committed middle level teachers who are following suit, nurturing and building on their students' interests, ideas, and questions to pursue learning opportunities that effectively change kids' lives and advance far more valid definitions of "accountability" and "excellence." These are also the teachers we must seek out, learn from, and encourage; they are the ones who will preserve the wisdom of the middle level concept that provoked the reform movement in the first place.

Back in the earliest days of middle level reform a now long-forgotten source caught our attention with a persuasive argument that middle level curriculum was urgently in need of major overhaul. The writer cautioned, however, that to simply replace ineffective programs in favor of all new designs would likely bring about certain catastrophe. The essay went on to encourage that educators resolve to build 15% of their curriculum around the expressed needs and interests of their students. We were advised to treat that modest 15% as professional inquiry conceived to better understand the studies and pedagogy that best served our students. The remaining 85% of our curriculum could remain unchanged for the moment. The crucial advice, however, was that we incorporate the insights drawn from the 15% into the remaining 85%, and thereby remake subsequent curriculum in ways that will be more closely aligned with the particular characteristics and needs of our students. In so doing, we affirm ourselves as professionals who adapt practices according to insights resulting from our inquiries. Young people like those reported in this chapter will thank us for our wisdom, actions, and courage.

References

Allen, R. (2003). The democratic aims of service learning. *Educational Leadership, 60*(6), 51-54.

Beane, J. A. (1993). *A middle school curriculum: From rhetoric to reality* (2nd ed.). Columbus, OH: National Middle School Association.

Beane, J. A. (2005). *A reason to teach: Creating classrooms of dignity and hope.* New York: Teachers College Press.

Bishop, P., & Pflaum, S. (2005a). *Reaching and teaching middle school learners: Asking students to show us what works.* Thousand Oaks, CA: Corwin Press.

Bishop, P., & Pflaum, S. (2005b). Student perceptions of action, relevance, and pace. *Middle School Journal, 36*(4), 4-12.

Bishop, P., Allen-Malley, G., & Brinegar, K. (2007). Student perceptions of integration and community: "Always give me a chance to shine." Volume 6 in V. Anfara (Ed.) *The handbook of research in middle level education.* (pp 91-120). American Educational Research Association's Middle Level Education Research Special Interest Group. Greenwich, CT: Information Age Publishing.

Chiaravalloti, L. A. (2009). Making the switch: Lightbulbs, literacy, and service-learning. *Voices from the Middle, 17*(1), 24-33.

Cook-Sather, A. (2002). Authorizing students' perspectives: Toward trust, dialogue and change in education. *Educational Researcher, 31*(4), 3-14.

Hamburg, D. A. (1993). The opportunities of early adolescence. *Teachers College Record, 94,* 466-471.

National Middle School Association. (2010). *This we believe: Keys to educating young adolescents.* Westerville, OH: Author.

Stevenson, C. (2002). *Teaching ten to fourteen year olds* (3rd ed.). Boston: Pearson Allyn & Bacon.

Valentine, J., & Collins, J. (2011, April). *Student engagement and achievement on high-stakes tests: A hierarchical linear modeling (HLM) analysis across 68 middle schools.* Paper presentation at the Annual Meeting of the American Educational Research Association, New Orleans, LA.

4

Multiple Learning Approaches
Educators use multiple learning and teaching approaches.

Barbara Brodhagen & Susan Gorud

Schools can be thought of as collections of opportunities to learn (Hammond, 1997). Student achievement is affected positively when those learning opportunities capitalize on students' cultural, experiential, and personal backgrounds. Teachers who consistently plan and implement instruction that honors the wide diversity among young adolescents are able to maximize student learning. Diversity has many facets that influence young adolescents and their learning environment: gender, socio-economic class, intellectual capacity, and linguistic and ethnic backgrounds among them. The way students learn is as individual as their fingerprints. By offering instructional approaches and learning experiences that offer multiple means of presentation, engagement, action, and expression, teachers give more students opportunities to learn and demonstrate their learning (Rose, Meyer, & Hitchcock, 2005; CAST). Evidence indicates that students who have positive affiliations with their teachers are more likely to achieve academically than those who do not (Anfara et al., 2003; Dilg, 2003; Wehlage, Rutter, Smith, Lesko, & Fernandez, 1989).

This chapter describes a sampling of developmentally responsive approaches to teaching and learning that respond to the diversity among today's young adolescents. Strategies include use of learning inventories, a variety of instructional/teaching approaches, question posing to and by young adolescents, projects, knowledge performance, and student reflection. Within each description, examples will show how these strategies can celebrate and address student diversity within a heterogeneous classroom in support of high levels of student learning. Finally attention will be given to professional development for educators who want to create a classroom environment that welcomes young adolescents' diversity and offers students access to academic and social success.

Inventories: Learning and Cultural

Teachers serious about responding to the diverse skills, abilities, and prior knowledge of young adolescents take time to learn about the range of students' multiple intelligences, learning styles, and individual experiences. Some teachers use formal inventories or assessments to help discover students' strengths, talents, learning preferences, and areas of challenge. Other teachers have students complete a questionnaire that might include open-ended statements such as the following:

» I learn best when I . . .

» In my spare time I really like to . . .

» I know when I really want to concentrate I have to . . .

» The best time for me to read is . . .

» When I think about making something with my hands I . . .

Still other teachers recognize that young adolescents have had many learning experiences in school and simply ask their students to describe how they believe they learn best. By posting a list of these strategies and activities, teachers are reminded to include them when planning.

An aspect of curriculum planning often neglected or overlooked is learning about and gaining information from cultural and learning inventories. Teachers can design beginning-of-the-year activities to enable students to share information about multiple aspects of their lives. Students could bring in photographs as a visual sampling of who they are as individuals. They could list their ethnic backgrounds and then display the information in a graph showing the entire class profile, and everyone can see the class diversity. The teachers can use the information to "ensure learning approaches and options that span the full range of culture-influenced possibilities" (Tomlinson & Eidson, 2003, p. 234).

Sometimes real cultural understanding comes only after a conflict has arisen in the classroom. A cultural inventory can be used to determine the social skills that need to be explicitly taught and modeled for students to forge relationships and effectively work together (Banks et al., 2005). Through studying the results of a cultural inventory, students can achieve a better understanding of their peers' cultural responses to conflict. The inventory might ask students to describe how close to them a person could stand without violating their personal space or what they consider a comfortable voice volume to use in class. Other inventory questions could address eye contact, appropriate physical contact, and sensitivity about personal property. Reading "Ann Landers-type" letters can focus discussions on addressing social and relational differences on cultural issues. A classroom addressing diversity must include explicit instruction that places intercultural relations in the forefront of classroom dialogue.

A cultural inventory helps teachers and students build on the strengths each brings to the classroom.

— Video, Scuola Vita Nuova, "First Graders"; Thurgood Marshall MS, "Art-Based Partnership"

Some middle school educators use narrative inquiry as a way to better understand their students' lives and their experiences. The stories the students tell can inform classroom planning that is more culturally relevant and includes students' voices (Lachek, and Gomez, 2011). With a good understanding of students' backgrounds, interests, and learning strengths and weaknesses, the teacher can more effectively plan differentiated units, daily lessons, and formative and summative assessments.

In addition to these strategies for gathering information about students' learning styles and cultural traits and preferences, it is a good idea to explain to students the reason for these inventories. By explaining the idea of multiple learning styles, students might be able to identify times when they have been unsuccessful in their learning or peer relationships and begin to articulate how other strategies might help them learn (Udvari-Solner & Kluth, 2008; Feinberg, 2004). A simple statement such as, "Please say it another way," cues the teacher into rephrasing or using visuals to give the direction. Some students might not want the entire class to become aware of language challenges or processing difficulties. If students write learning requests in a classroom journal that will be read only by the teacher, this

Find videos at www.amle.org/TWBinAction

happens in a safe and nonintrusive manner. Each of these strategies empowers students to advocate for themselves and their learning.

Teaching Approaches

This We Believe (2010) states that successful schools for young adolescents provide a curriculum that is challenging, explorative, integrative, and relevant. That section goes on to describe the kind of curriculum that young adolescents both need and deserve, including using teaching approaches that respond to student diversity (see Chapter 3). Teachers have always used a variety of teaching approaches—direct or whole group instruction, flexible grouping, and cooperative learning to name a few. Each of these approaches can have strengths and weaknesses, depending on the composition of the classroom learning community. A teaching approach or approaches should be selected by first determining the diverse learning needs present in the classroom and which approach will have more likelihood of increasing students' acquisition of skills and knowledge.

Presenting information through both visual and auditory means increases retention of material. The use of advanced organizers, anticipatory sets, or scaffolding (see Combs, 2004) helps students understand and remember more when new ideas or information are connected to prior learning. Connecting learning to real-life situations within multiple contexts makes learning more meaningful and accessible.

> Connecting learning to real-life situations within multiple contexts makes learning more meaningful and accessible.

Using "way in" books that create interest, initiate exploration, and connect to some student backgrounds can increase learning opportunities for young adolescents (Bintz, 2011).

Some underutilized teaching strategies offer possibilities that can tap into individual student learning strengths while responding to classroom diversity and learning challenges. Parallel teaching, station teaching, collaborative teacher-student planning, and the use of balanced literacy are only a few of the many strategies that teachers use to differentiate instruction in a responsive classroom (Tomlinson, McTighe, 2006; Udvari-Solner, Kluth, 2008).

Parallel teaching, where two teachers are teaching essentially the same content at the same time to two different groups, allows teachers to tailor the instruction to a specific group of students. Both groups of students would interact with essential and enduring concepts that are integral to the unit of study. For example, in a lesson on using metaphors and similes, one group of students could be introduced to advanced examples from a variety of texts, with students explaining and recording where the author used them and why. In the other group, visuals along with concrete examples are used with students who are linguistically challenged so these students could come to understand these literary structures without pressure of a text. Both groups could learn about metaphors and similes at their appropriate level of developmental readiness (Tomlinson & Eidson, 2003).

Station teaching allows students to encounter the essential and enduring concepts in a variety of ways. Within a unit about money and economics, "All About Franklin," small groups of students move between various stations where information about the four great ancient river civilizations and their contributions to economic development and the history of money are presented. The students would view videos, see pictures of artifacts, timelines, and read selections with students helping each other at each station. Station teaching allows opportunities for peer interactions and gaining knowledge through a variety of modalities. By learning at stations, students can see their own cultures' contributions. This practice allows the teacher to join groups of students who may need targeted teacher assistance.

Reading fluency and instruction are integrated throughout the curriculum.
— Video, William Thomas MS, "Reading for Fluency"

Collaborative teacher-student planning creates many opportunities to address diversity in the classroom. After students write questions, ideas, issues, or suggestions for resources in classroom journals that are read by teachers, they can share their ideas with their classmates during discussions. If some students are not comfortable making their ideas public, teachers can bring their suggestions to the group for them. Also, teachers can share their unit ideas with students and ask students to generate questions, activities, and even assessment strategies. There are numerous collaborative approaches that ensure all students have opportunities to offer input into the curriculum (Brodhagen, 1995). Diversity in the classroom is addressed when students' questions and ideas are included.

Efforts to improve and promote literacy should be present throughout the curriculum. A balanced literacy program gives students choice in readings connected to any important knowledge or skill being taught, teaches explicit reading strategies, and offers choice in trade books, especially when these books are intended to teach aspects of the larger curriculum. Teachers provide whatever instruction students need on reading and writing skills. Reading logs or journals enable students to answer comprehension questions and make connections to their lives or to other things they have read. Student groupings for reading or book groups change frequently, depending on the purpose for the groups. Occasionally, students who have similar skills might be in the same group; or there might be a need for gender-based groups; or there might even be a group who wants to read a particular author. Decisions like these are made to address the diversity of the classroom and to promote interaction and reflection among students. [Note: See themed issues of *Middle School Journal:* January 2004 "Teachers Speak Out on Creating Literate Young Adolescents" and November 2004 "Reading, Writing, and Poetry, Too."

Question Posing

Using multiple learning and teaching approaches that respond to students' diversity challenges educators to have students "acquire various ways of posing and answering questions . . . participate in decisions about what to study and how best to study the topics selected" (NMSA, 2010, pp. 22-23). To do this, students need an opportunity to ask questions relevant to their lives. Young adolescents might be asked to raise questions related to a teacher-selected theme, or they might be given the opportunity to generate questions for a chapter's focus. Or, the students' questions might become the focus for the curriculum (Brodhagen, 1995; Beane, 1993). Students can also collaborate in inquiry approaches to the curriculum (Wilhelm & Wilhelm, 2010). In each of these approaches, students draw on their background knowledge to pose essential questions to determine what else they need to learn.

The generation of essential questions demands critical thinking and problem solving, both of which are critical to success in the 21st century (Wagner, 2008; Wiggins & McTighe, 2005; Trilling, 2010). Questions should offer opportunities for ongoing debate and inquiry as well as opportunity for transfer from one discipline to another. Examples of two overarching essential questions that offer possibility for transfer might be "Did the Civil War ever really end?" or "What are the implications of a school or community 'going green'?"

Asking students to list or tell what it is they already know using the familiar K-W-L strategy reinforces their view about self as a successful learner, builds upon prior learning, and begins to provide the linkage to new learning that will be integrated into existing personal knowledge and understandings (Boomer, Lester, Onore, & Cook, 1994). This is supported by past and emerging research, which shows positive effects in the areas of mathematics, science, the arts, language arts, and social studies (Marzano, 2003; Cawelti, 1995).

Question posing need not be limited to core content areas. This strategy can be successfully employed in exploratory or encore classes as well. For example, in a French class studying the city of Paris, students collectively listed what they knew about the city and identified essential questions for which they needed answers. Students then determined which research methods to use, and, working in pairs, they found answers to their questions. They then created an all-class trivia game incorporating their work.

When young adolescents are invited to participate in the planning of their own learning, they suggest varied learning activities. They name activities they like and those in which they do well. This includes activities that are visual, auditory, kinesthetic, interpersonal, mathematical, or artistic. Young adolescents are quite skilled at naming a wide variety of activities that can be used to construct learning situations that build upon their learning strengths (Brodhagen, 1995; Storz & Nestor, 2003).

For example, a question raised in one of our student-planned themes was, "Who Am I?" Students' suggestions for activities that might be used to answer that question included (a) creating a life map that highlights events in their lives by either drawing pictures or using photos with captions explaining the events, (b) interviewing a couple of their relatives to recall what the student was like earlier in her or his life, (c) constructing a "trading card" highlighting important life statistics, and (d) completing a family tree including ancestral background. In a different theme, "Outer Space: The Mysteries Above and Beyond," the question "What is our solar system?" generated these suggestions: (a) make a model of our solar system in the classroom, (b) do a research project on all the parts of the solar system, (c) have a guest speaker, (d) visit the university Space Place, and (e) go to Kennedy Space Center.

> Young adolescents are quite skilled at naming a wide variety of activities that can be used to construct learning situations that build upon their learning strengths.

Students were unable to do the last of these, but the point is that the students themselves were able to generate many ideas for varied learning activities.

Projects

When students participate in naming or suggesting activities, they often suggest doing projects. Project-based learning has been a part of the educational scene for nearly a century (Kilpatrick, 1918). Projects are standard in many classrooms but most frequently and appropriately used in classrooms where curriculum integration or multidisciplinary curriculum approaches exist. Projects are authentically integrative as they use knowledge and skills from several disciplines. Projects can provide an enriched learning experience that responds to the needs of a diverse group of learners.

According to Blumenfeld, Soloway, Marx, Krajcik, Guzdial, and Palincsar (1991), there are two essential components of projects: "they require a question or problem that serves to organize and drive activities," and "these activities [must] result in a series of artifacts, or products, that culminates in a final product that addresses the driving question" (p. 370). The question itself can be determined by either the teacher or student, however, the students' freedom to generate artifacts is critical, because it is through this process of generation that students construct their knowledge; the doing and learning are inextricable. Artifacts are representations of the students' problem solutions that reflect their developing knowledge.

> Projects are authentically integrative as they use knowledge and skills from several disciplines

Once again we can see how students' learning styles and strengths and cultural backgrounds would be accommodated by their involvement in creating an artifact. A project plan implicitly or explicitly requires students to state or reflect upon what it is they already know about the question or problem that is the focus of their project. The new information learned builds or is constructed upon students' existing knowledge. Projects create numerous opportunities for differentiation to occur.

The detail and depth of information that a project requires can take several weeks of class time. During this time the young adolescent can sometimes lose focus or become frustrated.

To avoid this, teachers can plan project "pauses" for students to take a break and demonstrate the knowledge they have acquired thus far. For example, students can create an artifact, do a brief presentation of their work, create a trivia or board game, or, acting as teacher, present facts with visual support they have created. Project pauses allow students to reflect and support student motivation to complete their projects, and they allow the teacher to take an interim pulse of students' understanding of the project. Serving as formative assessments, student reflections can be recorded in process logs (Tomlinson & Eidson, 2003). Project pauses allow the teacher to effectively address diverse learning needs throughout the project.

Good projects should provide students opportunities to use multiple, multicultural resources and technology and popular culture that usually increase students' motivation to complete a project. Common experts, people in their personal community who know much about a topic, and school exploratory staff can also serve as resources for specialized knowledge.

Technology is an increasingly useful tool for both students and teachers.
— Video, Warsaw MS, "Differentiated Instruction"; Maranacook Community MS, "Curriculum Development"

Technology is a necessary tool in student- or teacher-designed projects and a tool that addresses young adolescents' learning requirements and preferences (DiBlasi, 2010). Using technology usually increases students' ability to access information. It allows them to get up-to-date facts such as weather and economic status reports; to access a wide range of databases; to correspond more quickly with other adolescents both at home and abroad; and to gain and respond to multiple viewpoints. Word processors and other applied technology allow for corrections and revisions in a less labor-intensive manner, making it especially appealing to students for whom writing does not come easily, or those students who can't physically write.

Projects also provide opportunities for interaction among students as well as between students and teachers. This interaction can be instructional and evaluative, and it can even be considered social. Beane and Lipka (1984) reported three features of schooling in which students said they "felt good about themselves at school." They are "I get to work with my friends," "we have fun," and "the teacher is nice." What young adolescents were talking about is a teacher who lets kids work in pairs, cooperative groups, or as peer tutors; a teacher who has them "do" things, like projects, plays, media productions, and so on; and a teacher who treats them with respect, which includes giving them challenging work (see Bishop & Pflaum, 2005). Fortunately, we now have many teacher accounts that include numerous examples of projects that we can refer to for ideas and guidance. Some of these are *Integrated Studies in the Middle Grades: Dancing Through Walls* (Stevenson & Carr, 1993), *Dissolving Boundaries* (Brazee & Capelluti, 1995), *Beyond Separate Subjects: Integrative Learning at the Middle-Level* (Siu-Runyan & Faircloth, 1995), *Whole Learning in the Middle School: Evolution and Transition* (Pace, 1995), *Learning Through Real-World Problem Solving* (Nagel, 1996), *Watershed: A Successful Voyage Into Integrative Learning* (Springer, 1994), *Soundings: A Democratic and Student-Centered Education*, (2006), and *Democratic Schools* (Apple & Beane, 1995).

Knowledge Performance and Student Reflection

Major learning activities or units should culminate in some kind of knowledge performance and student reflection (Anfara et al., 2003). Knowledge performance should be demonstrated through student-centered action and activity, such as projects, presentations, debate, drama, simulations, creative writing, art work, or use of technology (Beane, 1997). The essential and enduring knowledge or "big ideas" and skills must be apparent within each knowledge performance. When students create wind-up or summary projects, which are meaningful and personal, knowledge endures (Marzano, 2003).

To fairly and accurately assess students' learning within knowledge performance, teachers must consider students' learning strengths, cultural nuances, and other student learning characteristics when constructing and then completing evaluations (Rose, Meyer, & Hitchcock, 2005). In the evaluation process, different-looking projects could receive similar ratings, and because there is not one way to complete a project, each one can and probably will look different. As a result, students with special needs have opportunities to demonstrate their knowledge by employing the skills they do have, rather than failing because of those they do not have.

> Major learning activities or units should culminate in some kind of knowledge performance and student reflection.

To facilitate student reflection, a growing number of teachers have found that learning is enhanced when students participate in interaction and reflection about what is being learned.

In other words, having students talk about their learning can increase their understanding and mastery of new ideas. Whole class discussions serve as a forum for students to explain learning processes and to hear strategies used by others. Partners or triad groups can be used the same way. Journal writing and end-of-week "processing" sessions offer time for reflection about personal and whole-group learning experiences. When individual students are able to express their unique learning in multiple ways, diversity of learning is addressed.

When young adolescents are asked to explain what they have read in literature, to talk through how they have solved a math problem, to draw a web, to explain their position on a social studies issue, or to discuss a final integrating project about an issue or problem, we see them use critical thinking and processing skills, synthesize content, and make evident their meanings. This kind of interaction benefits both the speaker and the listener (McTighe & Wiggins, 2004; Marzano, 2003; Cawelti,1995). Culminating learning experiences that require knowledge performance and student reflection lend themselves well to standards-based assessments and student portfolios and, in turn, become authentic demonstrations of knowledge.

> Culminating learning experiences that require knowledge performance and student reflection lend themselves well to standards-based assessments and student portfolios.

Parents can benefit from students having opportunities to reflect on learning too. Reflection by students can improve at-home conversations when young adolescents actually have an answer to the question "what are you doing in school?" Parents would also observe student learning when invited to end-of-unit presentations, project fairs, and other culminating activities. Like other teachers, we have also found that student-led parent conferences are a powerful way of having students interact about and reflect on their learning. On these occasions, students explain to parents, guardians, or other significant adults what and how they have learned; how they have dealt with problems; how they have demonstrated their learning; and what goals they have set for further learning. These conferences are especially meaningful when they are a part of a comprehensive plan for students to assess their own work.

Professional Development

Student diversity within our schools continues to increase, while the cultural makeup of those who teach remains constant (Banks et al., 2005). Teachers are well intentioned and want all children to learn, but desire alone is not sufficient. Effective professional development supports cultural awareness and instructional approaches that honor and integrate the diversity found in today's classrooms. There are many resources available to help educators to develop and implement equity pedagogy (Banks et al., 2005), which in turn increases the likelihood of success for young adolescents. There is an extensive research base from which to draw; some teaching and learning strategies are better than others and using them effectively can result in improved student learning (Marzano, 2003).

School administrators, school boards, teachers' unions, and the wider community must realize, as was reported by the National Commission on Teaching and America's Future (1996), that good teachers are the most important element of successful learning. One of the best ways to improve student achievement is to continually improve the quality of the teaching staff. This means that teachers need adequate time to master new teaching and learning strategies. An hour in-service presentation is not enough for teachers to implement a new teaching practice. Professional development must be embedded and ongoing where teachers read research and determine whether a strategy can serve the needs of their students. Teachers need to come together to discuss what results or effects call for changes that they should implement in the classroom (Burnaford, Beane, & Brodhagen, 1994). In some districts, groups of teachers are able to meet throughout the year to study their own practice. Teachers might study teaching and learning strategies that respond to a diverse group of learners, curriculum integration, or numerous other topics related to their practice. However professional development is scheduled and organized, a premium should be placed on opportunities for teachers to share experiences and reflect together regarding promising classroom practices. Such collaborative professional development is greatly enhanced by the use of protocols and processes that focus and guide sharing and reflection (Easton, 2009; Larner, 2007; National School Reform Faculty. National Middle School Association has published a number of professional development kits that provide all the materials needed for a school-based, focused professional development experience whether by a team, faculty study group, or an entire faculty.

Conclusion

Five days a week, millions of diverse, rapidly changing young adolescents show up at schools all across the country—and no two of them are alike. This growing diversity places increased demands on all middle level educators. To meet these challenges we must recognize the need to continually learn about and implement multiple learning and teaching approaches that will best serve our diverse student population. By placing diversity in the forefront of our curriculum planning, we will afford all students the quality education they deserve. Our schools mirror our society. By honoring and celebrating the diversity in our classrooms, we are offering our nation's young people the best opportunity to become contributing members of their communities, the nation, and the world.

References

Anfara, V. A., Jr., Andrews, P. G., Hough, D. L., Mertens, S. B., Mizelle, N. B., & White, G. P. (2003). *Research and resources in support of This We Believe*. Westerville, OH: National Middle School Association.

Apple, M. W., & Beane, J. A. (1995). *Democratic schools*. Alexandria, VA: Association for Supervision and Curriculum Development.

Banks, J. A., Cookson, P., Gay, G., Hawley, W., Irvine, J., Nieto, S., et al. (2005). Education and Diversity. *Social Education 69*(1), 36–40.

Beane, J. A. (1993). *A middle school curriculum: From rhetoric to reality* (2nd ed.). Columbus, OH: National Middle School Association.

Beane, J. A. (1997). *Curriculum Integration: Designing the core of democratic education*. New York, NY: Teachers College Press.

Beane, J. A., & Lipka, R. P. (1984). *Self-concept, self-esteem, and the curriculum*. Boston: Allyn and Bacon.

Bintz, W. (2011). "Way In" books encourage exploration in middle grades classrooms. *Middle School Journal, 42*(3), 34–54.

Bishop, P. A., & Pflaum, S. W. (2005). Student perceptions of action, relevance, and pace. *Middle School Journal, 36*(4), 4–12.

Blumenfeld, P., Soloway, E., Marx, R. W., Krajcik, J. S., Guzdial, M., & Palincsar, A. (1991). Motivating project based learning: Sustaining the doing, supporting the learning. *Educational Psychologist, 26*(3 & 4), 369–398.

Boomer, G., Lester, N., Onore, C., & Cook, J. (1994). *Negotiating the curriculum: Educating for the 21st century*. London: Falmer.

Brazee, E. N., & Capelluti, J. (1995). *Dissolving boundaries: Toward an integrative curriculum*. Columbus, OH: National Middle School Association.

Brodhagen, B. L. (1995). The situation made us special. In M. W. Apple & J. A. Beane (Eds.), *Democratic Schools* (pp. 83–100). Alexandria, VA: Association for Supervision and Curriculum Development.

Burnaford, G., Beane, J., & Brodhagen, B. (1994). Teacher action research: Inside an integrative curriculum. *Middle School Journal, 26*(2), 5–13.

CAST. (n.d.) What is universal design for learning? Retrieved from http://www.cast.org/udl/index.html

Cawelti, G. (Ed.). (1995). *Handbook of research on improving student achievement.* Arlington, VA: Educational Research Service.

Combs, D. (2004). A framework for scaffolding content area reading strategies. *Middle School Journal, 36*(2), 13–20.

DiBlasi, H. (2010). Tools for schools: What's new with Web 2.0? *Middle Ground, 13*(3), 8–9.

Dilg, M. (2003). *Thriving in the multicultural classroom: Principles and practices for effective teaching.* New York, NY: Teachers College Press.

Easton, L. (2009). *Protocols for professional learning.* Alexandria, VA: Association for Supervision and Curriculum Development.

Feinberg, C. (2004, July 1). The possible dream: A nation of proficient schoolchildren. *HGSE News: The News Source of the Harvard Graduate School of Education.* Retrieved from www.gsc.harvard.edu/ news/features/ howard07012004.html

Hammond, L. (1997). The Right to Learn. *Social Education, 69*(1), 36–40.

Kilpatrick, W. H. (1918). The project method. *Teachers College Record, 19*, 319–335.

Lachuk, A., & Gomez, M. (2011). Listening carefully to the narratives of young adolescent youth of color. *Middle School Journal, 42*(3), 6–14.

Larner, M. (2007). *Tools for leaders.* New York: Scholastic.

Marzano, R. (2003). *What works in schools: Translating research into action.* Alexandria, VA: Association for Supervision and Curriculum Development.

McTighe, J., & Wiggins, G. (2004). *Understanding by design: Professional development workbook.* Alexandria, VA: Association for Supervision and Curriculum Development.

Nagel, N. G. (1996). *Learning through real-world problem solving.* Thousand Oaks, CA: Corwin.

National Commission on Teaching and America's Future. (1996). *What matters most: Teaching for America's future.* New York, NY: Carnegie Corporation.

National Middle School Association. (2010). *This we believe: Keys to educating young adolescents.* Westerville, OH: Author.

National School Reform Faculty. (n.d.) Protocols. Retrieved from http:www.nsrfharmony.org

Pace, G. (Ed.). (1995). *Whole learning in the middle school: Evolution and transition.* Norwood, MA: Christopher-Gordon.

Rose, D., Meyer, A., & Hitchcock, C. (Eds.). (2005). *The universally designed classroom: Accessible curriculum and digital technologies.* Cambridge, MA: Harvard Education Press.

Siu-Runyan, Y., & Faircloth, C. V. (Eds.). (1995). *Beyond separate subjects: Integrative learning at the middle level.* Norwood, MA: Christopher-Gordon.

Springer, M. (1994). *Watershed: A successful voyage into integrative learning.* Westerville, OH: National Middle School Association.

Springer, M. (2006). *Soundings: A democratic student-centered education.* Westerville, OH: National Middle School Association.

Stevenson, C., & Carr, J. E. (Eds.). (1993). *Integrated studies in the middle grades: Dancing through walls.* New York, NY: Teachers College Press.

Storz, M. G., Nestor, K. R. (2003). Insights into meeting standards from listening to the voices of urban students. *Middle School Journal, 36*(4), 4–12.

Tomlinson, C., & Eidson, C. (2003). *Differentiation in practice.* Alexandria, VA: Association for Supervision and Curriculum Development.

Tomlinson, C., & McTighe, J. (2006). *Integrating differentiated instruction and understanding by design.* Alexandria, VA: Association for Supervision and Curriculum Development.

Trilling, B. (2010). 21st century middle schools: What does success really mean? *Middle Ground, 10*(4), 8–11.

Udvari-Solner, A., & Kluth, P. (2008). *Joyful learning: Active and collaborative learning in inclusive classrooms.* Thousand Oaks, CA: Corwin Press.

Wagner, T. (2008). *The global achievement gap.* New York, NY: Basic Books.

Wehlage, G., Rutter, R., Smith, G., Lesko, N., & Fernandez, R. (1989). *Reducing the risk: Schools as communities of support.* London: Falmer Press.

Wiggins, G., & McTighe, J., (2005). *Understanding by design.* Alexandria, VA: Association for Supervision and Curriculum Development.

Wilhelm, J., & Wilhelm, P. (2010). Inquiring minds learn to read, write, and think: Reaching all learners through inquiry. *Middle School Journal, 41*(5), 39–46.

5

Varied Assessments

Varied and ongoing assessments advance
learning as well as measure it.

Sue C. Thompson & Dan French

∞∞∞∞∞∞∞∞∞∞∞∞∞∞∞∞∞∞∞∞∞∞∞∞∞∞∞∞∞∞∞∞∞∞

This We Believe: Keys to Educating Young Adolescents (National Middle School Association,
2010) urges educators to conduct continuous, authentic, and appropriate assessment and
evaluation measures in order to provide evidence about every student's learning progress.
The position paper states: "Such information helps students, teachers, and family members
select immediate learning goals and plan further education. . . . Grades alone are inadequate
expressions for assessing and reporting student progress on the many goals of middle level
education" (pp. 24-25).

It is important to understand the difference between assessment and evaluation because
the two are distinctly different functions. *This We Believe* (NMSA, 2010) emphasizes that
assessment is the process of estimating a student's progress toward an objective and using
that information to help students continue their learning. On the other hand, evaluation
is the process of using data and standards to judge the quality of progress or level of
achievement. Both assessment and evaluation have a role to play in determining the
academic growth of a student.

The Impact of No Child Left Behind

The advent of No Child Left Behind (NCLB) in 2001 has brought a new dimension to assessment and evaluation in schools. The federal mandate unleashed a flood of testing as the prime means of demonstrating educational accountability. Comprehensive definitions of accountability have been replaced in some states by one single, paper and pencil, on-demand high-stakes test. As educators know, it is impossible to truly understand what a student knows and can do based on information from one single test that inevitably focuses on a very narrow range of student output.

George (2002) stated, "Goals and results in NCLB, it should be noted, are limited to cognitive achievement as measured by standardized tests. Middle level leaders will need to supplement test data with other evidence of student achievement and growth that matches the full range of goals and expectations for young adolescents" (pp. 7-8). High-stakes testing programs in far too many districts and states have resulted in a movement away from the active, engaged learning experiences that truly prepare students for the world in which they live today and the world they will occupy as adults. Lounsbury (2004) further elaborates on this point:

> High-stakes testing programs moved middle schools away from the active, engaged learning experiences that truly prepare students for the world of today—and tomorrow.

> In a concerted effort to prepare students for standardized tests, in state after state the curriculum to be covered is being prescribed. These prescriptions, while seemingly sensible as a way to ensure accountability actually hinder middle level teachers in meeting the intellectual needs of their pupils. Courses of study with aligned and mandated curriculum are most likely to be counterproductive when presented to young adolescents. Teachers who know their students as individuals ought not be hampered unduly in exercising their professional judgment about what, when, and how to teach. In the current climate they are relinquishing much of their judgment and creativity and knuckling under [to] narrowly conceived and highly specific objectives that are purported to yield improved test scores. The best middle school teachers, however, are more nearly artists than technicians. (Lounsbury, 2004, p. xiv-xv)

Kohn (2004), an outspoken critic of standardized testing, points out that our students are being tested to an extent that is unprecedented in our history and unparalleled anywhere else in the world. Norm-referenced tests are not intended to measure the quality of learning or teaching. For educators who have a strong sense of social justice, one of the biggest concerns about standardized tests is that they are biased. "For decades, critics have complained that many standardized tests are unfair because the questions require a set of knowledge and skills more likely to be possessed by children from a privileged background" (p. 57).

In the midst of the testing emphasis, it is encouraging to note that the issue of social equity has managed to gain prominence through the work of organizations such as NMSA and the National Forum to Accelerate Middle-Grades Reform. In 1999 the Forum designed two criteria that specifically address assessment. One criterion states that students may use many and varied approaches to achieve and demonstrate competence and mastery of standards while the other states that the school continually adapt curriculum, instruction, assessment, and scheduling to meet its students' diverse and changing needs. There are two faces of standards in addressing educational equity.

In a society like ours that is stratified by race and income, we must have standards of what all students should know and be able to do upon moving from middle to high school and graduating from high school. The absence of standards virtually guarantees stratified resources and access to knowledge, based upon income, color of skin, and the community or neighborhood in which one lives. (French, 2003, p. 15)

Arhar (2003) took a critical look at the vision of education that is advocated through the *No Child Left Behind Act* (2001) and the vision of middle level education advocated by NMSA's *This We Believe* (1995, 2003), the National Forum to Accelerate Middle- Grades Reform (1994-2003a, 1994-2003b) and *Turning Points 2000* (Jackson & Davis, 2000). "One vision (NCLB) emphasizes accountability through standardized testing and parental choice and the other (National Forum to Accelerate Middle-Grades Reform) emphasizes becoming actively involved in helping children learn" (p. 47). This belief is supported by Pate (2004) who pointed out that appropriate and developmentally responsive assessment is an integral part of middle level education and stated, "Employing a variety of assessment practices will help ensure that teachers capture student learning, for no single method can possibly encapsulate all that students have learned. Assessment in middle schools should be ongoing and include both formative and summative measures" (p. 73).

> Assessment in middle schools should be ongoing and include both formative and summative measures.

Even middle school educators who are sensitive to working with young adolescents and their developmental needs and understand the value of varied assessments are in a state of confusion as a result of the emphasis on standardized test results and the sanctions being imposed on them based on these results. For example, one middle school states that it strives to incorporate the components reported as essential by the Association for Middle Level Education for its organizational structure. The population is divided into small learning communities through the use of interdisciplinary teams. On the other hand, each content area's standards and essential questions are examined and outlined within a curriculum map that is provided to each staff member. This map indicates month by month where teachers should be in their content areas. Teachers conduct common assessments in each content area to ensure that all students are learning the same information. There is no flexibility to deviate from the curriculum maps or the common assessments.

Equally troublesome, there is no representation of other content area teachers on these content-specific committees that develop the curriculum maps or the common assessment instruments. The way team time is used has been determined by the administration, and there is little opportunity or encouragement for members of the team to work collaboratively on interdisciplinary or integrated units. On the one hand, there stands what the school's vision statement says about instructional practice and assessment that will accommodate individual differences, interests, and abilities and staff members' commitment to understanding the uniqueness of each student. In tension with these is the district's expectation for a standardized curriculum and assessment plan. As Beane (2004) reminded us, "If the separate subject curriculum and lecture-worksheet regimen worked, middle level schools would have a very different history" (p. 57).

> Meaningful learning experiences occur through integrated thematic instruction that focuses on the questions, issues, and concerns of young adolescents in relation to their world.

Meaningful learning experiences occur through the complexity of integrated thematic instruction that focuses on the questions, issues, and concerns of young adolescents in relation to their world. Consequently, assessing these kinds of learning experiences should entail a wide range of authentic assessments, including projects where students are actually demonstrating what they know and can do through collaborating, exploring, making, investigating, acting, and being fully engaged in the learning experience. Such projects need not be subject-specific but may use skills and knowledge from several content areas.

Mark Springer, a strong proponent of integrative curriculum who designed a broad, successful integrative program at Radnor Middle School in Wayne, Pennsylvania, says he does not believe testing generally improves education. However, even Springer sees potential for teachers' using it in a positive way. In Paterson (2004), Springer says, "Confident, well-educated, experienced teachers will simply use the tests as yet another measure of performance. These teachers will continue to individualize instruction for their students and will continue to be creative and energetic and captivating. By doing so, they will continue to educate young thinkers who, by extension, will do well on tests" (p. 12).

> Using concepts to organize the curriculum, students can "demonstrate their strengths in a variety of ways so that assessment becomes integral to learning and not merely a post-instruction accountability tool."

Chirichello, Eckel, and Pagliaro (2005) wrote about an engaging, relevant, challenging, and thought-provoking unit on African cultures that is built around concepts. Concepts are big ideas that can be taught in a variety of ways to students who come to us with varied interests and ways of learning (also see Tomlinson, 1998). The authors explain, "Concepts connect topics, and essential questions can move the level of understanding to analysis, synthesis, application, and evaluation" (p. 39). Using concepts to organize the curriculum and standards, students can "demonstrate their strengths in a variety of ways so that assessment becomes integral to learning and not merely a post-instruction accountability tool" (p. 39).

Assessment and evaluation should reflect a curricular delivery model that is, like the curriculum itself, integrative, challenging, exploratory, and promotes learning through providing relevant and meaningful learning experiences for young adolescents.

Staying on the Right Track

While standardized, often high-stakes tests are a part of the landscape of American education, middle school educators who are concerned with meeting the needs of young adolescents must filter the assessment and evaluation processes and products of learning through varied and multiple procedures of assessment. There needs to be a clear distinction between standards and standardization. Standards should not lead to standardization of instruction or assessment. The tension created by high-stakes testing and other facets of standards based reform should not impede teachers' efforts to create relevant, integrated curriculum for young adolescents. This tension can be somewhat resolved when "the standards, concepts, and essential questions within the curriculum are the first sources for ideas about authentic assessment. Teachers and students can brainstorm together, then refine and adapt their ideas to fit the standards" (Jackson & Davis, 2000, p. 59).

National Middle School Association (2010) and the National Forum to Accelerate Middle-Grades Reform (2002) both call for multiple measures to assess students' progress. Authentic assessment practices such as portfolios, exhibitions, performances, and demonstrations provide a complete picture of student learning compared to that allowed by the exclusive use of standardized tests. Both learners and learning are complex. "The work of creating academically challenging, developmentally responsive, and socially equitable middle schools that serve a diverse range of students is much more complex and messy than merely measuring students using a high stakes standardized test" (French, 2003, p. 22).

National Middle School Association published a companion book for *This We Believe*, which provides practitioners with the research and resources that support its recommendations. *Research & Resources in Support of This We Believe* (National Middle School Association, 2010) provides specific citations to back up the association's advocacy of assessment and evaluation that will promote student learning. The book emphasizes that the goal is not to avoid accountability efforts, but to use assessment measures as tools for raising the achievement of students.

Goal Setting and the Empowerment of Young Adolescents

This We Believe . . . And Now We Must Act (Erb, 2001) emphasized the importance of using assessment to actively promote learning and encouraged student participation in all phases of assessment. In that volume, Vars (2001) stated, "Hence it is important to invite students to work with their teachers to make critical decisions at all stages of the learning enterprise, especially goal setting, establishing evaluation criteria, demonstrating learning, self-evaluation, peer evaluation, and reporting" (p. 79).

Williams (2002) shared the story of how she and her students changed their classroom environment from one that was teacher-directed to one that was a collaborative, educational team of learners where all voices were valued. She stated, "By providing different forms of assessment I learned to listen to all of my students more effectively. From reading their journal responses I realized the need to include the students more fully in their education" (p. 59). Through the self-assessments, a dialogue was started in class about learning and how to improve as learners.

Young adolescents need opportunities to reflect upon the work they are producing in order to develop the ability to do so. In the area of cognitive-intellectual development, young adolescents not only display a wide range of individual intellectual development, but they are increasingly able to think abstractly, not just concretely. Scales (2003) reported, "Middle level educators are in a unique position to help build many developmental assets such as feeling empowered and playing useful roles, building social competence, and developing a commitment to learning" (p. 51).

We get the kids very involved in owning responsibility for their test scores. We are very honest with them about what these tests mean.
— Brenda Tolbert, Lanugage Arts Teacher, Chapel Hill MS, "School-Wide Reading"

One way that young adolescents can be empowered is to provide opportunities for them to engage in self-reflection and grow in their ability to self-evaluate and value themselves as learners. As stated by Smith and Myers (2001), "Students need time to reflect on their work, to make connections between and among tasks, and to note improvements along the way. Such personal integration of knowledge is the key to good assessment" (p. 11). Students are able to not just study science or some subject but reflect on their work as scientists, or mathematicians, or historians.

Students may also consider their feelings about the learning tasks with which they are engaged. Good middle school teachers ask students to answer questions that give them opportunities to share work they are proud of, identify what they want to improve on, and evaluate what they gained from the learning activity. Students are learning to become critical consumers of their educational experiences and realize the impact these experiences have on their lives.

Student-Led Conferences
Meet Multiple Goals

Turning Points (Carnegie Council on Adolescent Development, 1989) recommended that middle grades schools "*reengage families in the education of young adolescents* by giving families meaningful roles in school governance, communicating with families about the school program and student's progress, and offering families opportunities to support the learning process at home and at the school" (p. 9). *Turning Points 2000* further advanced this idea and called for middle grades schools that involve parents and communities in supporting student learning and healthy development (Jackson & Davis, 2000, p. 24).

One challenge that middle level educators face is the commonly found declining degree of parent involvement as children progress from elementary to middle school. Student-led conferences are one of the ways to keep parents actively involved as students share important information about their learning. Students take ownership in the process as they select the work to share with the parent or conference attendee. Students come prepared to explain selected papers and may even determine questions they would like the attendee to ask them about their work. (See Berckemeyer and Kinney, 2005, *The What, Why, and How of Student-Led Conferences* and Kinney, Munroe, and Sessions, 2004, *A School-Wide Approach to Student-Led Conferences*.)

The benefits of student-led conferences are manifold and certain.

— Video, William Thomas MS, "Student-Led Conferences

According to Farber (1999), when the students on her middle school team switched from traditional parent-teacher conferences to student-led conferences, "The long-lasting improvement in students' intellectual focus was one of the main benefits of student-led conferences. But teachers point to many other advantages, including less stress, fewer complaints, and better parent attendance on conference day" (p. 21). Dyck (2002) identified these benefits of student-led conferences:

Find videos at www.amle.org/TWBinAction

» Encourage students to accept personal responsibility for their academic performance

» Help students recognize and take ownership for the things that interfered with their learning success

» Teach students the process of self-evaluation

» Develop students' oral communication skills and organizational skills

» Increase students' self-confidence

» Enhance communication between student and parents. (p. 38)

Enhancing communication between student and parents can be one of the most valuable benefits of student-led conferences. Increased conversations at home between children and their parents about schoolwork inevitably follow conferences. Parents and students are living in a fast-paced world, and conversations between them are all too often limited and fleeting and not typically about school. One student on the Alpha Team at Shelburne Community School in Vermont, a multiage group of sixth, seventh, and eighth graders stated, "You know, it's a ton of work and scary at first, but now I think it's kind of fun. You get to talk with your parents for as long as you want and no one interrupts you. We bring snacks because we talk about my work for so long" (Smith & Myers, 2001, p. 14). Technology has come into play with ways to keep home and school working together: Web sites and e-mail provide opportunities for parents, teachers, and students to connect electronically. For the foreseeable future, written reports will continue to be a tool used in communicating with the home and school, but other means are now available and are increasingly being used.

There are many ways students can demonstrate their learning.
— Video, Chapel Hill MS, "Hot Air Balloons," "School-Wide Reading"

Establishing Evaluation Criteria to Demonstrate Learning

"Teachers should specify the criteria for evaluation in advance in the form of a rubric that defines levels of quality" (NMSA, 2003, p. 27). Students should be involved in developing rubrics and should have examples of quality work available. Rubrics provide directions for how to recognize whether the student has reached a certain level of mastery related to skills, knowledge, and dispositions. By making teacher expectations clear, rubrics result in a higher quality of work and enhance student learning. Students are empowered when they can use rubrics to evaluate their own work. Rubrics take the guesswork out of grades. If students have a clear target to aim for, they are more likely to hit it.

There are many ways that students can demonstrate their learning including journals, demonstrations, peer feedback, teacher-designed tests, and audio or video evidence of learning. Portfolios include selections of student work and various artifacts that document students' efforts, progress, and achievements. Not only do portfolios show evidence of growth, they also stimulate a meaningful dialogue between a student and teacher as well as with parents.

One district uses cross-curricular portfolios to support integrated learning. All of the middle school teachers in this district determined the essential skills, knowledge, and dispositions they wanted their students to have acquired by the end of each of the three years in middle school. The work reflected, collectively, the beliefs and mental models the middle school teachers had about curriculum and assessment in the district's middle schools. Four common strands and definitions were identified:

Communication: A piece of student work that demonstrates effective written and oral student expression.

Problem Solving—Critical Thinking: A piece of student work that demonstrates problem solving and critical thinking skills that could originate in any discipline. The skills might include identifying and solving problems, applying perspective, using manipulatives, making connections to real life, understanding one's own learning style, or gathering, processing, and producing data.

Academic Development—Integrated Studies: A piece of student work that reflects the standards for the disciplines represented in middle school and shows the connection between the disciplines. Students demonstrate their ability to use skills and knowledge across disciplines to complete projects, exhibitions, and other assignments.

Personal and Social Awareness: A piece of student work that demonstrates evidence of application to the life skills of appreciation of others, common sense, cooperation, effort, flexibility, goal setting, integrity, patience, respect, sense of humor, leadership experiences, caring, community service, curiosity, empathy, friendship, initiative, moral courage, perseverance, responsibility, and organization and time management.

The standards reflected the teachers' knowledge and understanding of current cognitive research and the needs and characteristics of the young adolescent learner. The strands also indicated that the teachers valued the integrated curriculum delivery model. (Thompson, 2002, pp. 169-170)

The teachers also recognized the difficulties in trying to assess the life skills of the students under the Personal and Social Awareness strand and developed a self-assessment checklist, so students could rate themselves and their growth in this area—another example of student empowerment and valuing student voice.

Conclusion

Middle schools today face tremendous pressures related to assessment and evaluation. These tensions can either be used to create meaningful dialogue about the role and nature of assessment and evaluation in middle schools or can result in schools' simply giving in to pressures. Educators and parents should have opportunities to view students' progress through multiple lens, ones that reflect their growth and development in several dimensions.

In developmentally responsive middle level schools, assessment procedures also reflect the unique characteristics of young adolescents. Assessment should emphasize individual progress rather than comparison with other students and should not rely on extrinsic motivation. The goal is to help students discover and understand their own strengths, weaknesses, interests, and aptitudes. Students' self-assessment helps develop a fair and realistic self-concept. Young adolescents' concern with peer approval is another reason to emphasize individualized assessments rather than comparisons with others. (NMSA, 2010, p. 26)

Schools, however, in expedient attempts to raise test scores, are promoting all kinds of incentive programs, from special treats for those students who do well on tests, to certificates indicating the achievement of certain students to the exclusion of others. Valuable time away from learning is being used for All-School Assemblies—pep rallies—to "pump" students up for testing days. But as Kohn (1993) points out, "Punishment and rewards are not opposite at all; they are two sides of the same coin. And it is a coin that does not buy very much" (p. 50).

The Association for Middle Level Education (AMLE) understands that successful schools for young adolescents are undergirded by an interdependent web of beliefs and characteristics that do not operate independently. When all of the characteristics of This We Believe (2010) are in place and working in concert, the sum is greater than the parts. Every decision made in a successful middle school should support what is in the best interests of students. A broad program of assessment and evaluation, therefore, is a necessary component of a successful middle level school.

Sue Swaim (2005), former executive director of National Middle School Association, now AMLE, has stated well the need to avoid evaluating schools and students on the basis of a test:

> No one argues the importance of accountability in our schools and classrooms, nor does anyone dispute the fact that, when appropriately developed and implemented, tests are important tools for evaluating schools' progress in achieving academic excellence. Today, however, school success is too often defined solely by the results of high-stakes tests. This is a mistake. When considered by themselves, test scores are an inadequate yardstick by which to measure a person's education or a school's success. We must acknowledge the serious limitations of standardized tests in evaluating the adequacy of an individual's education and the competency of a faculty. Middle school accountability must be based on a broader database. (p. 5)

References

Arhar, J. (2003). No Child Left Behind and middle level education: A look at research, policy, and practice. *Middle School Journal, 34*(5), 46–51.

Beane, J. (2004). Creating quality in the middle school curriculum. In S. Thompson (Ed.), *Reforming middle level education: Considerations for policymakers* (pp. 49–63). Greenwich, CT: Information Age.

Berckemeyer, J., & Kinney, P. (2005). *The what, why, and how of student-led conferences.* Westerville, OH: National Middle School Association.

Carnegie Council on Adolescent Development. (1989). *Turning points: Preparing American youth for the 21st century.* New York: Carnegie Corporation.

Chirichello, M., Eckel, J., & Pagliaro, G. (2005). Using concepts and connections to reach students with integrated curriculum. *Middle School Journal, 36*(5), 37–43.

Doda, N. (2004). Creating socially equitable middle grades schools. In N. Doda & S. Thompson (Eds.), *Reforming middle level education: Considerations for policymakers* (pp. 65–84). Greenwich, CT: Information Age.

Dyck, B. (2002). Student-led conferences up close & personal. *Middle Ground, 6*(2), 39–41.

Erb, T. O. (Ed.). (2001). *This we believe . . . And now we must act.* Westerville, OH: National Middle School Association.

Farber, P. (1999). Speak up: Student-led conference is a real conversation piece. *Middle Ground, 2*(4), 21–24.

French, D. (2003). The new vision of authentic assessment to overcome the flaws of high stakes testing. *Middle School Journal, 35*(1), 14–23.

French, D. (2004). The role of accountability in middle level schools. In S. Thompson (Ed.), *Reforming middle level education: Considerationsn for policymakers* (pp. 85–107). Greenwich, CT: Information Age.

George, P. (2002). *No child left behind: Implications for middle level leaders.* Westerville, OH: National Middle School Association.

Jackson, A. W., & Davis, G. A. (2000). *Turning points 2000: Educating adolescents in the 21st century.* New York: Teachers College Press and Westerville, OH: National Middle School Association.

Kinney, P., Munroe, M., & Sessions, P. (2000). *A school-wide approach to student-led conferences.* Westerville, OH: National Middle School Association.

Kohn, A. (1993). *Punished by rewards: The trouble with gold stars, incentive plans, A's, praise, and other bribes.* Boston: Houghton Mifflin.

Kohn, A. (2004). *What does it mean to be well educated?* Boston: Beacon Press.

Lounsbury, J. (2004). Introduction: Policymakers, please think on these "things." In S. Thompson (Ed), *Reforming middle level education: Considerations for Policymakers* (pp. xiii-xvii). Greenwich, CT: Information Age.

National Forum to Accelerate Middle-Grades Reform. (1994-2003b). *Policy on High Stakes Testing.* Retrieved from www.mgforum.org/highstakes/page1.htm

National Forum to Accelerate Middle-Grades Reform. (1998). *Vision Statement.* Retrieved from www.mgforum.org/about/vision.asp

National Forum to Accelerate Middle-Grades Reform. (1999). *Schools to Watch Criteria—Social Equity.* Retrieved from http://www.mgforum.org/improvingschools/STW/STWcriteria.asp

National Forum to Accelerate Middle-Grades Reform. (2002, July). *High Stakes Testing Policy Statement, Issue 3.* Retrieved from http://www.mgforum.org/highstakes/page1.ht

National Middle School Association. (1995). *This we believe: Developmentally responsive middle level schools.* Columbus, OH: Author.

National Middle School Association. (2003). *This we believe: Successful schools for young adolescents.* Westerville, OH: Author.

National Middle School Association. (2010). *Research & resources in support of This We Believe.* Westerville, OH: Author.

Pate, E. (2004). Middle school curriculum, instruction, and assessment through the 1970s, 1980s, and 1990s. *Middle School Journal, 35*(5). 70–74.

Paterson, J. (2004). Looking on the bright side? Considering the positives of increased assessment. *Middle Ground, 7*(3), 10–13.

Scales, P. C. (2003). Characteristics of young adolescents. In National Middle School Association, *This we believe: Successful schools for young adolescents* (pp. 43–51). Westerville, OH: National Middle School Association.

Smith, C., & Myers, C. (2001). Students take center stage in classroom assessment. *Middle Ground, 5*(2), 10–16.

Swaim, S. (2005). Perspective: Time for serious problem solving. *Middle Ground. 8*(4), 5.

Thompson, S. (2002). Reculturing middle schools to use cross-curricular portfolios. In V. Anfara & S. Stacki (Eds.), *Curriculum instruction and Assessment* (pp. 157–179). Greenwich, CT: Information Age Publishing.

Tomlinson, C. A. (1998). For integration and differentiation choose concepts over topics. *Middle School Journal, 30*(2), 3–8.

Vars, G. (2001). Assessment and evaluation that promote learning. In T. O. Erb (Ed.), *This we believe . . . And now we must act* (pp. 78–89). Westerville, OH: National Middle School Association.

Williams, C. (2002). We chose another road: Empowering students. In N. Doda & S. Thompson (Eds.), *Transforming ourselves, transforming schools: Middle school change* (pp. 57–73). Westerville, OH: National Middle School Association.

6

Shared Vision

A shared vision developed by all stakeholders guides every decision.

Sue Swaim

∞∞

How do you begin the journey of implementing a successful middle school? It starts with a vision . . . *a shared vision* developed and implemented under the guidance and nurturing of school leaders in collaboration with all the various stakeholders: students, teachers, parents, administrators, board of education members, central office personnel, and community members. The importance of a shared vision should not be underestimated. Idealistic and uplifting, the vision "reflects the very best we know and lights the way toward achieving a truly successful middle level school. It reveals how research and practice can work in harmony to provide the foundation for building a school in which every student can succeed" (National Middle School Association, 2010, p. 27).

Without a shared vision that is understood and supported by its stakeholders, middle level school improvement efforts will be seriously flawed from the onset and potentially short-lived because "ownership" rests more with a single leader rather than the school community as a whole. Instead, the school community should collaboratively build a strong and enduring vision—one that reflects the very best we can imagine about all the elements of schooling, including student achievement, student-teacher relationships, and community participation. The "heart" of the shared vision must focus on the nature and needs of young adolescent learners. We have learned that when middle school educators implement practices based on their knowledge of learning and human development, students make measurable gains in academic achievement while moving forward in becoming healthy, ethical, and productive citizens.

Developing and Implementing a Shared Vision

In order to develop a shared vision, many districts begin with the formation of a task force. Actually, the development of a school-wide shared vision can also begin with a school-based task force. However, it is important to note that the resulting shared vision and its accompanying mission statement must evolve out of the lives and philosophies of the educators involved, not just out of a committee consensus that is then announced to the larger community for its acceptance.

> A shared vision must evolve out of the lives and philosophies of the educators involved, not just out of a committee consensus.

The task force is usually comprised of representatives from all stakeholder groups who need to work together if schools are to grow and change. The task force process needs to be collaborative to help develop educational partnerships among the stakeholders that are crucial to the long-term success of any school's program. As young adolescent learners have many different learning styles, so do the members of a task force. Therefore, extensive opportunities are provided to enable task force members to build a common knowledge base and philosophy. This involves both individual study and give-and-take dialogue among members of the group.

Fidelity to a school-wide shared vision has ensured that student achievement continues to improve even as students move into the district and new teachers join the staff.

— Chapel Hill MS, "Shared Vision"

In addition to NMSA's (2010) *This We Believe: Keys to Educating Young Adolescents* and *Research & Resources in Support of This We Believe* (2010), consider several other resources as foundational reading. They include *Turning Points 2000: Educating Adolescents in the 21st Century* (Jackson & Davis, 2000), the National Forum to Accelerate Middle-Grades Reform's Vision Statement and Schools to Watch Criteria (1998), and National Association of Secondary School Principals' *Breaking Ranks In the Middle* (2006). Collectively, these documents, based upon research and practice, "speak with one voice" regarding the characteristics of successful middle schools. Additional resources such as Thompson's (2004), *Reforming Middle Level*

Education: Considerations for Policymakers, Doda and Thompson's (2002) *Transforming Ourselves, Transforming Schools: Middle School Change*, and Dickinson's (2001) *Reinventing the Middle School* should be examined. Shared literature study must allow ample discussion time and be a part of the information-gathering and digesting process.

Seeing something in action is also an important part of the process. Visiting schools with strong middle level programs in place is especially valuable. However, before embarking on school visits, it is important to be clear about what the team needs to see. Consider using the 16 characteristics in *This We Believe* (NMSA, 2010) as a framework for the visits. How are these recommended characteristics implemented in the school being visited? Are the characteristics being implemented in concert with one another, or has the school chosen to deal with a few while ignoring others? How does the school's professional development initiative focus on these issues? Are people working together in study groups focused on learning results and analyzing student work with the goal of improving student achievement? These are examples of questions that can be addressed by using *This We Believe* to help guide the visit and follow-up discussions.

> Shared literature study plus ample discussion and answer sessions must be part of the information-gathering and digesting process.

Visitors observe various programs in action and confer with teachers, administrators, parents, and students about what is happening in that school. Team members should include representatives of all stakeholder groups. This enables members to see things from different viewpoints, continue discussions upon return, and be responsive to the constituency each person represents.

Likewise, attending middle level conferences and workshops provides opportunities for people to confer with others in the field and to directly benefit from others' experiences and ideas. It is best for teams of stakeholders to attend these events so several representatives can hear the same message at the same time, ask questions of the presenters, and return to school to continue discussion. These activities give the task force an opportunity to develop a common knowledge and set of questions that must be addressed within its own community to help middle schools become all they should and can be.

The middle level task force reaches out to involve the community during the development process. Members identify key people in the community who have a direct interest in early adolescence such as pediatricians or other health professionals, youth club leaders, social workers, juvenile law enforcement personnel, or religious leaders. As leaders they become resource people in addressing the community's expectations for the middle school, and they can help articulate the vision throughout the community.

Ongoing communication is vitally important. The developmental characteristics of young adolescents, how developmentally appropriate middle schools lead to improved academic achievement, and financial considerations of implementing the middle school concept are among topics that need to be addressed and shared with the community.

Effective schools involve all stakeholders in creating vision, defining mission, and establishing consistent expectations and common language for the learning community.

— Video, Thurgood Marshall MS, "School Climate"; Chapel Hill MS, "Shared Vision"; Warsaw MS, "Common Language"

It is important to have a plan for sharing and disseminating information regarding the mission and resources needed to implement a successful middle school. A variety of formats may be used such as guest speakers at highly publicized public meetings, special briefings for reporters and editors, school district policy sessions, pamphlets disseminated to parents, coffees hosted by principals, and open forums for community input. Teachers, parents, and students should be directly involved in these events, for they are the ones who will implement the shared vision.

Developing and Implementing an Operational Mission Statement

Once the vision for middle level education has been developed and articulated at the district and the school level, each school community needs to create its own mission statement. When the shared vision and mission statement work in concert, they provide the foundation (a) for setting a clear course for school growth and improvement; (b) for supporting and developing the skills, talents, and academic growth of all members of the learning community; and (c) for creating a school organization that supports rather than inhibits teaching and learning.

Find videos at www.amle.org/TWBinAction

While the middle school mission statement takes into account the district's philosophy and goals as well as relevant state guidelines, it should be "personalized" and unique to its own situation. Too often mission statements are quickly developed by relatively few, approved routinely by a faculty, and consequently remain merely rhetoric. All stakeholders must actively participate in the process of formulating a mission statement if it is to guide the school's course.

One of the challenges is developing a mission statement that is succinct while reflecting the top priorities and beliefs of each school. Long, wordy mission statements soon disappear from consciousness, while a succinct mission statement is remembered and used as a guidepost when making specific decisions about programs and practices.

An operational mission statement is revisited as the school community grows and learns through doing and as new research and practices emerge. One responsibility of a school leader is to keep listening to all members of the school's community and regularly ask for input on the school's vision and mission statement.

An operational mission statement constantly raises the question, *Is what we are doing best for our students based on what we know about the human growth and development of youngsters ages 10 to 15?* When contradictory policies coexist, school supporters will be able to effectively advocate for what is best for their school and its students. For example, a middle school comprehensive health committee might question the presence of soda machines in the school as being a direct contradiction to the school's commitment to the health and well-being of its students. The mission statement as a guide for the school's policies, goals, and operational procedures is an important tool for addressing policy inconsistencies.

Without a shared vision and operational mission statement that is understood and supported by all the stakeholders, a sense of aimlessness may prevail and limited harmony may exist. Uninformed and uninvolved people can easily open the door to criticism of the school, especially if a change takes place without adequate understanding or advance communication. Ultimately, the sincere efforts and hard work of those involved can be undermined if a shared vision and mission statement do not exist or are underused.

Communicating the Shared Vision
and Operational Mission Statement

One of the most important aspects of developing and implementing a shared vision and the related mission statement is how to communicate these to the wider audiences who need to hear and understand the message. Three important audiences are (a) elementary and high school staffs, including support personnel; (b) all parents; and (c) the community at large, including its news media, business leaders, civic organizations, and religious leaders. Building understanding and support for your middle school is an ongoing process that does not end once a shared vision and mission statement have been developed. If they are expected to support the school and help sustain its commitment to young adolescents, new middle level parents, teachers, policymakers, community members, and others need to understand the foundational pieces of your middle school's policies and practices. Therefore, developing a planned, ongoing communication program is important. This communication program helps a variety of audiences understand the rationale for middle level education as set forth in *This We Believe: Keys to Educating Young Adolescents* (NMSA, 2010) as well as become familiar with the characteristics of this age group. They need to see how putting the shared vision and mission statement into action will increase student achievement and better meet the developmental needs of 10- to 15-year-olds.

Educating young adolescents is a complex undertaking. National Middle School Association's (2010) *This We Believe: Keys to Educating Young Adolescents* succinctly delineates the multifaceted issues that should be addressed if we are to implement schools that truly focus on the academic growth and well-being of all our students. Implementing the 16 characteristics in harmony with one another, consistently over time, must become our collaborative commitment. The journey starts by developing a shared vision and a related operational mission statement to guide the way.

References

Dickinson, T. S. (Ed.). (2001). *Reinventing the middle school.* New York: RoutledgeFalmer.

Doda, N. M., & Thompson, S. C. (Eds.) (2002). *Transforming ourselves, transforming school: Middle school change.* Westerville, OH: National Middle School Association.

Jackson, A. W., & Davis, G. (2000). *Turning points 2000: Educating adolescents in the 21st century.* New York: Teachers College Press and Westerville, OH: National Middle School Association.

National Association of Secondary School Principals. (2006). *Breaking ranks in the middle.* Reston, VA: Author.

National Forum to Accelerate Middle-Grades Reform. (1998). *Vision Statement.* Retrieved April 11, 2005, from www.mgforum.org/about/ vision.asp

National Forum to Accelerate Middle-Grades Reform. (1994-2003). *Criteria for Schools to Watch.* Retrieved April 11, 2005, from www.mgforum. org/ImprovedSchools/STW/STWCriteria.asp

National Middle School Association. (2010) *This we believe: Keys to educating young adolescents.* Westerville, OH: Author.

Thompson, S. C. (Vol. Ed.). (2004). *Reforming middle level education: Considerations for policymakers.* In V. A. Anfara, Jr. (Series Ed.), *Handbook of Research in Middle Level Education.* Greenwich, CT: Information Age Publishing and Westerville, OH: National Middle School Association.

7

Committed Leaders

Leaders are committed to and knowledgeable about this age group, educational research, and best practices.

Candy Beal & John Arnold

∞∞∞∞∞∞∞∞∞∞∞∞∞∞∞∞∞∞∞∞∞∞∞∞∞∞∞∞∞∞∞∞∞∞∞

Since the inception of No Child Left Behind, when speaking of education, people normally talk abstractly of "raising standards" while giving little thought to the substantial support that would be needed for all students to meet those elevated standards. *All too often, holding high expectations of students comes down to admonitions about raising their test scores on mandatory, statewide tests or improving their behavior, accompanied by strategies for teaching to these tests or firming up discipline.* This simplistic approach is unrealistic and, ultimately, ineffective, given the fact that it ignores the reality that each child is at his or her own place on the learning continuum and brings a wealth of personal experiences to the learning landscape (Dewey, 1916, 1933, 1961, 1968). Moreover, such an approach does not begin to deal with the important aspects of growth and learning and, thus, overlooks a whole host of developmental factors influencing how we teach and how our students learn. In addition, this approach does not encourage an individual's intellectual curiosity, initiative, divergent thinking, risk taking, or the capacity to work with others in a respectful and ethical manner—all critical to preparing our students with the skills and attitudes to be 21st century global citizens (Gardner, 2008). Serving the "standardized testing monster" often relegates teachers to lessons seeking spit-back answers, leaving them short on time to teach for application of those facts. Using an approach that does not differentiate for levels or interests deadens instruction that should be rich with choice and able to show students the connection of their subjects, one to another, as well as how what they are discovering applies to the real world.

Leaders committed to and knowledgeable about young adolescents go far beyond these facile interpretations of holding high expectations. Such leaders see and appeal to the best in young adolescents in all their diversity, making sure that those high expectations are achievable, realistic, and ones that promote ways to help them realize their potential in every realm of development. Further, they extend to the teachers, counselors, administrators, parents, and community members who work to support this development (Garbarino, 1985). This chapter will elaborate on how that looks in real-life schools.

Importance of High Expectations

It is well documented that expectations, relative to students, become self-fulfilling prophecies. As one student commented, "My teacher thought I was smarter than I was . . . so I was." Positive expectations promote positive attitudes and motivation to achieve; negative expectations can result in a student's alienation, discouragement, and lack of effort. In the classic study, *Pygmalion in the Classroom* (Rosenthal, 1968), teachers were assigned groups of students with similar IQs and past school performances. Some teachers were told that their students had high IQs, other teachers were not told this. Students in the "supposed" high IQ groups outperformed the other students by a significant margin. In studies cited by George (1988) and Wheelock (1994), students with the same abilities, when grouped together, tended to regard themselves and their classmates as "dumb" if placed in a "low" group but "smart" if placed in a "high" group. Teachers' curriculum strategies differed markedly depending upon their perceptions of student ability. Clearly, adult expectations have a profound effect upon students' performances and attitudes. Studies cited by Sanders, Field, and Diego (2001) indicated that not only are teachers' and administrators' expectations highly correlative with academic achievement, parents' academic expectations for their children significantly influence academic achievement as well.

> "My teacher thought I was smarter than I was . . . so I was."

The value and importance of positive expectations for young adolescents is magnified because of the negative stereotypes about them present in our society. "Popular wisdom" regards them to be innately full of storm and stress, opposed to adult values, dominated by peer opinion, and disinterested in any intellectual concerns. These characterizations are demonstrably untrue and highly destructive. While early adolescence is a difficult time for some, it is not unduly so for the vast majority. Studies show that young adolescents exhibit no more neurotic behavior than any other age group (Peterson, 1987); they choose friends whose parents' values are consonant with those of their parents (Bandura, 1964), rely on significant adults in making important decisions (Lamb, Ketterlinus, & Fracasso, 1992), and are intellectually curious and alert (Keating, 1990).

> We must be the advocates for the power and promise of young adolescents. If we don't, who will? Who has?

Predominant negative stereotypes are based largely on media images of "in your face" adolescent behavior and psychiatric accounts of disturbed youth. They fail to realize that, while puberty is undeniably a biological phenomenon, "adolescence" as we know it today is, to a great extent, the result of social forces that have increasingly isolated young people from the adult world and have created a youth culture. The starting point for high expectations and developmentally responsive middle schools, then, is ridding ourselves of negative stereotypes about young adolescents and becoming proactive supporters of our youth. We must be the advocates for the power and promise of young adolescents. If we don't, who will? Who has?

Knowledgeable Leaders

Middle grades leaders who are knowledgeable about young adolescents, relevant research, and best practices provide their students with opportunities and support to achieve far more than most of us ever imagine. Three classic examples powerfully illustrate that crucial fact.

> Students in Alan Haskvitz's seventh grade class at Suzanne Middle School, a large Los Angeles County school that is 60% Mexican American, proposed legislation that enables California to save billions of gallons of water annually; persuaded the county sheriff of the need to fingerprint all area children so that runaways and kidnapped children could be traced more easily; and helped the county registrar rewrite voter instructions when they discovered those at the polls were written on a college level of readability.

> In Sam Chattin's seventh grade science classroom in William H. English Middle School, Scottsburg, Indiana, students ran the largest animal refuge shelter in the Midwest. While nursing animals back to health, they studied about living creatures, environmental policies, and a host of other biological issues. They have

shared their work and insights through presentations in ten states and as special guests of the International Animal Rights Convention in Russia.

For more than two decades, seventh and eighth grade students of Erick Mortensen and Larry O'Keefe in the Paradise Project at Edmunds Middle School, Burlington, Vermont, traveled an average of 40,000 miles a year. All details of each trip were planned and carried out by students, and twice yearly they published a literary journal about their learning adventures. Further, they engaged in an "achievement program," learning practical skills and teaching them to one another. To advance to level six of this Boy Scout-type program, one student organized a weekend cleanup of the Lake Champlain waterfront that mobilized some 1,000 citizens, and another student made all arrangements for a month's stay in the school by a blind artist-in-residence. (Arnold, 1990)

It is noteworthy that in all of these examples, students' test scores *skyrocketed*, though test scores had not been the focus of attention. Haskvitz's students' average scores jumped from around the 20th to higher than the 90th percentile; Chattin's students, through special testing by the National Science Foundation, achieved scores in the upper 90th percentiles in knowledge of science information and interest in science; and the Paradise students outperformed non-project students by large margins.

You can do and you can re-do, but you can't "not do"—and that has become a norm.

— Joyce Southern, Counselor, Chapel Hill, MS, "Shared Vision"

More recent examples from three Raleigh, North Carolina, middle schools drive home the fact that "All those who serve as school leaders—whether administrators, teachers, or other staff members—must possess a deep understanding of the young adolescents with whom they work and the society in which they live" (National Middle School Association, 2010, p 28).

Recapturing the history of their school, a formerly all-black high school desegregated in the 1970s, became the mission of students at Ligon Middle School. They tracked down and interviewed graduates, published alumni memoirs, and produced a video of graduate biographies. They also used Geographic Information Systems (www.gis.com) to trace the ongoing development of the black community surrounding the school and built a community Web site to share historical information. Students were empowered by their mission as "keepers of the history" and learned firsthand about life in the Jim Crow era (Alibrandi, Beal, Wilson, & Thompson, 2000; Alibrandi et al., 2001). School leaders used their knowledge of the unique developmental needs of their students to advance their learning and growth.

Knowledge and understanding of research and best practices led middle school leaders in North Carolina to implement a North Carolina State curriculum integration-research project involving 5,000 students. As part of North Carolina's Sixth Grade Goes to Russia, Natalie Bates's social studies students at Dillard Drive Middle School chose their fields of inquiry and formulated "Big (research) Questions" about Russia. Merging individual findings with interview data gleaned from Russian citizens via an interactive project website, they formulated answers to their questions. Bates and her students also planned and hosted a statewide Global Connections Conference for North Carolina students to share their culminating projects—original dances to Russian classical music, handmade matrushka dolls, "Faberge" eggs and balalaikas, scale models of cathedrals, and newly composed folk tales. Research showed that Bates's students showed improved academic achievement, decreased absences, and an increased appreciation of social studies. Of special note were students' journal entries that stated that Bates's belief in their ability to achieve extraordinary results made the difference in their interest and participation levels (Beal, 2002; Beal, Cuper, & Dalton, 2004; Beal & Bates, 2010).

> In Karen Rectanus's seventh grade class at Exploris Middle School in Raleigh, North Carolina, students engage in a service project every Friday. Projects such as: making sandwiches for shelters, cleaning up the environment, planning a pocket park, and teaching lessons on healthy eating to college students enable middle schoolers to practice democratic citizenship. In addition, when revolts occurred in Egypt, Rectanus, her team, and students used a day to simulate the "overthrow" and redevelop the power system at their school. Their Tweets about this activity were picked up by a national news feed and went viral. Students were interviewed by NBC news about what they found out about politics and government in action. "It's hard work, and you have to keep trying to get it right and be fair," was the typical student response. Rectanus's students, and Exploris as a whole, regularly score in the 95th percentile on the North Carolina state tests and are recognized by the state each year as a School of Excellence. Rectanus credits the curriculum integration process used in grades 6–8 for their school's success. The teachers and students use no textbooks (except in math) and teach to themes in this school of great academic, social, and physical diversity. Rectanus describes the learning process as empowering for the students and "messy," but rewarding for the teachers.

As these examples indicate, leadership that's informed by sound educational research and proven best practices can lead to amazing growth and development for young adolescents and their teachers. When you believe in the power and promise of middle schoolers, they, too, believe.

It's not all about test scores, as the citizens of Ireland will attest. Twenty years ago during the era of the Celtic Tiger, dot com companies located in Ireland, and entry level computer jobs were plentiful. Those jobs have since been outsourced to China and India, so Ireland is restructuring its schools to cope with the reality that teaching to the test does not prepare one with the 21st century skills needed to be a major player in the global workplace. Vowing that not one more of Ireland's students will be sacrificed to spit-back learning, Educate Together, an Irish education group with government endorsement, is taking to the junior school level their decades-tested, successful, primary school model that uses curriculum integration as the teaching and learning approach. These researchers and educators believe in their young people. They see them as capable of becoming reflective thinkers and collaborators who use 21st century skills to become intellectually engaged with others around the world. Belief in the power of young adolescents is what will enable Ireland's students to realize their promise.

Effective schools expect and help students develop the range of capacities necessary for responsible citizenship.

— Video, Chapel Hill MS,
"School-Wide Reading," "Physical Fitness"

We all must recognize that no matter what system of education is in place, learning is not just all about academics. From the start, NMSA, as a supporter of young adolescents, has stressed the importance of educating the whole child, focusing on their social, psychological, and moral development as well as their academic growth.

This We Believe: Keys to Educating Young Adolescents (2010) further states that "…it is the middle school principal who has the central role [in developing successful schools], ensuring that policies and practices exist to …nurture, sustain, and advocate for a comprehensive, student-centered education program" (pp. 28–29). Principals must hold high expectations for all their students without having the same expectations for all their students. It should also be noted that an administrator's high expectations, support, and praise for teachers develops a highly motivated faculty with a can-do attitude.

Find videos at www.amle.org/TWBinAction

A Developmentally Responsive Approach

A developmentally responsive approach to teaching and learning necessarily implies one that is differentiated and personalized, taking into account individual needs, interests, and abilities. Such an approach is characterized by

» **Starting where students are, gearing instruction to their levels of development and understanding**. In all middle level classrooms, there will be a diverse group of learners. Some will have limited capacity for complex, abstract reasoning, others will be facile with it, and a majority will be somewhere in between as they transition from concrete to more abstract modes of thinking. To deal with this spectrum, teachers must be keen observers who provide a rich variety of materials, opportunities for hands-on and experiential learning, and tasks that appropriately stretch students toward the next level.

» **Varying degrees of structure**. Some students will need, at least initially, very explicit, straightforward assignments; others can handle choices from a limited menu; and others will be capable of initiating projects on their own. The aim is to help students, when ready, move toward increasing autonomy.

» **A varied pace of learning**. A friend once commented, "In business, we expect employees to do high-quality work but vary the time needed to accomplish it. In education, you seem to vary the quality, but hold time constant." Where learning is self-paced, or the amount of time students have to complete certain assignments is flexible, students are often able to improve the quality of their work considerably (see Bishop & Pflaum, 2005).

> When students are enabled to make decisions and increasingly take control of their own learning, their motivation and achievement flourish.

» **A variety of teaching and learning strategies**. Tomlinson (1999, 2001, 2008) noted that teaching today requires teachers to differentiate their instruction, assignments, and assessment methods. Multiple approaches that involve whole groups, small groups, and individuals are needed to meet the different learning styles and types of intelligences that exist in middle level classrooms. In general, most effective strategies are activity-oriented and inquiry-based (Beane, 1993, 1997, 2005; Bishop & Pflaum, 2005). They include integrative learning, cooperative learning, independent study, peer tutoring, service-learning, apprenticeships, and a host of other approaches.

» **A curriculum that is rich in meaning, one that helps students make sense of themselves and their world.** Among other things, this implies that the content of what is studied deals with substantive issues and values, is related to students' own questions, opens doors to new learning, and is integrative in nature (Bishop & Pflaum, 2005). Studies on alternatives to tracking (Oakes, 1985; Wheelock, 1994; Beane, 1997; Beal, 2002; Beal & Bates, 2010) indicate that a curriculum rich in meaning enhances student performance at all levels.

» **Significant opportunities for students to assume initiative and responsibility with regard to curriculum and school life.** When students are enabled to make decisions and increasingly to take control of their own learning, their motivation and achievement flourish. The common ingredient in the innovative programs described earlier is that students "own" the programs.

Effective principals engage administrators, teachers, parents, and the community at large as they set the tone, promote positive relationships, and keep the focus on student needs, development, and learning. Their influence is critical when building a school program whose hallmark is unconditional belief in the power and promise of middle schoolers.

References

Alibrandi, M., Beal, C., Wilson, A., & Thompson, A. (2000). Reconstructing a school's history using oral histories and GIS mapping. *Social Education, 6*(3), 134–140.

Alibrandi, M., Beal, C., Wilson, A., Thompson, A., Mackie, B., Sinclair, N., et al. (2001). Students reclaim their community's history: Interdisciplinary research with technological applications. In M. Christenson, M. Johnston, & J. Norris (Eds.), *Teaching together: School/university collaboration to improve social studies education* (pp. 61–70). Washington, DC: National Council for the Social Studies.

Arnold, J. (1990). *Visions of teaching and learning: 80 exemplary middle level projects.* Columbus, OH: National Middle School Association.

Arnold, J. (1993). A curriculum to empower young adolescents. *Midpoints Occasional Paper, 4*(1). Columbus, OH: National Middle School Association.

Bandura, A. (1964). The stormy decade. Fact or fiction? *Psychology in the Schools, 1*, 224–231.

Beal, C. (2002). To Russia with technology. *Social Education, 66*(3), 166–172.

Beal, C. & Bates, N. (2010). Crossing digital bridges for global understanding. *Middle School Journal, 41*(5),19–26.

Beal, C., Cuper, P., & Dalton, P. (2004). The Russia research project: Building digital bridges and meeting adolescent needs. *The International Journal of Social Education, 19*(2), 1–18.

Beane, J. A. (1993). *A middle school curriculum from rhetoric to reality.* Columbus, OH: National Middle School Association.

Beane, J. (1997). *Curriculum integration: Designing the core of democratic education.* New York, NY: Teachers College Press.

Beane, J. (2005). *A reason to teach. Creating classrooms of dignity and hope.* Portsmouth, NH: Heinemann.

Bishop, P. A., & Pflaum, S. W. (2005). Student perceptions of action, relevance, and pace. *Middle School Journal, 36*(4), 4–12.

Dewey, J. (1916). *Democracy and education.* New York, NY: Macmillan.

Dewey, J. (1933). *How we think.* Boston, MA: D. C. Heath.

Dewey, J. (1961). *Democracy and education.* New York, NY: Macmillan.

Dewey, J. (1968). *The child and the curriculum, the school and the society.* Chicago, IL: University of Chicago Press.

Gardner, H. (2008). *Five minds for the future.* Boston, MA: Harvard Business Press.

Garbarino, J. (Ed.). (1985). *Adolescent development, an ecological perspective.* Columbus, OH: Charles Merrill.

George. P. S. (1988). Tracking and ability grouping. *Middle School Journal, 20*(1), 21–28.

Keating, D. (1990). Adolescent thinking. In S. S. Feldman & G. I. Elliot (Eds.), *At the threshold: The developing adolescent* (pp. 54–89). Cambridge, MA: Harvard University Press.

Lamb, M., Ketterlinus, L., & Fracasso, M. (1992). Parent-child relationships. In M. Bornstein & M. Lamb (Eds.), *Developmental psychology: An advanced textbook* (pp. 465–518). Hillsdale, NH: Lawrence Erlbaum.

National Middle School Association. (2010). *This we believe: Keys to educating young adolescents.* Westerville, OH: Author.

Oakes, J. (1985). *Keeping track: How schools structure inequality.* New Haven, CT: Yale University Press.

Peterson, A. (1987, September). Those gangly years. *Psychology Today, 21,* 28–34.

Rosenthal, R. (1968). *Pygmalion in the classroom: Teacher expectations and pupils' intellectual development.* New York, NY: Holt, Rinehart, and Winston.

Sanders, C., Field, T., & Diego, M. (2001). Adolescents' academic expectations and achievement. *Adolescence, 36,* 795–802.

Tomlinson, C. (1999). *The differentiated classroom: Responding to the needs of all learners.* Alexandria, VA: Association for Supervision and Curriculum Development.

Tomlinson, C. (2001). *How to differentiate instruction in mixed ability classrooms.* (2nd ed.). Alexandria, VA: Association for Supervision and Curriculum Development.

Tomlinson, C. (2008). *The differentiated school: Making revolutionary changes in teaching and learning.* Alexandria, VA: Association for Supervision and Curriculum Development.

Wheelock, A. (1994). *Alternatives to tracking and ability grouping.* Alexandria, VA: Association for Supervision and Curriculum Development.

8

Courageous & Collaborative Leadership
Leaders demonstrate courage and collaboration.

Patti Kinney & Linda Robinson

∞∞∞

The word courage is derived from the French word coeur, meaning heart. This is fitting for at the very center of every successful school for young adolescents beats the heart of a courageous, collaborative leader. And while "leaders demonstrate courage and collaboration" is but one of the characteristics described in *This We Believe: Keys to Educating Young Adolescents* (NMSA, 2010), it is particularly pivotal as a school weaves together all sixteen characteristics into the tapestry of a high-performing middle school.

Being an effective middle level leader is not for the fainthearted. *Research and Resources in Support of This We Believe* (Caskey et al., 2010) defines courageous leadership "as the ability to 'step outside the box and take chances' to help the school establish appropriate and defensible goals, and collaborative leadership as the ability to include all stakeholders in decision making" (p. 36). To do this, one must be a master juggler with the ability to work with people, solve problems, listen, communicate, organize, laugh at oneself, and be patient—just to name a few essential qualities. It also requires being an instructional leader with the best interests of students at heart; establishing a culture in which teachers, parents, community members, and students work together to turn a shared vision of high expectations into reality; and continually challenging the status quo to bring about school improvement. And all this must occur while simultaneously dealing with the never-ending responsibilities of school management such as budgeting, staff supervision, student discipline, district office requirements, and more.

An effective principal such as Mr. Barillas nurtures a school climate that promotes teamwork, encourages debate, and values democratic participation.

— Video, Thurgood Marshall MS, "School Climate"

Not surprisingly, research continues to support the critical nature of principal leadership in transforming schools. In *Turning Points 2000,* Jackson and Davis (2000) found "One of the most consistent findings in educational research is that high-achieving schools have strong, competent leaders" (p. 156). They further state, "No single individual is more important to initiating and sustaining improvement in middle grades school students' performance than the school principal" (p. 157). These conclusions were confirmed in a study published by the Wallace Foundation (Leithwood, Louis, Anderson, & Wahlstrom, 2004), which reports school leadership is "second only to teaching among school-related factors in its impact on student learning" (p. 3). Their follow-up study (Wallace Foundation, 2010) concludes

> that there are virtually no documented cases of troubled schools being turned around without a powerful leader. One reason is that a good principal is the single most important determinant of whether a school can attract and retain high-quality teachers. The principal is also uniquely positioned to ensure that excellent teaching spreads beyond isolated classrooms in his or her building. The bottom line is that investments in good principals are a particularly cost-effective way to improve teaching and learning. (p. 3)

Given the crucial nature of leadership to the success of a middle school, it is disturbing to note that very few middle level principals have had formal coursework in middle level education (Valentine, Clark, Hackmann, & Petzko, 2002, p. 63) or have received training in shared leadership and decision making (Jackson & Davis, 2000, p. 157). (See also Chapter 1 in this volume for further discussion of this point) So then, what characteristics combine to create a courageous, collaborative leader at the middle level?

Find videos at www.amle.org/TWBinAction

It Begins with a Vision

The road to a successful school for young adolescents begins with a vision. While this vision must be developed, nurtured, and shared with others before it can become a full-fledged reality, it begins in the mind and heart of a school leader who holds a firm conviction that each student is able to achieve a high level of learning. The vision must also be based on a set of sound educational beliefs that speak to the dignity, equality, and uniqueness of the young adolescents served by the school. The leader must be able to clearly articulate these beliefs and demonstrate by both actions and words that he or she holds firm to them. This is not always an easy or comfortable undertaking, as it requires courage to challenge long-held practices that are detrimental to students or to deal with issues or conditions that are out of alignment with the school's vision.

Drawing on this vision to set direction for the school then becomes a significant component of a leader's job; for as Warren Bennis states, "Leadership is the capacity to translate vision into reality." Using the 16 tenets found in *This We Believe: Keys to Educating Young Adolescents* (NMSA, 2010) as guiding principles will help develop a firm foundation for school decision making and help put the vision into action. Yogi Berra once said, "If you don't know where you are going, you will end up somewhere else." A leader who demonstrates courage and collaboration has a vision that makes it clear what is the ultimate destination

A Culture of Collaboration and Shared Decision Making

A school's culture—the way the school does business and how the people in the school interact with one another—is most often a reflection of the school leader's beliefs and actions. In the February 2011, Kappan, authors Louis and Wahlstrom write, "School culture matters. It's a critical element of effective leadership, and there is increasing evidence…that organizations with stronger cultures…are more effective in achieving their goals" (p. 52). They later characterize a weak culture as one that has "a single leader who directs the work of others from a position of authority" (pg. 53). Building a culture of collaborative leadership and shared decision making can be a significant challenge for a school leader. He or she must clearly promote collaboration by both words and actions and understand that school improvement is a joint effort—a single individual simply cannot know what is best for all or do everything that is needed to ensure that each student is successful. In the Learning Leader, Doug Reeves summarizes this well: "Distributed leadership is based on trust, as well as the certain knowledge that no single leader possesses the knowledge, skills, and talent to lead an organization. . ." (2006, p. 28).

Perhaps Helen Keller said it best: "Alone we can do so little; together we can do so much." The nature of leadership has changed significantly over the past few decades, and the traditional role of the principal as the manager of all aspects of the school is no longer acceptable for building and maintaining a successful middle school program. To sustain ongoing and enduring change, a principal must nurture a school culture that fosters teamwork; encourages debate on effective middle level programs, practices, and policies; and values input from all members of the school community, including students. But as written in *Voices of Experience: Perspectives from Successful Middle Level Leaders* (NMSA/NASSP 2010):

> Building the culture necessary to create a shared vision does not happen overnight. The principal must be willing and able to relinquish tight control and genuinely involve the staff in most phases of the school's operation. The belief that a collaborative process, although at times less efficient, is in the best interest of the students and the school supports this sharing. High levels of trust must exist and have been earned by repeated actions and behaviors that reflect the leader's character and leadership style. A realization that the collaborative process takes time—and may even require a reshaping of one's mind-set—must be accepted. (p. 13)

But how then does this happen? The leader must build the leadership capacity of others, empowering them to make decisions and enact changes. The job of today's principal is to ask questions rather than provide answers, to facilitate the process of school improvement rather than prescribe how it should be done, and to collaboratively explore alternatives to ineffective policies and practices rather than dictate the ones that will be used. Only when this culture of collaboration and shared decision making is in place can a school create the shared vision necessary for student success and turn it into a reality.

Just as the role of the principal has evolved into more than manager of school business, the roles and influence of teachers have also grown beyond the classroom. In truly successful schools for young adolescents, teachers are no longer isolated individuals working behind closed doors, but are active leaders in the school learning community. In 2008, Doug Reeves reported the results of a research study that examined the impact of teacher leadership saying, "Teachers not only exert significant influence on the performance of students, but they also influence the performance of other teachers and school leaders" (pg 2). These teacher-leaders participate in spirited discussions within learning communities that reflect on their instructional practices to ensure success for all students. They are involved members of their teams, eagerly seeking ways to make their curriculum integrative, relevant, and challenging for their students; they share instructional strategies to help meet the needs of each student; and they carefully study the results of student assessments

Middle level leaders must possess a deep understanding of the students entrusted to their care.

— Video, Thurgood Marshall MS, "School Climate"; Central MS, "Smart Teachers"; Warsaw MS, "Common Language"

and discuss their finding with their colleagues. As committed members of the school staff, they collectively share their expertise to help the school solve problems, make decisions, and set policy and direction.

It is a memorable experience to visit a school for young adolescents where the leader understands the power of collaboration and has ensured that it has permeated the school culture. A leader who values the voice of the entire school community and has involved them in all aspects of the school has courageously tapped into the power of collaboration and created a school that is far greater than the sum of its parts.

A Passion for Young Adolescents

All leaders at the middle level must possess a deep understanding of the students that have been entrusted to their care. They must recognize students' strengths, appreciate their mercurial nature, and celebrate their uniqueness. They must demonstrate a deep love for their students by being around them, talking with them, and building genuine connections, because middle school students can spot a phony in a minute. Such leaders develop a safe, inviting environment that supports academic growth and personal development, encouraging students to become active members of their school and of their local and global communities. It is this unwavering devotion to the education and well-being of each student in their school that moves a leader beyond *competent* to *exemplary*.

Find videos at www.amle.org/TWBinAction

This passion for middle level students and their needs must also play out in the decisions school leaders make on a daily basis. To effectively keep the best interests of the students at the heart of all decisions, a leader needs a firm foundation in the elements of middle level education such as teaming, student advocacy, and flexible scheduling as well as a sound understanding of pedagogy, curriculum, instruction, and assessment practices as applied to the middle level. This knowledge, combined with a passion for middle level students, creates a school leader who is truly an advocate for young adolescents and can be confident that decisions held up to the standard of "Is it best for all students?" can be answered with a resounding yes.

A leader's zeal for young adolescents must also extend beyond the schoolhouse door. We are past the time when advocacy was an option—it is now an imperative, and school leaders desiring to sustain school improvement must build support for middle level education at all levels. This can start by simply keeping the superintendent and school board informed of research on effective middle level practices; they can be key allies only if they know and understand what one is trying to accomplish at the middle level. Advocacy efforts also need to be directed at other stakeholders—parents, key community members, policymakers, and state and federal officials included in the education process. It takes courage to step forward and be a passionate advocate, but it is a vital component of successful middle level leadership.

> Being a courageous, collaborative leader means putting yourself in the line of fire.

A Role Model for Risk Taking and Reflective Learning

Being a courageous, collaborative leader means putting oneself in the line of fire; for as Albert Schweitzer said, "Example is not the main thing in influencing others. It is the only thing." Your actions will speak much louder than your words and those around you will watch closely to see if you hold true to your convictions. This type of leader recognizes that risks are embedded in the very nature of teaching and learning. Middle school students take a risk every time they ask a question, venture an answer, or attempt a new task. Teachers face a risk every time they walk into the classroom; they do not magically know what they will need to do in order to help a struggling student be successful, and they do not automatically know how to handle every situation that arises during a day.

Leaders often encourage others to try something new, take a chance, or stretch their comfort zone. But is the leader modeling this behavior? Do students and staff see their leaders trying new things or admitting they do not have the solution for every problem that comes their way? Do they see them making mistakes and learning from them? Do their actions send the message that it is okay not to know something, but it is NOT okay to not seek out the answer? A school leader who demonstrates courage and collaboration understands and appreciates that it is the very action of taking the risk, rather than its result, that creates the opportunity for personal growth. And since the very definition of risk implies a chance of harm or loss, the leader must always be prepared to model how best to handle the consequences of a failed endeavor.

School leadership sometimes requires standing strong for effective middle grades practice in the face of conflicting policies.

— Video, Central MS, "Professional Development"

Reflective leaders are risk takers. These leaders are willing to try something new in order to learn something new. They regularly reexamine and challenge their professional practices because they understand that education at its best is ongoing and dynamic, changing and adapting to the needs of the learners. They take charge of their own learning and lead the way in establishing the school as a learning community for both adults and students. As Reeves states, "Reflective leaders take time to think about the lessons learned, record their small wins and setbacks, document conflicts between values and practice, identify the difference between idiosyncratic behavior and long-term pathologies, and notice trends that emerge over time" (2006, p. 49).

A courageous, collaborative leader's modeling of risk taking and reflective learning is a key element in the process of school improvement. At its heart, school improvement is about people improvement—challenging, changing, refining, and strengthening the pedagogy, beliefs, and values of those who work together in a school. An effective leader infuses professional development into the school routine as evidenced by the sharing and discussion of professional articles, the creation of professional learning communities, the exchange of new ideas learned through professional growth offerings, and participation in professional organizations. Additional evidence includes staff members who engage in action research, the constant presence of formal and informal discussions regarding best practices for young adolescents, and most of all, the school's utter commitment to student success.

A leader of this caliber must also serve as a role model for life-long learning. He or she stays abreast of the latest research and trends in the field of middle level education; the information is not kept secret but rather used to spark conversations, challenge ineffective practices and ensure the school is on track in preparing their students for the 21st century. This leader is adept in strategically using current technology not only to improve instruction and enhance learning, but as a tool to facilitate school operations and augment communication. He or she understands that while electronic means are not a replacement for face-to-face communication, Web 2.0 tools such as blogs, wikis, podcasts, videocasts and social networking sites can be effectively used to develop collegial networks; disseminate school information; collect and respond to concerns from members of the school community; build support for school programs and practices; and reinforce advocacy efforts on behalf of the young adolescents served by the school.

Accepting Responsibility for Student Achievement

While at first glance it may seem at odds with a culture of shared decision making, a leader who demonstrates courage and collaboration must assume the ultimate responsibility for the academic growth and well-being of the school and students. There can be no pointing of fingers or pushing the blame on to others. These leaders must be mindful of the sign that President Harry Truman kept on his desk—"The buck stops here."

For the teacher it means accepting full responsibility for the success of students in his or her classroom. Stricken from the vocabulary are statements such as *My students don't want to learn; I teach them, they just don't do the work; My students don't speak English; or If only the parents were more supportive.* While some of these reasons may indeed make the challenge of teaching more difficult, they cannot be used as excuses for students not learning. The effective teacher accepts that he or she is the key to student success and uses formal and informal assessment data to drive planning and instruction, learns all he or she can about the special needs of the population of students in the classroom, seeks out information on up-to-date effective professional practices, and never gives up on students. Most important, he or she realizes that ultimately it is his or her skills and attitude coupled with holding high expectations for each student that make the difference between student success and failure.

The principal must accept an even broader range of responsibility for school success. Just as the teacher is responsible for the growth and development of students within the classroom, so is the principal accountable for the growth and development of the school staff—and this responsibility begins with hiring teachers who are highly effective in working with middle level students. This requires the principal and the interview team to hire teachers who understand the development of young adolescents, who are highly knowledgeable in their content area(s), and who are skilled in the instructional strategies that work best with middle level students. These teachers also need to be committed to their own professional growth and development and be willing to participate as a collaborative, contributing member of both their team and the school. A principal focused on student achievement must also accept the responsibility to ensure that these new teachers are effectively inducted into the school culture through mentorship and professional development. In addition to hiring and developing effective teachers, the leader must also address retention concerns through a systematic plan that provides teachers with the support and nourishment needed for long-term commitment and success.

Accepting responsibility for the instructional leadership of a school is another sign of a courageous, collaborative leader. This role does not require the principal to be an expert in every area of instruction but rather to make certain that the school's teachers have the skills, knowledge, and resources necessary to make effective learning-based decisions. Leaders of this caliber will regularly be found building the capacity of the instructional staff to improve student learning by providing feedback that promotes effective instruction, by analyzing and using data to drive student achievement, and by keeping the school focused on maintaining high expectations for every student.

A story is told of a chicken and a pig discussing the preparation of a special breakfast for the farmer. The chicken suggested bacon and eggs to which the pig replied, "That's easy for you to say. For you, that's only a contribution, for me it's a total commitment!" Many stakeholders in the educational process today contribute to school reform efforts, but it is the total commitment to the education of young adolescents that distinguishes the courageous, collaborative leader.

Getting to the Heart of the Matter

Being a leader in a school for young adolescents is a daunting task; add courageous and collaborative to the description, and the bar is raised even higher. But it can be done. The recipe? Take committed people with organizational skills, add in liberal doses of intelligence and common sense, throw in hard work, mix in a love of young adolescents with a commitment to stay the course, and stir with a passionate heart. Author and speaker Robert Cooper may well have had a middle school leader in mind when he said, "Leadership is doing all you can to have the heart of a lion, the skin of a rhino, and the soul of an angel." Measuring one's self against this standard of leadership may cause one to feel more like the cowardly lion than the king of the jungle, but take heart and begin the journey. There are many, many fine courageous, collaborative leaders found in middle level schools around the world. Some indicators that reveal the presence of such a leader include:

» Interacting consistently and frequently with adults and students both inside and outside the classroom.

» Communicating with parents and the community to inform them of issues pertaining to the education of young adolescents and to keep them involved in school affairs.

» Developing a leadership team focused on school improvement.

» Creating a school governance system that allows input from all stakeholders.

» Articulating a clear vision that drives a well-developed improvement plan that adapts to the shifting needs of the school.

» Using data effectively to tie curriculum, instruction, and assessment to results in student learning.

» Providing ongoing, embedded professional development that increases student success.

» Promoting and modeling best practices for young adolescents.

» Developing the leadership skills of others.

» Employing effective adult learning practices.

» Having a sense of humor that allows one to laugh at oneself —and with others.

» Listening well and knowing when and who to ask for help.

» Keeping a finger on the pulse of the school and having the knowledge and ability to respond accordingly.

But what should an aspiring leader do if a critical look in the mirror indicates one does not quite merit the description of courageous and collaborative? Put your heart into it and take action with the following measures:

» Educate yourself on the middle school concept. Begin with *This We Believe: Keys to Educating Young Adolescents* (NMSA, 2010).

» Find a mentor—someone you can observe, question, and learn from.

» Engage in professional reading. A few suggestions to start with: *Voices of Experience: Perspectives from Successful Middle Level Leaders* (Kinney & Swaim, 2010), *Leadership that Makes a Difference: Revitalizing Middle Schools* (Clark & Clark, 2008), *The Learning Leader* (Reeves, 2006), *The Six Secrets of Change: What the Best Leaders Do to Help Their Organizations Survive and Thrive* (Fullan, 2008).

» Join local, state, and national professional organizations and take advantage of their services.

» Participate in professional development activities—attend workshops, conferences, and classes.

» Visit successful middle level schools.

» Stay current in the field by reading professional journals and recently published resources.

» Admit freely you need to learn more and invite others to join you on the journey.

The human body is comprised of many systems working together in harmony and so is a successful school for young adolescents. The 16 characteristics of effective middle level schools described in *This We Believe: Keys to Educating Young Adolescents* (NMSA, 2010) must not be looked at individually, but rather as an integrated system functioning as a whole. But just as the heart gives life to the body, a leader who demonstrates courage and collaboration gives life to the school. This leader is the heartbeat of the school, and the goal is clear—every middle level school deserves to be led by a courageous, collaborative leader with a heart that beats loud and strong for young adolescents.

References

Caskey, M., Andrews, P.G., Bishop, P., Capraro, R., Roe, M., & Weiss, C. (2010). *Research and resources in support of This We Believe*. Westerville, OH: National Middle School Association.

Clark, S., & Clark, D. (2008). *Leadership that makes a difference: Revitalizing middle schools*. Westerville, OH: National Middle School Association.

Fullan, M. (2008). *The six secrets of change: What the best leaders do to help their organizations survive and thrive*. San Fransisco: Jossey-Bass.

Jackson, A.W., & Davis, G. (2000). *Turning points 2000: Educating adolescents in the 21st century*. New York: Teachers College Press and Westerville, OH: National Middle School Association.

Kinney P., & Swaim, S. (2010). *Voices of experience: Perspectives from successful middle level leaders*. Westerville, OH: National Middle School Association and Reston, VA: National Association of Secondary School Principals.

Leithwood, K., Louis, K., Anderson, S., & Wahlstrom, K. (2004). *How leadership influences student learning*. New York: The Wallace Foundation.

Louis, K., & Wahlstrom, K. (2001). Principals as cultural leaders. *Phi Delta Kappan, 92*(5), 52.

National Middle School Association. (2010). *This we believe: Keys to educating young adolescents*. Westerville, OH: Author.

Reeves, Doug. (2006). *The learning leader: How to focus school improvement for better results*. Alexandria, VA: Association for Supervision and Curriculum Development.

Reeves, Doug. (2008). *Reframing teacher leadership to improve your school*. Alexandria, VA: Association for Supervision and Curriculum Development.

Valentine, J., Clark, D., Hackmann, D., & Petzko, V. (2002). *A national study of leadership in middle level schools*. Reston, VA: National Association of Secondary School Principals.

Wallace Foundation. (2010). *Education leadership: An agenda for school improvement*. Retrieved from www.wallacefoundation.org

9

Professional Development
Ongoing professional development reflects best educational practices.

Candy Beal & John Arnold

∞∞∞

There is much to learn about the tools and strategies that enable us to stay up-to-date about the developmental needs of young adolescents, and we must use them. If we hope to help students fulfill our high expectations, we must also have high expectations for ourselves as learners. The National Staff Development Council (n.d.) recommends that teachers spend 25% of their work time learning and collaborating with colleagues. The 25% may appear high and difficult to achieve in this time of slashed school budgets, a less-is-more mentality, and daily challenges to teams who are trying to stay true to the middle school vision. Perhaps, instead of the percentage of time on task, teachers should focus on the intent of the recommendation: *learning and collaborating with colleagues.*

Using Data

This We Believe: Keys to Educating Young Adolescents (National Middle School Association, 2010) states, "A growing body of research and practice tells us effective professional development programs are those based on data collected about that school and the identified needs of teachers" (p. 30). Types of data include observations and videotapes of teaching practice, teachers' journals, transcriptions of teacher conversations, student work, and student attitudes toward learning—data informing professional development include, but should not be limited to, students' standardized test scores.

Data can improve professional development when used as the focus of workshops or faculty study groups in which educators study student work and analyze the instructional practices used to facilitate that work. Data are also useful for helping to determine professional development resource allocation, content, and delivery. One type of professional development based on data analysis is lesson study. Historically used by the Japanese, lesson study is a model for teacher learning in which teachers take a set of concrete steps over time to improve their teaching.

> Data that informs professional development includes, but should not be limited to, students' standardized test scores.

Lesson study: Using data to improve practice

In lesson study, teachers work collaboratively on a small number of "study lessons." Working on these study lessons involves planning, teaching, observing, and critiquing the lessons. To provide focus and direction to this work, the teachers select an overarching goal and a related research question that they want to explore. This research question then serves to guide their work on all the study lessons.

While working on a study lesson, teachers jointly draw up a detailed plan for the lesson, which one of the teachers uses to teach the lesson in a real classroom as other group members observe the lesson. The group then comes together to discuss their observations of the lesson. Often, the group revises the lesson, and another teacher implements it in a second classroom, while group members again look on. Then the group reconvenes to discuss the observed instruction. Finally, the teachers produce a report of what their study lessons have taught them, particularly with respect to their research question. Teachers refine their practice based on evidence of what works best with their students in their particular teaching situations rather than implementing typical educational research that works in a global sense but may or may not apply to particular circumstances.

The research question that focuses the lesson study is derived by determining the gap between an aspiration for students and students' actual development. An example of a "gap" and its development into a goal is

1. Wanting students to be curious about math—to realize it is inherently interesting and be motivated to learn it in school, from their peers, and in their non-school environment.

2. Noticing students don't seem to care about mathematics. They have no apparent curiosity about numbers or what they could mean. They don't ask questions or really want to discover the answers to questions in class.

3. Facilitating a discussion about the gap with colleagues in a study group.

4. Setting a group goal of developing students who are curious about mathematics and who will engage in mathematics to satisfy their curiosities (Ertle, Chokshi, & Fernandez, 2002).

A somewhat less formal and less involved procedure for examining and learning from student work has taken hold in recent years. While still following exacting protocols, this very professional strategy uses an example from an already-taught lesson rather than one developed specifically for trials and discussion. A teacher presents the materials to teammates for discussion and analysis, usually during common planning time. This strategy uses protocols to ensure productive discussions about the student work or teacher assignment under consideration. *Looking at Student and Teacher Work to Improve Students' Learning* (Association of Illinois Middle-Level Schools, 2005) fully details and discusses this approach. This professional development kit, published by NMSA, contains all the materials needed by a team, a study group, or even an entire faculty to conduct a low-cost, school-based professional development experience.

In the examples the data informs teachers' thinking about engaging students in their learning rather than serving as a "final measure" or grade of students' performance. As Chris Toy pointed out, "Gathering data is more like what a physician would do when examining a patient during a physical rather than pronouncing whether the patient is dead or alive" (personal communication, April 30, 2011). To a degree, teachers have always "studied students' work," if only as they were grading it, but the processes suggested here are a far cry from what typically had been a solitary activity. The models used in the examples value collaboration and draw on the wisdom of colleagues in refining thinking and practice.

The complexity of using data

The use of data to drive professional development can involve complex decision making. For example, Trends in International Mathematics and Science Study (TIMSS) data on math and science achievement might indicate that U.S. math and science teachers need content-related professional development such as graduate courses, summer workshops, or classroom help from content specialists with emphasis on teaching for understanding and for inquiry learning. However, the data might also indicate the need to account for cultural and socioeconomic differences among countries, measuring improvements brought about by interventions, and the provision of meaningful feedback to schools in time to actually guide improvement (National Education Association Foundation for the Improvement of Education, 2003). Using multiple forms of data; verifying accuracy, validity, and reliability; revisiting key questions; and making meaning of the data are all essential parts of the process. Highly skilled, knowledgeable professionals must be the influencers of policies impacting what goes on in classrooms, not corporations or "non-profit arms" of corporations. And to support those who know our children best— those h*ighly skilled, knowledgeable professionals who must influence the policies that impact what goes on in our classrooms*—we must focus on providing timely professional development that they, themselves, have identified as most needed.

> To support those who know our children best, we must focus on providing timely professional development that they themselves have identified as most needed.

Characteristics of Effective Professional Development

In their comprehensive report on professional development, Darling-Hammond, Wei, Andree, Richardson, and Orphanos (2009) showed that effective professional development (a) is intensive, ongoing, and connected to practice; (b) focuses on student learning and addresses the teaching of specific content; (c) aligns with school improvement priorities and goals; and (d) builds strong working relationships among teachers. As Chris Toy said,

> Effective professional development looks and feels a lot like effective classroom practices and curriculum design. I'd even venture to say (although I won't insist) that the model and implementation of ineffective professional development looks an awful lot like stand up and deliver, sit n' git, teacher-centered classroom instruction, and it feels the same to teachers as it does to kids! (personal communication, April 30, 2011)

Effective teaming can greatly assist teachers in their professional growth. Ongoing research at North Carolina State University (NCSU) is examining the role played by teachers' generational differences in determining team success when teams are made up of varying age members. How do personal characteristics and work ethic beliefs that are shaped by growing up in one era or another affect a teacher's attitudes and views, and therefore, a team's dynamics and effectiveness? What role does "teammate fit" play in establishing a supportive teacher work environment, one that is then translated to a positive learning environment for children? Early findings suggest the need for teams to be carefully chosen and, when formulated, helped to examine and discuss views and beliefs about how children learn, how to effectively use a variety of teaching methods, and team expectations for its teacher members—especially with regard to after school activities, daily team meetings, interactions with parents and administrators, and working with middle schoolers.

Teachers must be able to honestly discuss the differences in their backgrounds and beliefs and address how compromises might need to be made for the group to work together effectively. helped to examine and discuss views and beliefs about how children learn, how to effectively use a variety of teaching methods, and team expectations for its teacher members—especially with regard to after school Greater understanding leads to less friction and a more cohesive team in both structure and operation.

Once the team has a better understanding about itself, members can use their collective knowledge and insights about middle schoolers to inform their discussions about learners on their team. The sharing of insights and recommendations to achieve success for every student becomes the team's primary focus. Discussing and assessing students systematically, teams can learn exponentially about adolescents' development, learning styles, backgrounds, and interests; collaborating on curriculum, they can learn new strategies and refine familiar ones that meet student needs. Colleagues who work closely together with the same students have a powerful support system and the opportunity to learn a great deal from one another.

> Discussing and assessing students systematically, teams can learn exponentially about adolescents' development, learning styles, backgrounds, and interests.

It is well known that effective principals are essential to successful schools, doing much to set the tone, promote positive relationships, and keep the focus on student needs, development, and learning. When principals have high expectations of teachers and support them in their efforts, teachers are much more likely to respond to students in a similar manner. Comer (2004) stated the case when he quoted a parent saying, "Teachers don't feel celebrated and rewarded enough. And in some ways, I think that is a reflection of their inability to offer praise, at times, [to children]" (p. 36).

In the same way that teams support each other, educators can form learning communities or study groups to discuss professional readings and workshops or programs focused on specific school improvement practices. Development can also come in the form of local or national conferences, mentors, university courses, and formal or informal web-based offerings.

When teams collaborate on curriculum, they can learn new strategies and refine familiar ones that meet student needs.

Schools Around the World http://cct2.edc.org/saw2000/, with its international database of student math and science work, provides teachers with a basis for meaningful discussions about teaching and learning. Teachers can compare work from their own classrooms to that found on the database to decide if the work meets high standards; the analysis process gives them insight into interventions that could be used for low achievers.

Technology-Related Professional Development

In her book *Teaming Rocks,* Jill Spencer urges educators: "Take charge of your team's own professional development," to avoid the problems with, and then abandonment of, new technological devices deployed by schools without adequate professional development for their integration into instruction. A team visit (in person or virtually) to a school successfully using the technology, Web research, e-mail dialogs, and the study of educational technology blogs are some of her recommendations for continuously upgrading a team's ability to use the power of electronic devices in the classroom.

Middle level educators participating in listservs can easily and quickly share their expertise, clarify their thoughts and feelings about their interactions with their students on a daily basis, and offer support to each other. *(CAUTION: Be extremely careful about what you say about your students or colleagues on any social network site. You never know who will see what you have to say and how your words may be interpreted.)* Topics include whatever middle level educators are interested in on a daily basis: transitioning students into and out of middle school; motivating students; debating acceptance of late work; and sharing links to compelling videos, articles, and educational blogs with thought-provoking content. For example, one middle school math teacher and professor teaching preservice middle grades educators said this of NMSA's listserv, MiddleTalk:

MiddleTalk is the opportunity to bounce ideas and concerns off each other. It is the best professional development, and it can't be any more authentic. We get ideas from all over and share ours. Remember, we learn more from each other than just reading or listening to lectures. Thanks to all of you, we have made a great listserv for the middle grades.

Posted October 27, 2009

Another post reads:

MiddleTalk is an amazing collection of people: colleagues, mentors, coaches, family, and friends. This group fills the void that many of us find in our own professional development or school community. We can ask questions of the group and offer suggestions to those who need help. We can pose hypothetical situations and receive the honest feedback that helps us move our dreams forward to reality. We can take intellectual risks, all with the protection, support, and guidance of the community.

Posted October 28, 2009

Teacher Educators

Up-to-date knowledge about young adolescent development, pedagogy and methodology, curriculum, and school organization is surely important, but this knowledge must be modeled and applied in the educator's own teaching if it is to be effective. And it is critical to inspire aspiring teachers to care deeply about young adolescents and to be advocates for their full development.

> Students academically and socially empowered to make better choices because they understand what is going on in their lives is a recipe for middle grades success.

Data from both focus groups and nationwide surveys indicate that Generation Y educators (those born between 1977 and 1995) want sustained, constructive, and individualized feedback, including peer review, to test instructional strategies and improve practice. And Gen Y, like their predecessors, highly value the opportunity to collaborate and learn from their colleagues (Coggshall, Ott, Behrstock, & Lasagna, p. 14). Research into generations and teaming at NCSU would support the conclusions by Coggshall and associates.

In addition, Gen Ys who have heard praise for their efforts, large and small, throughout their lives find a school culture that does not support collaboration and positive feedback to be one in which they do not choose to stay. It is little wonder that newly minted teachers who come into a traditionally run school and find a "go-it-alone" culture may adopt a "one-and-done" attitude.

Help Yourself, Yourself

Help Yourself, Yourself (HYY) (Beal, Dalton, & Ross, 2003; Beal, 2011), a study begun several years ago at NCSU, takes a novel approach to teacher education. Preservice teachers study child development theories and their application to teaching and learning and are then teamed with practicing classroom teachers knowledgeable about all aspects of adolescent development. Both then work together to teach development theories to middle grades students in hopes that this information will enable the students to make improved academic and social choices. After all, why keep this useful information a mystery from those who need it most—the middle grades students, themselves, who are experiencing the changes of adolescence?

Through discussions, journals, and other methods, all parties discuss questions such as these: Were they more deliberate when a moral issue presented itself? Did they better understand what was going on socially in their lives? Did understanding their style of learning and types of intelligence (Gardner & Boix-Mansilla, 1994) make it easier for them to choose assignments that played to their strengths? Did they stick with difficult problems and concepts long enough to explore their complexities? Were they empowered to make changes at home and school, and did that give them some measure of control in directing their own lives? Did they have the tools to take responsibility for their own learning?

Results from a decade of implementation are extremely positive. Those teachers using HYY have found that the academic work, test scores, and behavior of their students have all improved. This program is successful with all students at all academic ability levels. In addition, HYY is considered by middle grades students to be their favorite self-help program. Teachers, too, found that with improvement in student behavior, their job became much more enjoyable. HYY requires that teachers know development theories so that they can share them with their students. And that's the challenge the program faces; most teachers' last exposure to development theories was in their college courses when many simply learned a list of characteristics, not how the theory worked in application. When teachers know and understand these theories and how they are manifested in the context of a middle school classroom, they are far better able to inform their own teaching practices. Students academically and socially empowered to make better choices because they understand what is going on in their lives is a recipe for middle grades success (Beal, 2011).

Pen Pal Program

When 13 of her 15 preservice teachers indicated they would not teach in urban schools, Dr. Lori Wilfong of Kent State University partnered with Casey Oberhauser, an urban middle school teacher at Maple Heights City Schools in Ohio, to create the Pen Pal Program. Components of the program included preservice teachers exchanging letters with students in a diverse school setting; middle grades students engaging in literacy practice while learning of another culture; and preservice teachers learning theories and practices from coursework with students in a controlled environment.

Through the Pen Pal Project, preservice teachers

» Benefited from the positive role modeling (professional demeanor, obvious kindness and caring for students) of the urban classroom teacher.

» Developed relationships with students from a background unlike their own and discovered from their letter exchanges that the students "were just like them."

» Experimented with questioning students, choosing literature, and creating a line between being an authority figure and being a friend to students.

The program benefited the urban middle grades students. They learned

» Reading doesn't have to be a solitary task, as demonstrated by the friendships they built around sharing a book.

» Ways to form book clubs and reading partnerships.

» Adults other than teachers read and enjoy books outside school.

» Characteristics of successful college students (Wilfong & Oberhauser, 2010).

Learning Through Teaching

Learning through Teaching in a Pedagogical Laboratory [L-TAPL] brings together educational researchers and master teachers, who demonstrate good teaching practices to novice teachers. These novice teachers, in turn, learn and practice teaching in an after-school lab environment "coaching" a select group of urban middle schoolers. The middle grades students' achievement levels rise more than they would from the regular academic school programs alone, thanks to the added instructional time; and novice teachers learn and practice best teaching strategies for children in urban environments. New teachers benefit from observing accomplished teachers in actual classrooms. They can engage in reflection and analysis of the effectiveness of teaching strategies they used when they meet to collaborate with their peers and master teachers. Researchers who study both the labs and the middle grades children in their actual classrooms give feedback to teachers on the engagement of these students in all their lessons and shed light on what practices are working best in the actual classroom situations. Used primarily to raise the achievement levels of African American and Latino middle grades students and, at the same time, train urban teachers, the L-TAPL pedagogical lab model indicates that teachers are eager to learn and apply the lessons from data that is derived from their own practice and their own students' work. Researchers concluded that all types of partnerships formed involving schools, communities, and universities can adopt and benefit from this model (Onafowora, 2008).

We base our whole school on expectations—high expectations for the administration, faculty, staff, clerks, parents, students—high expectations permeate this school

— Bill Foster, Principal, Chapel Hill MS, "High Expectations"

Closing

Holding high expectations for all and translating them into meaningful actions is surely no simple task. It is an ongoing effort that changes and grows as we meet new challenges and have fresh insights. As in all aspects of middle level education, the key to success lies in keeping our eyes on the prize: the growth and development of young adolescents. Stevenson (2002) has poignantly and powerfully reminded us of this potential:

> My middle school teaching experience has left me with immutable optimism about the potential of young adolescent children. Given learning opportunities that truly challenge, the responsibility to exercise meaningful choice, and respect for their ideas and dignity, youngsters are capable of tremendous commitment and dazzling originality. Underneath the confounding, frustrating, often exhausting surface, there lies an indomitable human spirit, capable of the exceptional. (pp. 331–332)

Holding high expectations for professional development for all educators—teachers, principals, assistant principals, athletic directors, curriculum directors, superintendents, and technology personnel—is not an empty exhortation. Disaggregating groups of educators and ensuring they are "walking the talk" about consistently applying best practices for teaching and learning for everyone is the bedrock of our efforts to create schools that truly honor young adolescents, schools that help them to become all that they can be.

References

Association of Illinois Middle-Level Schools. (2005). *Looking at student and teacher work to improve students' learning*. Westerville, OH: National Middle School Association.

Beal, C., Dalton, P., & Ross, M. (2003, November). *Forming a Help Yourself, Yourself (HYY) club: Teaching development theory to your students to help them better understand their own adolescence and take responsibility for their futures*. Paper presented at the annual conference of the National Middle School Association, Atlanta, GA.

Beal, C. (2011, May). *The Help Yourself, Yourself Program. From Re-imagining adolescence: Yes, you can! Yes, we can! Yes, they can!* Invited speaker at Re-imagining Conference, Educate Together, Limerick, Ireland. Retrieved from https://sites.google.com/site/ncreimaging (select Beal, then HYY).

Coggshall, J. C., Ott, A., Behrstock, E., & Lasagna, M. (2011). "Retaining teacher talent: The view from Generation Y." Learning Point Associates and Public Agenda, retrieved from http://www.learningpt.org/expertise/educatorquality/genY/Gen%20Y%20report.pdf

Comer, J. (2004). *Leave no child behind. Preparing today's youth for tomorrow's world*. New Haven, CT: Yale University Press.

Darling-Hammond, L., Wei, R. C., Andree, A., Richardson, N., & Orphanos, S. (2009). *Professional learning in the learning profession: A status report on teacher development in the United States and abroad*. Dallas, TX: National Staff Development Council.

Ertle, B., Chokshi, S., & Fernandez, C. (2002). Lesson Study Research Group. Retrieved from http://www.tc.columbia.edu/lessonstudy/doc/Goal_Selection_Worksheet.pdf

Gardner, H., & Boix-Mansilla, V. (1994). Teaching for understanding—and beyond. *Teachers College Record, 96,* 198–218.

National Education Association Foundation for the Improvement of Education. (2003). Using data about classroom practice and student work to improve professional development for educators. Retrieved from www.nfie.org

National Middle School Association. (2010). *This we believe: Keys to educating young adolescents*. Westerville, OH: Author.

National Staff Development Council. (n.d.). *NSDC resolutions*. Retrieved from http://www.nsdc.org/connect/about/resolutions.cfm

Onafowora, L. (n.d.). Assessing Learning through Teaching in a Pedagogical Laboratory. Retrieved from http://coedpages.uncc.edu/ncare/Preceedings2008/Abstracts/NCARE_2008_Proceedings_Onafowora.htm

Schools Around the World http://cct2.edc.org/saw2000/

Spencer, Jill. (2011). *Teaming rocks!* Westerville, OH: National Middle School Association.

Stevenson, C. (2002). *Teaching ten to fourteen year olds* (3rd ed.). Boston, MA: Pearson Allyn & Bacon.

Wilfong, L. G., & Oberhauser, C. (2010, November). *We have a lot to learn from each other: Preservice teacher and middle school student pen pal project.* National refereed presentation at National Middle School Association Annual Conference, Baltimore, MD.

10

Organizational Structures
Organizational structures foster purposeful learning and meaningful relationships.

Deborah Kasak & Ericka Uskali

ooooooooooooooooooooooooooooooooooooooooooooooooooo

The operative word for middle grades education has long been flexibility. Young adolescent learning needs and characteristics defy rigidity. Successful schools for young adolescents are places that design their practice to reflect an understanding of young adolescent growth and development so that the odds of optimum results are increased. Organizational structures that facilitate learning and nurture relationships have to feature flexible, small learning communities, so the needs of students can be recognized and adjustments made in form and function to maximize learning. The best schools are ever-changing learning organizations that carefully and thoughtfully address academic excellence through developmental responsiveness for all their students (National Forum to Accelerate Middle-Grades Reform, 1998).

The 21st century presents educators with shrinking resources and demands for increased accountability through No Child Left Behind (NCLB). The pressure of meeting adequate yearly progress has schools racing to demonstrate academic progress by satisfactory test scores.. Times dictate tough choices. Regrettably some schools and districts have taken the pathway that dismantles the very organizational structures that have the best chance of building meaningful relationships and improving learning. (Juvonen, Le, Kaganoff, Augustine, & Constant, 2004; American Institute for Research, 2005). *This We Believe: Keys to Educating Young Adolescents* (NMSA, 2010) provides the beacon for making the social context and organization of schooling supportive of high performance.

The hallmark of an effective middle level school rests in its capacity to personalize learning. Small learning communities or learning teams hold remarkable possibilities for student development when teams are high functioning and well implemented. When schools are organized into small learning communities, close relationships between students and adults can be established and more individualized attention given to all learners (Arhar, 1990; Arhar & Kromrey, 1995). Team organizational structure alters and personalizes the working relationships between students and teachers, therefore enhancing the context wherein good instruction can thrive.. Teams, it has been found, have contributed to greater student contact and increased personalization. Teams establish shared responsibility for student learning that reduces the stress of isolation among students and teachers. Finally, teams are the platform for creating greater coordination, collaboration, and integration of learning opportunities (Alexander & George, 1981; Arhar, Johnston, & Markle, 1988, 1989; Carnegie Council on Adolescent Development, 1989; Dickinson & Erb, 1997; Erb & Doda, 1989; Felner et al., 1997; Flowers, Mertens, & Mulhall, 1999, 2000a, 2003; George & Alexander, 2003; George & Oldaker, 1985; Gruhn & Douglass, 1947; Johnston, Markle, & Arhar, 1988).

> Small learning communities or learning teams hold remarkable possibilities for student development when teams are high functioning and well implemented.

Over the past three decades, middle level schools and their teams have experimented with many variations of interdisciplinary team organization. Full and vigorous implementation is the expectation, and yet the level of implementation varies greatly and is a school-by-school reality sometimes even a team-by-team situation. Depending on local fiscal and human resources, all manner of adaptations have been made when it comes to the actual implementation and function of small learning communities. Research does indicate that well established interdisciplinary teams are truly beneficial, so the question becomes, *How do schools implement teams in ways that create high-performing learning communities for their students?*

Team Operation, Tasks, and Needs

What constitutes an effective team? What resources must a team have if it is to improve students' academic outcomes? How can we create effective teams that share a commitment to improving student, team, and school performance? Research-based answers to these questions should guide practice and increase the chances for success.

The work of teaching teams is significant and complex, but well worth the effort. Five characteristics of effective teams have been proposed by one group as:

(a) having a culture of discourse at their center,

(b) having a clearly defined purpose that guides their work and specific measurable goals that they achieve,

(c) being able to define and commit to norms that guide how the team operates,

(d) being disciplined in maintaining their focus, and

(e) communicating effectively within the team and with those outside the team (Center for Collaborative Education, 2001).

Teams in their early stages of implementation focus on coordinating class work, tests, student behaviors, parent contacts, and special team activities. Experienced teams progressively take on tasks that integrate and connect curriculum, concepts, essential questions, and instruction; experiment with blocks of time; develop service learning projects; hold individual student conferences; and plan strategies to increase parental involvement (McQuaide, 1994).

During common planning time teams manage their time well, establish performance goals, and engage in four broad sets of tasks: (a) curriculum coordination; (b) coordination of student assignments, assessments, and feedback; (c) parental contact and involvement; and (d) contact with other building resource staff (Shaw, 1993). Each of the four broad areas of team function is composed of different activities. The depth of team functioning is progressive. Teams cannot do everything at once, but as teams mature in their development and improve the quality of their practice they will perform the multitude of tasks with greater ease and frequency. Even "good functioning" teams cannot accomplish their objectives, tasks, and goals without sufficient time to plan and reasonable conditions within which to operate (Flowers, Mertens, & Mulhall, 2000a, 2000b, 2003; Warren & Muth, 1995).

> Experienced teams progressively take on tasks that integrate and connect curriculum, concepts, essential questions, and instruction.

Conditions to make teaming effective

The presence of certain structural resources makes team effectiveness more likely and supports their contribution to the overall developmental responsiveness of a school. Information first released in 1997 from a longitudinal study of reforming middle level schools in Illinois identifies several necessary conditions for modifying instruction to improve student achievement (Erb & Stevenson, 1999; Felner et al., 1997; Flowers, Mertens, & Mulhall, 1999; 2000a). These studies have identified conditions needed for teams to make optimum changes and improve student performance:

1. **Common planning time in excess of four times per week for an equivalent of 40 or more minutes per day.** This common planning time is in addition to a teacher's individual preparation period. To successfully influence instruction and improve student performance, teams of teachers need sufficient time for team "work" and to accomplish team tasks.

2. **Team sizes of fewer than 120 students with smaller teacher-to- student ratios.** Small communities for learning must be just that—small. Teacher teams of two, three, and four members produce more positive outcomes for students. Homeroom class sizes on the smaller teams (25 or fewer students) increase results and overall team performance.

3. **The length of time a team has been together.** Stable team composition contributes to productivity since teams learn how to improve their performance and function as they improve their teaming practices. Higher order team operations occur when teams move beyond the beginning stages of learning to work together. Stable teams make discussions about instruction and assessment a major activity for team planning. (Flowers, Mertens, & Mulhall, 2000a; Spencer, 2011))

> All high-performing teams, whether in middle schools, business, or athletics, function best where there is time to collaborate, refine practice, reflect, invent, and work together

The evidence for the benefits of collaboration is unmistakable. If teams operate under these conditions, the likelihood of the team's improving instruction and achievement is greatly enhanced. If teams function with less than these threshold conditions, their impact is ultimately diminished. All high-performing teams, whether in middle schools, business, or athletics, function best where there is time to collaborate, refine practice, reflect, invent, and work together. The clear relationship between collegiality and improvements for both teachers and students is evidenced in these ways:

(a) remarkable gains in achievement;

(b) higher quality of solutions to problems;

(c) increased confidence among all school community members;

(d) teachers' ability to support one another's strengths and to accommodate weaknesses;

(e) the ability to examine and test new ideas, methods, and materials;

(f) more systematic assistance to beginning teachers; and

(g) an expanded pool of ideas, materials, and methods

(Little, 1990)

As studies continue to demonstrate that students in schools with teams that have dual planning time outperform students in schools without such planning time (Flowers, Mertens & Mulhall, 2003; Mertens & Flowers, 2003), policymakers and principals must take heed of this now well-established reality.

These are necessary conditions, however, but even in and of themselves, not sufficient. There are schools that provide teams with adequate common planning time, desirable team size, and longevity, yet do not attain high levels of performance. Flexible organizational structures provide the *opportunity* for high performance to occur; but, the structure must be matched with high doses of vision, will, and creativity to make teams perform well.

> Flexible organizational structures provide the opportunity for high performance to occur; but, the structure must be matched with high doses of vision, will, and creativity to make teams perform well.

Common planning time must be used well by every set of teachers in a building, and everyone must be held accountable for results. Just because teams have been created does not mean they perform well. Disappointing results may result when a school adopts the team or house structure and then fails to minimally implement it. In those situations, teams with common planning time are not expected to meet; or if they do meet, there is no organization or agenda to guide their meetings. Time is wasted on excessive conversation about matters that cannot be changed or have been discussed repeatedly with no resolution, or members violate the norms of acceptable team functioning by arriving late, grading papers, or missing the meeting altogether. Such teams, even with the best of organizational structures will under-perform, and the school will not likely meets its goals (Anfara & Lipka, 2003; Roney, Anfara, and Brown, 2008).

Being a member of a great team entails far more and leads to highly satisfying results. In Chicago, during the era of the championship Bulls, a billboard read: *Players Play, Teams Win.* Interdisciplinary teams will make our schools win when they are done well, when they capitalize on opportunities to adjust time and student groupings to meet varied needs. Katzenbach and Smith (1993) described high-performing teams in these words:

> Groups become teams through disciplined action. They shape a common purpose, agree on performance goals, define a common working approach, develop high levels of complementary skills, and hold themselves mutually accountable for results. (p. 45)

To be successful at making the organizational structure serve its ultimate purpose, a school community needs to keep its vision of exemplary middle grades education clearly focused, examine all of its practices to align them with its vision, and hold each and every student and teacher accountable for the attainment of its vision and results.

When implementing flexible organizational structures, the key element is daily designated time to collaborate and work on instructional goals. Common planning time is pivotal. Without it, when in the course of a jam-packed day could teachers find the time to collaborate, engage in conversations about student work, or evaluate the quality of their assignments? Common planning time is the "placeholder." Without it, teachers have fewer chances for success. Of course, there are some schools that attempt to implement organizational structures with less than ideal conditions. Such schools may even report improvements in coordination, but their impact is severely limited. Schools and districts that seek to improve student achievement cannot escape the need to provide sufficient common planning time for teams.

Organizational options abound in successful middle schools. Looping promotes learning at Thurgood Marshall MS; ongoing professional development has strengthened the math department at Central MS; and young adolescents learn their own lessons by tutoring first graders at Scuola Vita Nuova, a K-8 school.

High-performing teams spend two or more days a week in common planning time engaged in curriculum discussion, planning, and professional development. The use of instruments such as a weekly curriculum connections chart and "looking at student and teacher work" protocols add depth and dimension to discussions that may have once focused on misbehaving or challenged students but now focus on important curriculum and instructional issues. Formally looking at student work has proven to be a meaningful exercise.

> Looking at student work is a process. This highly meaningful strategy involves having teachers use their team time to examine a chosen piece of student work, talking about what the piece reveals about the student's learning, understanding, and possibly misconception of a particular skill, item, or assignment. (Association of Illinois Middle- Level Schools, 2005, p. 7)

Although teams may question the value of looking at student and teacher work in a concentrated process, most teachers admit that once tried, they would never return to their old formats for assignment discussions. The benefits are numerous. Gaining a greater understanding of what students know and are able to do, embedding professional development into a daily school schedule, and fostering a sense of community among the staff are just a few of those benefits. Looking at student and teacher work is perhaps the most effective form of professional development available to teachers today. Dennis Sparks (1998), executive director of the National Staff Development Council remarked, "The image of the future would be a group of teachers sitting around a table talking about their students' work, learning and asking, "What do we need to do differently to get the work we would like from kids?" (p. 19).

Many teams are now successfully using "Backward Design" models of curriculum development to focus their interdisciplinary units into more purposeful units of study for their students. These types of protocols and models for the effective use of common planning time directly relate to the quality of student work, a primary priority for having mutual team planning time.

Applying Team Tasks and Needs to Responsive School Structures

When establishing teams, the strengths and distinctive characteristics of the faculty members need to be considered. Some schools have teachers prioritize their strengths and liabilities, do inventories or learning styles ratings, and even ask for confidential feedback as to whom they could effectively work with on a team. Diversity within a teaching team is valued because of the wide array of tasks a team must perform in order to be effective. A good team presents a balanced lineup with good role players held together by their common commitment to the education of their students (Erb & Doda, 1989).

The size of teams varies, ranging from two to five members. The implications of the NCLB definition of "highly qualified" have direct bearing on small teams, those learning environments that best foster relationships, and learning. There is no argument with the fact that middle grades teachers should be highly qualified, but they must be rich in content knowledge *and* skilled at teaching young adolescents. The research has shown that smaller teams get better results; so even with NCLB, schools must encourage dual content preparations to support smaller teams (Flowers, Mertens, & Mulhall, 2000a).

It has been standard to establish teams composed of a teacher from each of the four core subject areas and sometimes a reading teacher. In small schools the composition of teams is then largely pre-determined. Teachers were more comfortable viewing team membership through their "discipline" lens. Before too long, it became common for schools to experiment with smaller teams of two or three members. Why was that? As teachers became adept at teaming and began to recognize the benefits associated with smaller more flexible teams, their view of teaching more than one discipline changed. Curriculum integration, a practice

> Curriculum integration can be more easily accomplished on smaller teams where teachers have wider responsibility for multiple subjects.

that matures with time, can be more easily accomplished on smaller teams where teachers have wider responsibility for multiple subjects. (Alexander, Carr, & McEvoy, 2008; Bishop & Allen-Malley, 2004). Some schools begin with smaller teams at the sixth grade and increase the size of teams toward the exit grade level.

Staff teaching assignments on a team need not be rigidly prescribed. A team of teachers can review the curriculum they are accountable for in a given year and then determine who on the team will teach what topics with an eye on the requirements for highly qualified teachers. Teams may decide to remain with their students for more than one year to optimize student advancement and capitalize on long-term teacher-student relationships. Looping with students builds long-term relationships with students and families as well and strengthens a teacher's knowledge and awareness about the learning needs of individual students.(George & Lounsbury, 2005). Both partner (two person) teams and looping, as already implied, are becoming more common.

In addition, various staff members need to be involved in teaming. Support staff such as special education or gifted teachers are often assigned to work with teams in a collaborative fashion. These staff members, in consultation with the team, decide if a set of students will be pulled out for instruction or whether the special education teacher will co-teach in the increasingly practiced inclusion model. Some schools include a unified arts or exploratory teacher on the teams either for a quarter, semester, or year (see Smith, Pitkin, & Rettig, 1998).

Deciding what and how many teachers are assigned to a team, as well as the relationship of the specialty staff are both done in collaboration with the building leadership team. Once school staffs decide to implement a team structure and provide adequate time and resources for teams to function, they need to provide "up-front" time prior to implementation for initial team development. This often occurs during professional development days or in the summer prior to implementation. Teams normally progress through a series of stages tha may take weeks even months. They begin with deciding on the nuts and bolts of team operation. Team goals are set, roles and responsibilities are identified and assigned, operating procedures are established, and team process needs are addressed. All of these items are agreed upon by team members with the caveat that periodic adjustments may be necessary as each team begins to work. To successfully complete these initial steps, schools may hire a consultant, send staff members to conferences or institutes, engage in school visitations, provide relevant books and examples gathered from other schools, or join forces through a reform network.

> Deciding what and how many teachers are assigned to a team, as well as the relationship of the specialty staff, are both done in collaboration with the building leadership team.

The school also needs to prepare its students and the community for teaming. Clear and concise messages about the benefits of this team or house structure and examples of successful implementation are instrumental in the adoption of this organizational structure. Parents need to be assured that their students will be better served through this structure. As a part of that assurance, visible evidences of the team in action are important Team newsletters, Websites, open houses, sharing of team rules and expectations, team recognitions, and phone calls to parents are ways to provide evidence.. The team organizational structure creates a community of learners that parents as well as students can quickly identify with.

Flexible Use of Time to Enhance Instruction

In flexible organizational structures, teachers can see possibilities for further actions since instructional time is directly under the purview of the team. Since teams have a large block of time with their students, teachers are able to adjust and rearrange the instructional time as they see necessary in order to achieve the team's instructional goals (Hackmann & Valentine, 1998; Noland, 1998; Seed, 1998; Smith, Pitkin, & Rettig, 1998; Ulrich & Yeamen, 1999). The most flexible teams adjust the schedule on a week-by-week or even at times on a day-by-day basis depending on learning needs identified during common planning time. Academic priorities take precedence over regular, rigid period lengths and ringing bells.

But there is no chaos in this flexible arrangement. On the contrary, teachers on the team are attentive to where each student is at a given time and the reason for a student's placement. Since the team's classrooms are located in a designated section of the building and the teachers communicate regularly, even during the day , the students are actually held to a higher level of accountability than in rigid school structures with fixed periods, bells, and passing periods.

Even within an individual teacher's classroom, flexible grouping is the norm rather than the exception. Teachers differentiate instruction through the application of strategies such as collaborative learning, elaborated helping arrangements, progress-based grading, challenge activities, and graphic and learning organizers. The classroom teacher identifies individual learning strengths, needs, and styles then modifies instruction accordingly. Differentiating teaching for a broad range of abilities appears to occur more often as team functioning becomes more proficient. In schools that implement the teaming structure well, teachers and students indicate that they are engaged more often in classroom instructional strategies that are interactive, hands-on, and challenging (Felner et al., 1997). In schools without flexible team structures or ones lacking time for common planning, classroom practices are less likely to be altered, and teachers find it more difficult to implement strategies for heterogeneous classes.

Adequate team work and common planning time not only magnifies a team's operating potential, but also contributes to adoption of desirable teaching strategies. Common planning time within the school day serves as a vehicle for ongoing professional development through team dialogue and problem solving, a natural outgrowth of quality team functioning

(Kain, 1995; Powell & Mills, 1994, 1995). In common planning time teachers share effective teaching strategies and support one another as they learn to expand their teaching repertoires. The learning culture established within high-performing teams includes identifying outcomes for improvements in curriculum, instruction, and assessment.

Organizational Structure Is Critical

The organizational structure a school adopts helps or hinders what can occur in a learning community. The traditional, well-entrenched departmentalized structure   clearly hinders efforts to personalize and differentiate instruction. Savvy leaders work to create the flexible, interdisciplinary team organization as a framework that will give life to a developmentally responsive middle school. The existence of such a team structure is not the end-all and be-all, but structural improvements greatly increase the chances that desired instructional changes will occur. The flexible use of time, staff, space, and instructional grouping sets up relationships whereby students learn and teachers teach in a more responsive, effective manner. Through the skillful guidance of committed teams of teachers acting in the best interests of their students, young adolescents have a better chance for a lifetime of possibilities and successes.

References

Alexander, W. M., & George, P. S. (1981). *The exemplary middle school.* New York, NY: Holt, Rinehart and Winston.

Alexander, W., Carr., & McEvoy, K. (2006). *Student—oriented curriculum: A remarkable journey of discovery.* Westerville,,OH: National Middle School Association.

Anfara, V. A., Jr., & Lipka, R. P. (2003). Relating the middle school concept to student achievement. *Middle School Journal, 35*(1), 24–32.

American Institute for Research. (2005). *Works in progress: Key issues facing middle schools and high schools.* Washington, DC: Author.

Arhar, J. M. (1990). The effects of interdisciplinary teaming on social bonding of middle school students. *Research in Middle Level Education, 14*(1), 1–10.

Arhar, J. M., Johnston, J. H., & Markle, G. C. (1988). The effects of teaming and other collaborative arrangements. *Middle School Journal, 19*(4), 22–25.

Arhar, J. M., Johnston, J. H., & Markle, G. C. (1989). The effects of teaming on students. *Middle School Journal, 20*(3), 24–27.

Arhar, J. M., & Kromrey, J. (1995). Interdisciplinary teaming and demographics of membership: A comparison of students belonging in high SES and low SES middle-level schools. *Research in Middle Level Education, 18*(2), 71–88.

Association of Illinois Middle-Level Schools. (2005). *Looking at student and teacher work to improve students' learning.* Westerville, OH: National Middle School Association.

Bishop, P., & Allen-Maelly, G. (2004). *The power of two: Partner teams in action.* Westerville, OH: National Middle School Association.

Carnegie Council on Adolescent Development. (1989). *Turning points: Preparing American youth for the 21st century.* New York, NY: The Carnegie Corporation.

Center for Collaborative Education. (2001). *Guide to collaborative culture and shared leadership.* Boston, MA: Author.

Dickinson, T., & Erb, T. (1997). *We gain more than we give: Teaming in middle schools.* Columbus, OH: National Middle School Association.

Erb, T. O., & Doda, N. M. (1989). *Team organization: Promise—practices and possibilities.* Washington, DC: National Education Association.

Erb, T. O., & Stevenson, C. (1999). What difference does teaming make? *Middle School Journal, 30*(3), 47–50.

Felner, R. D., Jackson, A. W., Kasak, D., Mulhall, P, Brand, S., & Flowers, N. (1997). The impact of school reform for the middle years: A longitudinal study of a network engaged in Turning Points-based comprehensive school transformation. *Phi Delta Kappan, 78*, 528–532, 541–550.

Flowers, N., Mertens, S. B., & Mulhall, P. F. (1999). The impact of teaming: Five research-based outcomes. *Middle School Journal, 31*(2), 57–60.

Flowers, N., Mertens, S. B., & Mulhall, P. F. (2000a). What makes interdisciplinary teams effective? *Middle School Journal, 31*(4), 53–56.

Flowers, N., Mertens, S. B., & Mulhall, P. F. (2000b). How teaming influences classroom practices. *Middle School Journal, 32*(2), 52–59.

Flowers, N., Mertens, S. B., & Mulhall, P. F. (2003). Lessons learned from more than a decade of middle grades research, *Middle School Journal, 35*(2), 55–59.

George, P. S., & Alexander, W. M. (2003). *The exemplary middle school* (3rd ed.). Belmont, CA: Thomson/ Wadsworth Learning.

George, P., & Lounsbury, J. (2000). *Making big schools feel small: Multiage, looping, and schools within a school.* Westerville, OH: National Middle School Association.

George, P. S., & Oldaker, L. (1985). *Evidence for the middle school.* Columbus, OH: National Middle School Association.

Gruhn, W., & Douglass, H. (1947). *The modern junior high.* New York, NY: Ronald Press.

Hackmann, D. G., & Valentine, J. W. (1998). Designing an effective middle level schedule. *Middle School Journal, 29*(5), 3–13.

Johnston, J. H., Markle, G. C., & Arhar, J. M. (1988). Cooperation, collaboration, and the professional development of teachers. *Middle School Journal, 19*(3), 28–32.

Juvonen, J., Le, V., Kaganoff, T., Augustine, C., & Constant, L. (2004). *Focus on the wonder years: Challenges facing the American middle school.* Arlington, VA: RAND Corporation.

Kain, D. L. (1995). Adding dialogue to a team's agenda. *Middle School Journal, 26*(4), 3–6.

Katzenbach, J. R., & Smith, D. K. (1993). *The wisdom of teams: Creating the high-performance organization.* New York, NY: Harper Business.

Little, J. W. (1990). The persistence of privacy: Autonomy and initiative in teachers' professional relations. *Teachers College Record, 91*(4), 526–27.

McQuaide, J. (1994). Implementation of team planning time. *Research in Middle Level Education, 17*(2), 27–45.

Mertens, S. B., & Flowers, N. (2003). Middle school practices improve student achievement in high poverty schools. *Middle School Journal, 35*(1), 33–43.

National Forum to Accelerate Middle-Grades Reform. (1998). *Vision statement.* Retrieved from www.mgforum.org/about/vision.asp

National Middle School Association (2010). *This we believe: Keys to educating young adolescents.* Westerville, OH: Author.

Noland, F. (1998). Ability grouping plus heterogeneous grouping: Win-win schedules. *Middle School Journal, 29*(5), 14–19.

Powell, R. R., & Mills, R. (1994). Five types of mentoring build knowledge on interdisciplinary teams. *Middle School Journal, 26*(2), 24–30.

Powell, R. R., & Mills, R. (1995). Professional knowledge sharing among interdisciplinary team teachers: A study of intra-team mentoring. *Research in Middle Level Education, 18*(3), 27–40.

Roney, K., Anfara, V., & Brown, K. (2008). *Creating organizationally healthy and effective middle schools.* Westerville: OH: National Middle School Association.

Seed, A. (1998). Free at last: Making the most of the flexible block schedule. *Middle School Journal, 29*(5), 3–13.

Shaw, C. C. (1993). A content analysis of teacher talk during middle school team meetings. *Research in Middle Level Education, 17*(1), 27–45.

Smith, D. G., Pitkin, N. A., & Rettig, M. D. (1998). Flexing the middle school block schedule by adding non-traditional core subjects and teachers to the interdisciplinary team. *Middle School Journal, 29*(5), 22–27.

Sparks, D. (1998). Professional development. *AEA Advocate, 24*(18), 18–21.

Spencer, J. (2011). *Teaming rocks! Collaborate in powerful ways to ensure success.* Westerville:OH: National Middle School Association.

Ullrich, W. J., & Yeamen, J. T. (1999). Using the modified block schedule to create a positive learning environment. *Middle School Journal, 31*(1), 14–20.

Warren, L. L., & Muth, K. D. (1995). Common planning time in middle grades schools and its impact on students and teachers. *Research in Middle Level Education, 18*(3), 41–58.

11

School Environment
The school environment is inviting, safe, inclusive, and supportive of all.

Marion Johnson Payne

cooooooooooooooooooooooooooooooooooooooooooooooooooooo

Successful schools for young adolescents are universally characterized by a culture that is inviting, safe, inclusive, and supportive of all. The social and educational atmosphere, the ambience of a school, can make or break the school program. A positive school atmosphere is rooted in a vision that all stakeholding groups were involved in from its inception.

As schools get larger and as youth spend less time under the supervision of adults in their out-of-school lives, it becomes increasingly important that schools provide a stable atmosphere characterized by positive, long-term relationships. And middle schools have a special responsibility to provide protective custody, or what might be likened to a cocoon, as these vulnerable young people move beyond their limited lives as children and experience the option-oriented and sometimes precarious life of young adolescents. When their school is viewed as a safe haven, students are more willing to ask questions, take risks, and try out unfamiliar things, which their new exploratory nature urges them to do.

What to Look for

Inviting, safe, and supportive buildings give one a sense of warmth. The school decor makes an immediate statement about the caring commitment of its faculty and staff, and the prominently displayed student work attests to the student-centeredness of the school's programs. Attractive and welcoming, the physical plant is alive with visual messages and stimuli reflecting a sense of pride. Students, staff, and even visitors feel that they belong. Their sense of safety and security is strong, as measures are in place to ensure that students and adults are indeed safe and secure. Attendance is typically quite high in such schools.

National Middle School Association (2010) described such an atmosphere in these words:

> The essence of a happy, healthy school is reflected in the talk one hears. Staff members are cordial to each other, teachers and administrators call students by name, and students interact comfortably and respectfully with adults and peers. Statements of encouragement and positive feedback substantially outnumber disciplinary or correctional comments. Interactions among staff members and between students reflect fairness and mutual respect. Teachers, staff, and students learn and put into practice the skills of direct feedback, mediation, healthy and appropriate confrontation, problem solving, positive risk taking, and personal and collaborative goal setting. (p. 33)

Strahan, L'Esperance, and Van Hoose (2009) employed a musical metaphor to depict a school: "A successful school is much like a symphony. As the harmonizing of many parts results in powerful music, so, too, the appropriate blending of many factors in school results in powerful experiences for students" (p. xiii). Having an inviting, supportive, and safe environment is not just desirable, it is a prerequisite for maximizing student achievement. Schools with such environments encourage students and teachers to take risks, to explore, and to create. Consequently, critical thinking is refined, and productivity increases. Students and teachers take pride in the school as problems are identified and solutions are pursued.

> Having an inviting, supportive, and safe environment is not just desirable, it is a prerequisite for maximizing student achievement. Schools with such environments encourage students and teachers to take risks, to explore, and to create.

Lily Hope Wilkinson, an eighth grader at Frank Strong Middle School in Durham-Middlefield, Connecticut, spoke convincingly about the importance of relationships at the 2005 New England League of Middle Schools conference. She said,

> I will never as long as I live forget my experience in middle school. It is the most vital part of any person's development, and I feel personally that . . . Strong Middle School shaped me as a person. It's at middle school where you are first

faced with adult responsibility, and for the first time we form adult relationships outside our family. Whether it is the coach that pushed you to improve your jump shot, the teacher that opened your eyes and made you want to make a difference, or the friend who was always there for you, the relationships made in the middle school have an impact on you forever.

The National Forum to Accelerate Middle-Grades Reform has articulated a vision of academic excellence, developmental responsiveness, and social equity that would lead to high-performing middle level schools' becoming the norm rather than the exception.

The foundation of Central Middle, why we are doing so well, is that the staff members bring a family environment to the school

— James Harrison, Security Guard, Central MS, "Safe Environment"

That vision recognizes the importance of a positive, supportive climate. The Forum believes all students are capable of achieving at high levels. Through its Schools to Watch Program now operating in 19 states, schools that are meeting the nationally recognized criteria are providing models and mentors (see www.schoolstowatch.org).

Determining the Presence of an Inviting, Supportive, and Safe Environment

A successful middle grades school is one that links students, staff, parents, and the community in a variety of ways. All stakeholders are involved in evaluating the environment just as they had been in determining the mission. To evaluate a program, midpoint in the year conduct an informal survey by holding one-on-one conversations or by contacting stakeholders by phone, e-mail, or other means. At year's end, conduct a written survey of a random sample of school and community members to check the current perceptions of various individuals and groups. Evidence of a positive school climate includes

» A high degree of community involvement (parents, volunteers, and community business partners).

» A higher than usual attendance rate.

» Positive attitudes of teachers, students, and parents apparent in informal conversations.

» Expressions indicating pride in the school.

» High degree of participation in school-wide and system-wide activities.

» A positive tenor of media coverage.

» Recognition of high academic expectations for every student.

» Ability to handle and spring back from adversity.

A particularly strong indicator of a school's supportive environment is its handling of adverse situations. A school with a positive climate is able to approach each day and each situation as an opportunity for growth and community building. When faced with the sudden death of a student, for instance, Mount View Middle School in Marriottsville, Maryland, was forced to come together with the community and work through this death. From the onset of the tragedy, the school became a place to gather for comfort, information, planning, discussion, and grieving. Individuals in the community dealt with all aspects of this traumatic experience. Staff members were given released time to either meet with a counselor or take time for themselves. A cadre of parents established a highly comforting presence while not permitting the media to interfere with the safe haven within. One family chartered a bus to provide transportation for any students who wanted to attend the funeral. This unfortunate incident revealed that the positive school climate had depth and was strengthened significantly by people pulling together in a time of need.

Strong leadership that promotes healthy, respectful relationships is the foundation on which a school creates a safe and secure environment.

— Video, Central MS, "Safe Environment"

When determining the prescence of an inviting, supportive, and safe environment, look for five key conditions that indicate a supportive and inviting environment:

» The environment promotes creativity, responsible risk taking, and critical thinking.

» The environment fosters mutual trust and respect.

» Staff and students feel safe at school and in work-related activities.

» Staff, students, and parents report that the learning environment is academically stimulating.

» Students advocate and practice the safe, legal, and responsible use of information and technology.

Find videos at www.amle.org/TWBinAction

Everyone in an inviting school works proactively to eliminate harassment, verbal abuse, bullying, and name calling. Students and teachers understand that they are part of a community where differences are respected and celebrated. A couple of facts highlight the need for a proactive approach:

» The fear of bullying may keep as many as 160,000 students out of school on any given day.

» In a study prepared for the American Psychological Association, 80 percent of middle school students admitted to bullying behavior in the prior 30 days. (Borba, March 3, 2011.)

Successful middle schools make interpersonal communication/conflict resolution and the rights, challenges, and responsibilities of living in a democracy part of their ongoing programs. Important ideas for middle school students to discuss are

» Similarities and differences among people.

» The uniqueness of each individual.

» Understanding and appreciating diversity.

» Prejudice, stereotyping, name calling, misinformation, and rumors.

» Each person's role in creating fair and respectful communities.

The multiple incidents of increased terrorism worldwide and the heightened sensitivity to individual and personal security in the United States have resulted in all schools paying greater attention to safety measures. The presence of uniformed school resource officers or security guards, and even metal detectors at entrances, has become a reality in many places. Uniforms for students, required student and staff picture identification badges, and more sophisticated sign-in and sign-out procedures are ways many schools have responded to the need for a safe environment. Given such conditions, special efforts to maintain a warm, friendly environment became even more critical.

Maintaining an Inviting, Supportive, and Safe Environment

Like the young adolescents themselves, the climate of developmentally responsive middle level schools requires constant nurturing. A positive school climate encourages students' interest in learning, and, ultimately, they become lifelong learners. Likewise, teachers who work in a positive environment feel good about themselves and their work, a condition students readily note. In fact, improving school climate may depend more on the behavior of adults than any other single factor. Change takes time and effort, but it is possible if all adults work together toward a common goal. The law of positive reinforcement makes clear the influence of positive leaders: "In the absence of positive reinforcement from appointed leaders, negative human attitudes and behaviors are most likely to emerge from the group being led" (DeBruyn, 1996, p. 1). Maintaining a positive school climate is, therefore, an ongoing process requiring almost daily reaffirmation from all parties.

In *If You Don't Feed the Teachers, They Eat the Students*, Connors (2000) wrote, "Every day, students from all walks of life arrive at school hoping they will be safe, fed, and assisted in realizing dreams. . . . To ensure that teachers are supportive of all students, we must create professional, safe, secure, and encouraging environments where everyone feels appreciated, listened to, and respected" (p. 12). This is a message school leaders must not miss. The best leaders actively focus on providing a climate in which teachers are encouraged to take risks and willingly serve as coaches, guiding students through the trials and tribulations of early adolescence.

> The best leaders actively focus on providing a climate in which teachers are encouraged to take risks and willingly serve as coaches, guiding students through the trials and tribulations of early adolescence.

Inclusiveness

A positive, student-centered, inclusive, supportive environment grounds a successful urban science magnet school in St. Louis. Formed in response to overcrowding and court-ordered desegregation, Compton-Drew Investigative Learning Center Middle School has a majority (60%) of low-income students, and 12% of its students have disabilities. On average, students in this school performed better in major academic areas in 2000 than students in other magnet schools. Sixth grade students enter the school with the same content and reading scores as sixth graders in the other magnet schools, however, by eighth grade, students in this school outperform other magnet school students in the major content areas. And students with disabilities show similar trends. Students with disabilities are included in regular classroom learning, with appropriate forms of support (Morocco, Clark-Chiarelli, Aguilar, & Brigham, 2002).

Heterogeneous classroom grouping, cooperative peer learning, and teaming are important components of the school. Compton-Drew ILC students are formally grouped in pods that stay together across different subject classrooms and usually have a common task and a common product. Students are expected to help one another answer any question that arises in the group and call on the teacher as a group if they cannot solve an issue on their own. These peer structures are designed to provide academic support for individual students, particularly students with disabilities or other special needs that affect their learning.

Students in this school are members of an investigative learning community, where they explore big scientific and social questions (e.g., What is culture? Why does pollution happen, and what can we do about it?) Invariably, when you walk into a classroom at Compton-Drew ILC, students are engaged in an investigative curriculum unit that spans several or all subject areas … students may be engaged in cross-talk—a formal, student-managed discussion format. They may be using computers to write essays about their learning or working in their pods.

One researcher observed:

> On one particular day, we observe four sixth grade students from one pod sprawled on the hallway floor, just outside their classroom. Two of the students are African American two are Anglo/European, and they have a wide range of learning abilities. One of the students has specific disabilities that affect her reading, writing, information processing, and attention to learning activities. All four are actively participating in preparing for a read-aloud performance of a West African folk tale, "He-Lion." They chose to research West Africa as part of a 12-week World Cultures unit. Each pod in the sixth grade selected a culture and is studying it through reading folk tales, history, and geography. (Morocco, et.al, 2002)

Compton-Drew is organized around three core beliefs. The first is that students can build knowledge through cooperative investigations of rigorous scientific and social questions. The second is that students need to build socially responsible identities in our culturally diverse, global society. The third is that content-rich curricula and instruction are necessary to academic excellence. And *all* students are included.

Transition Programs

Effective middle schools plan and implement effective transition programs in cooperation with elementary and high schools to ensure students successfully integrate into their new schools and maintain their academic and social progress (National Middle School Association, 2010).

Transitioning issues involve safety, curriculum information, and connectedness. Students and parents new to a school want assurance that the students will be able to show up each day and not fear physical or emotional violence, whether it's the extremely rare occasion of a stranger with a weapon or the more likely event of physical intimidation or name calling. And to make a successful transition, students also need to know the more usual concerns of what classes they have to take, where those classes are, what rules are important, what opportunities and activities are available, and where they have to be when.

> The more connected students become to their new school, the better they will do in all the measures that are important in tracking their success: grades, test scores, attendance, and discipline.

The more connected students become to their new school, the better they will do in all the measures that are important in tracking their success: grades, test scores, attendance, and discipline. There is no one transition activity or program that will suffice. Once students start the middle grades, several events and activities over a period of a month are needed to achieve a successful transition. In the years prior to their entering and leaving the middle grades, there are other activities and events that can facilitate transitioning. Schools must look at their students, their staff, and their community for active participation in building a program that ensures successful transitioning into and out of the school.

Most successful transition programs incorporate some or all of the following approaches: student orientation, parent orientation, older student mentoring, brief periods of faculty exchanges, student letter exchanges, peer mediation and conflict resolution programs, and ongoing parent connections.

A Word of Caution

Middle level reform in recent decades has helped to shift schools from being bureaucratic organizations to being communities of learners. Although many middle school classrooms still exist as independent entities operating in isolation from each other, Purkey and Strahan (2002) pointed out that everything in the school really is connected. To illustrate this, they present the Jell-O Principle:

> The school and everybody in it are like one big bowl of Jell-O: if you touch it anywhere, the thing jiggles; everything is connected to everything else. Understanding the Jell-O principle helps the teacher to remember that everything—temperature, time of day, color of walls, how the teacher dresses—adds to or subtracts from positive classroom discipline. No effort to make the school more inviting is wasted. (p. 42)

Thus, school climate and academic mission are inextricably linked. Although middle schools have continued to improve, it is clear that many thousands of young adolescents continue to attend middle schools where the programs and practices do not reflect what is known about exemplary middle level teaching and learning nor what has been advocated by National Middle School Association (now the Association for Middle Level Education) for more than 30 years. Indeed, in "The Status of Programs and Practices in America's Middle Schools: Results from Two National Studies," a report of two national studies of programs and practices in the nation's middle schools conducted in 2009, Kenneth McEwin and Melanie Greene found in comparing highly successful and randomly selected middle schools, that

A school's environment is revealed through its activities, relationships, programs, and decisions.

— Video, Scuola Vita Nuova, "Coffee House"; Warsaw MS, "Common Language"; Thurgood Marshall MS, "School Climate"

» Successful middle schools follow the middle school concept/philosophy more faithfully and implement recommended middle school components (e.g., interdisciplinary teaming, advisory programs, common planning time for core teachers).

Find videos at www.amle.org/TWBinAction

» Middle schools authentically following the middle school concept/philosophy are more likely to be associated with higher scores on achievement tests and other positive student outcomes.

McEwin and Greene concluded that much has been accomplished toward creating developmentally responsive middle level schools. Despite difficulties encountered along the way (e.g., negative political climates, devotion to tradition of some educators and a segment of the public), the middle school concept has survived and remains a valid model for organizing the schooling of young adolescents. But there is a significant gap in many schools between the levels of principal support for recommended middle level components and the actual implementation of those same programs and practices. Standardized testing pressures, opposition from traditionalists, and economic factors might impact the use of developmentally responsive practices (McEwin & Greene, 2010).

> There is a significant gap in many schools between the levels of principal support for recommended middle level components and the actual implementation of those same programs and practices.

Middle grades teachers still rely heavily on direct instruction methods and coverage, less often using strategies such as investigations and cooperative learning groups. The existence of a positive school environment is a prerequisite for achieving such reforms. A personalized school environment strengthens students' commitment to school, enhances their engagement in learning, and paves the way for faculty and staff to move the middle school beyond its organizational successes and tackle the difficult but critical matter of curriculum and instruction. Without the catalyst of an inviting, supportive, and safe environment, organizational changes seldom result in positive curricular and instructional changes.

In Summary

With increased student achievement on tests and accountability as the current educational priorities, establishing and maintaining a positive school climate is crucial. A school's administrators have the major responsibility of creating the desired atmosphere to carry out the school's mission; it cannot be achieved without their active leadership. As many misguided efforts to implement easy but unproven practices are undertaken to meet the requirements of No Child Left Behind, maintaining an emphasis on collaborative problem solving is especially important. Attempts to separate school climate issues from the academic mission are doomed to fail in the long run. Schools that are warm, safe, and positive are environments in which young adolescents have the opportunity to succeed in all aspects of their education.

References

Borba, M. (2011, March). When your child is bullied and bullying intensifies. Retrieved from http://www. micheleborba.com/blog/2011/03/03/what-to-do-when-bullying-wont-stop-or-intensifies/

Campbell, M. B., & Jacobson, M. (2008). From survive to thrive: The importance of transition. *Middle Ground, 11*(3), 10–12.

Collins, J. (2001). *Good to great.* New York, NY: HarperCollins.

Connors, N. (2000). *If you don't feed the teachers they eat the students.* Nashville, TN: Incentive.

DeBruyn, R. L. (1996). *Why administrative assistance and positive reinforcement are necessary on a weekly basis for teachers.* Manhattan, KS: The Master Teacher.

Jackson, A. W., & Davis, G. (2000). *Turning points 2000: Educating adolescents in the 21st century.* New York, NY & Westerville, OH: Teachers College Press & National Middle School Association.

McEwin, C. K., & Greene, M. W. (2010). Results and recommendations from the national surveys of randomly selected and highly successful middle level schools. *Middle School Journal, 42*(1), 49–63.

Morocco, C. C., Clark-Chiarelli, N., Aguilar, C. M., & Brigham, N. (2002). Cultures of excellence and belonging in urban middle schools. *Research in Middle Level Education Online, 25*(2). Retrieved from http:// www.nmsa.org/Publications/RMLEOnline/tabid/101/Default.aspx

National Middle School Association. (2010). *This we believe: Keys to educating young adolescents.* Westerville, OH: Author.

National Forum to Accelerate Middle-Grades Reform. (1998). *Vision Statement.* Retrieved from www.mgforum. org/about/vision.asp

Partners Against Hate. (n.d.). *Building community and combating hate: Lessons for the middle school classroom.* Retrieved from www.partnersagainsthate.org/educators/middle_school_lesson_plans.pdf

Purkey, W., & Strahan, D. (2002). *Inviting positive classroom discipline.* Westerville, OH: National Middle School Association.

Strahan, D., L'Esperance, M., & VanHoose, J. (2009). *Promoting harmony–Young adolescent development and classroom practices.* Westerville, OH: National Middle School Association.

12

Adult Advocate
Every student's academic and personal development is guided by an adult advocate.

Ross M. Burkhardt & J. Thomas Kane

∞∞∞

Advocacy:

The particular role that middle level educators play as active supporters of and intercessors for young adolescents. While each student should have an adult who is primarily responsible for the academic and personal growth of that individual, advocacy should be inherent in the school's culture and in shared responsibility.

(Lounsbury & Brazee, 2004, p. 11)

The idea of being known and noticed and cared about in a place is a reason to stay.

(Shulkind, 2007)

"Mr. B., I got a 93 on my test!" Marisa rushed into my classroom between second and third period to tell me the good news. For several weeks we had been discussing her lack of success in math. An honor student in seventh grade, Marisa was unexpectedly receiving Cs and Ds on her eighth grade algebra tests. She had considered a tutor or possibly dropping to a lower ability level; recently she had begun attending math extra help sessions. In my dual role as Marisa's advisor and teacher, I saw her four times daily—morning advisory, English, advisory lunch, and social studies. Once a month I had a 40-minute advisory conference with Marisa to discuss school issues and life in general. An accomplished actress who was learning to play lacrosse, Marisa regularly shared with

me the joys and the woes of being 13. And math was one of her burdens. I listened sympathetically as she voiced her frustrations; she knew that I believed in her eventual success. After hearing her plight, I suggested the math extra help sessions. That is about all I did, besides listening to her. Marisa did the rest.

Advocacy lies at the heart of middle level education, and every middle level educator needs to be an advocate for young adolescents. National Middle School Association (2010) in its position paper *This We Believe: Keys to Educating Young Adolescents* asserted that successful schools for young adolescents are characterized by, among other things, an adult advocate for every student, one "who is knowledgeable about young adolescent development in general, who self-evidently enjoys working with young adolescents, and who comes to know students well as individuals" (p. 35).

As young adolescents navigate the transition from elementary school to middle school, as their bodies grow and change, as they develop new interests and expand peer relationships, as they probe boundaries and test limits both at home and in school, as they explore a rapidly changing world through the Internet and social media, as they are subjected to daily bombardments of enticing advertisements on television and in magazines, as they consider alluring messages embedded in the lyrics of current popular songs, as they confront sensational headlines, and as they edge tentatively yet inexorably toward maturity, advocating for young adolescents is necessarily problematic. Some of these youngsters weather the turbulence with few upsets; others inhabit self-centered lives redolent with roller-coaster drama, still others experience pain and suffering resulting from abusive settings or unhealthy choices, or both. All experience momentous changes when growing from ages 10 to 15.

Clearly, educating young adolescents is as great a challenge as it ever was, and middle level teachers "are engaged in the most important work on the planet" (NMSA, 1996, p. 3). J. H. Lounsbury put it this way:

> As young adolescents undergo the many changes that occur in this transition stage of life, they need the support and guidance of adults who understand them and can put into perspective their occasionally belligerent ways, their often silly manner, their sometimes hurtful nature, and their incessant questioning. Young adolescents want desperately to talk to adults, to engage in informal conversations about issues that interest them, and to hear the opinions of adults they like. Middle school teachers are in a unique position to be the advocates these vulnerable youth need; for, as professional educators, they understand

human growth and development, have an established relationship with them, and are present among them and their peers in the ongoing life of school. Middle school teachers cannot and should not try to escape the critical responsibility they inevitably carry as significant others in the lives of these young people who quite literally are making up their minds about the values, attitudes, and dispositions that will direct their behavior in the years to come. It is an awesome responsibility and an opportunity to influence lives that must be taken willingly and seriously. I firmly believe that fulfilling this role well will lead to increased academic achievement. (Personal communication, December 30, 2004)

Many middle level schools respond to this "awesome responsibility" by instituting advisory programs designed to address the affective needs of young adolescents while supporting their academic development. Most advisory programs share several common attributes: (a) a designated staff member responsible for a small group of students, (b) regularly scheduled meetings of the advisory group, (c) ongoing individual conferences between advisor and advisees during the school year, (d) administrative support for advisory activities, (e) parent contact with the school through the child's advisor, and, most important, (f) an adult advocate for every young adolescent.

Advocacy and advisory are closely related. If advocacy is an operational mindset, an attitude about how to engage with and support young adolescents during these important years of growth, then advisory refers to specific programs designed by middle level educators to address the needs and interests of kids. In From Advisory to Advocacy, James and Spradling (2002) offered this distinction:

> An advocacy program is not a curriculum printed in a manual. It is a process developed through a set of experiences that establishes rapport between adults and students, students and adults, and students and students—practices those students can internalize and use with others over a lifetime. (pp. 5–6)

According to *This We Believe* (NMSA, 2010), one obligation of a successful middle level school is to provide "an attitude of caring that translates into action when adults are responsive to the needs of each and every young adolescent in their charge" (p. 35). Successful schools demonstrate "a continuity of caring and support that extends throughout a student's middle level experience" (p. 36). An advisory program enables such a "continuity of caring" to take root. Schools that have instituted and maintained successful advisory programs note greater academic achievement, fewer alienated students, increased attendance, less vandalism, more student-centered learning activities, and a better educational climate permeating the building. As Galassi, Gulledge, and Cox (1998) pointed out:

> Research indicates that students who receive adequate support become better adjusted to middle school and have a more positive self-concept, decreased feelings of depression, and greater liking of middle school (e.g., Dubois, Felner, Meares, & Krier, 1994; Dubois & Hirsch, 1990). (pp. 58–59)

In a watershed research report on the impact of the 1989 *Turning Points* recommendations, Felner and associates (1997) reported that small teams and teacher-based advisory programming in particular . . . appear to enable students to make the transition into middle grades schools without the pronounced declines in socio/emotional well-being and academic achievement that have been reported in some studies of students moving into middle grades schools and junior high schools. (p. 549)

Doda (2003) spoke to the importance of middle level educators creating caring schools for young adolescents:

> Advisory, or whatever we choose to call it (i.e., Home Base, Prime Time, Morning Meeting, etc.), is our commitment to creating caring schools—schools dedicated to building community where our children are actively respected, valued, taken seriously, understood; where they can learn to care about each other, develop compassion, participate in a model democratic, humane community; where they can be encouraged, coached, supported; and where student voice can be at the forefront of curriculum. . . . If we embrace advisory . . . as a powerful opportunity to enhance our efforts to reach and teach our young people, then affect and achievement become codependent, and no middle school should be without it. (p. 21)

In its 1989 landmark publication *Turning Points: Preparing American Youth for the 21st Century*, the Carnegie Council on Adolescent Development advanced eight recommendations for transforming the education of young adolescents and middle grades schools. The first recommendation endorsed the creation of smaller communities of learning and called for an adult advisor for each student. "The effect of the advisory system," noted the report, "appears to be to reduce alienation of students and to provide each young adolescent with the support of a caring adult who knows that student well. That bond can make the student's engagement and interest in learning a reality" (p. 41).

At Warsaw Middle School, every student is a part of a focus group, three from each grade 5–8, that stays together over their middle school years.
— "Focus Group"

This recommendation—"smaller learning communities"—was reaffirmed in *Turning Points 2000: Educating Adolescents in the 21st Century* (Jackson & Davis, 2000, p. 24).

In 1981 when Joan Lipsitz visited Shoreham-Wading River (SWR) Middle School to conduct research for her acclaimed book *Successful Schools for Young Adolescents*, she encountered a phenomenon, the absence of alienation, when she was told by a seventh grade girl, "They absolutely know me here" (Lipsitz, 1984, p. 129). Would that every middle school student in every middle level school could make the same declaration!

That notion—students being known and knowing that they are known by the adults in the building—is at the heart of advocacy. The two most important jobs middle level educators have are to know the students they teach and to address their learning needs. The National Board for Professional Teaching Standards is unambiguous on this point: "Accomplished [middle level] generalists draw on their knowledge of early adolescent development and their relationships with students to understand and foster their students' knowledge, skills, interests, aspirations, and values" (National Board for Professional Teaching Standards [NBPTS], 1994, p. 9). If teachers expect students to become engaged learners, they must communicate to those students that they are welcomed, respected, and appreciated. Young adolescents need affirmation and support.

At Thurgood Marshall Middle School all students and teachers are looped and spend two years together. "They know me, I know them. I know their stories. I know what to expect of them, and they know what to expect of me."

— Renee Robinson,
Teacher, "Introduction"

They need to know that those who are charged with educating them are also concerned about them. Advisory programs help to make this concern an everyday reality for students.

And yet, some schools that initiated advisory programs during the past four decades lost sight of this concern. Too many programs floundered because advisory was seen as a curriculum to be covered rather than a relationship to be nurtured. And while it is more difficult to develop positive relationships than it is to conduct scripted activities, one goal of every middle level educator ought to be the creation of a more intimate school setting for students. J. Burns recently remarked:

> Advisory means attentive relationship-building work with kids. We have recently coined the term "relational work" between teachers and students. Advocacy means knowing who young adolescents are and speaking out for them and their interests. However, this does not mean defending the student right or wrong.

It is not about that. I am seeing advocacy more as what we do with kids across the day. Teachers also bring parents into it, bring the community into it. In my conversations with students, I have been told the things they really like in advisory are food and time to socialize. What they really dislike in advisory are pencil and paper activities, because they get so much of that elsewhere during the day. Both advisory and advocacy are about relationships that grow as people figure out what really matters in school achievement. (Personal communication, January 11, 2005)

Advocacy speaks to a dynamic relationship between middle level educators and those they serve—the emerging adolescents in our schools. Knowles and Brown (2000) asserted that "advisors must be willing to develop a relationship with students different from the one they experience as a regular classroom teacher—one characterized by caring, not authoritarianism" (p. 153).

> The relational sense of caring forces us to look at the relations. It is not enough to hear the teacher's claim to care. Does the student recognize that he or she is cared for? Is the teacher thought by the student to be a caring teacher? When we adopt the relational sense of caring, we cannot look only at the teacher. (Noddings, Caring in Education, 2005, p.1)

In his seminal work, *A Middle School Curriculum: From Rhetoric to Reality*, Beane (1993) argued, "The central purpose of the middle school curriculum should be helping early adolescents explore self and social meanings at this time in their lives" (p. 18). Teachers who serve as advisors to sixth, seventh, and eighth graders receive daily, if not hourly, reminders of what it is like to be a young adolescent in today's fast-paced world. Through conversation and contact with their charges, teachers gain useful insights into early adolescence that they can then weave into the ongoing classroom experience over the course of the school year.

Teachers and staff make a point of talking with students outside of class, attending performances and sporting events, and generally being available.

— Video, Warsaw MS, "Focus Group";
Scuola Vita Nuova, "Community Liaison";
Maranacook Community MS, "Ice Fishing"

Young adolescents are concerned about issues other than school, and they need assistance in facing the future. Rubinstein (1994) observed,

Find videos at www.amle.org/TWBinAction

Often, the predominant question teens have while trying to exist in the larger, more anonymous middle schools is whether life is really worth living. If we want them to answer this question with "Yes, life is worth living," then we must find the ways and time to give them the personal attention and support they need to grow up as healthy people in both body and mind. Support must come before challenge to help young people grow. (p. 26)

Advisory programs that focus on the needs of young adolescents provide such attention and support. As the adage goes, "Kids don't care how much you know until they know how much you care."

Initiating Advocacy

How to begin? One useful approach is to have a faculty committee frame a mission statement that describes the nature and purpose of advocacy. In 1973 a group of advisors at SWR Middle School drafted the following passage, which served for more than three decades as the basic definition of its nationally recognized program:

Advisory is essentially a comprehensive, school-oriented, one-to-one relationship between the advisor and the ad- visee for the purposes of communication and direction. . . . Advisory enables each student to have an adult advocate in the school; the advisor is a person who can champion the advisee's cause in student-teacher, student-administrator, and student-student interactions. (SWR Middle School, 2004)

Advisors need to know what is expected of them as they advocate for young adolescents. A staff committee can compile a list of responsibilities, a job description, that may include taking attendance, disseminating school announcements, collecting lunch money, handling minor discipline issues, and communicating with the families of advisees. This We Believe described the advisor as "the primary liaison between the school and family [who] often initiates contact with parents, providing pertinent information about the student's program and progress, as well as being ready to receive calls from any parent with a concern" (NMSA, 2010, p. 36). When teachers "make themselves available to counsel and advise students on a wide range of issues

> Constructive relationships provide teachers with a window to see more sharply aspects of students' character, values, interests, and talents.

from academic progress to peer relationships to extra-curricular opportunities," they form "constructive relationships," which support students in becoming better learners and more responsible citizens. Such relationships provide teachers with "a window to see more sharply aspects of their students' character, values, interests, and talents that might otherwise be overlooked" (NBPTS, 1994, pp. 9–10).

How does a teacher learn to be an effective advisor? Staff development sessions are helpful, especially when veterans share their experiences with beginning advisors. Also, a positive attitude can lead to expertise over time. Jane Wittlock, a former teacher and administrator at SWR Middle School, responded to the question "What kind of training should an advisor have?" in the following manner: "I don't think training could really help. If you don't love 10- to 14-year-olds initially, *nothing* could help you become an advisor. If you think this age group is *truly special*, then you'll be a good advisor" (SWR Middle School, 1989). This response emphasizes the attitudinal nature of advocacy—a positive relationship between the advisor and the advisee.

Chris Stevenson described the Alpha Program in Shelburne, Vermont, which has educated young adolescents for more than four decades, as "a community of adults and young adolescents who willingly learn, work, and live together in a harmonious climate driven by high expectations, initiative, individual choices, and remarkable degrees of responsibility and accountability well beyond what is even expected, much less accomplished through conventional school practices" (Kuntz, 2005, p. vi). Advocacy thrived at Alpha largely because of

> …teachers who believed that teaching involved making connections with each student on many levels: intellectual, personal, social. They defined successful teaching as "getting to know the hopes, fears, and potential of each student." They did not follow a standard approach to learning or teaching; they individualized expectations and activities for students. They were as concerned about student identity and self-understanding as they were about the content presented and activities planned. (p. 39)

Administrative support is one key to a vibrant advocacy program in middle school. The school principal must engage in three activities that support advisory activities: mentoring, monitoring, and maintenance. The principal, as mentor, ensures that new staff members understand the school's philosophy and mission statement on advisory. Initially, new teachers can be paired with successful veteran advisors. To enhance their in-depth understanding of the role that advocacy plays in a caring school community, the principal can supply novice advisors with pertinent reading materials.

The principal should monitor advisory experiences that take place in the school through dialogue with staff members and students by witnessing, from a distance, the interactions that occur between advisors and advisees and by orchestrating sharing sessions for teachers at faculty meetings. Such occasions provide a venue for exchanging tales of success and failure that can inform future advocacy activities.

Maintenance of a middle school's program begins with the principal's keeping current his or her own expertise regarding early adolescence and advocacy by reading timely journal articles and new publications focused on advocacy. The principal can propose advisory program enhancement opportunities as teachers design their yearly personal professional development plans.

Through mentoring, monitoring, and maintaining a school's relational work with young adolescents, principals become visible witnesses for advocacy and promoters of the advisory program. They understand the long-term gains that an advisory program can provide. MacLaury (2002) reported:

> Many principals perceive supportive advisory programs to also have a long-term, positive effect by helping to prevent students from dropping out of school. George and Oldaker (1985) determined that 93% of such exemplary schools had advisory programs for all their students and that 62% of these children enjoyed "consistent academic improvement," while schools reported an 80% reduction in referrals for behavioral problems. (p. 17)

A school's priorities show up in the master schedule. For effective advisor-advisee relationships to blossom, the schedule must allow time for advisory activities to occur. Group meetings, individual conferences, parent conferences, program evaluation—all of these will appear in the school calendar where and when there is genuine commitment to making advisory work.

When creating advisory groups, remember that smaller is better. If every educator in the building serves as an advisor, the load is shared evenly, and more students are better served. An ideal advisory group contains 10 to 12 students. Advocacy takes time; the smaller the group size, the more effective the advisor can be.

For many parents of middle school children, early adolescence is a developmental labyrinth. Confused about what makes their child tick, parents do not always fully grasp the format, design, and intent of a developmentally responsive middle level school. This is especially true when parents are, themselves, products of a traditional junior high school experience.

If parents are to become genuine partners with and supporters of their child's middle school, every effort should be made to educate them regarding the format and functioning of an effective middle school. Parents should have a clear picture of how a middle school operates and, as part of their orientation to the early teen years, understand the importance of advisory and advocacy. Back to School Night provides an annual opportunity to inform parents. The *first* stop on such an evening should be a meeting with their child's advisor. After explaining the program to parents, advisors can engage them in an advocacy exercise that will help them appreciate how advisory can serve their child.

Advocating for students includes collaboration between home and school.

— Video, Warsaw MS, "Focus Group"

Whether beginning an advisory program from scratch or evaluating one that has been in place for many years, staff members need regular occasions to discuss and modify the operational aspects of the program. Faculty meetings are useful for this purpose. The following set of questions may prove helpful:

1. What does the school's mission statement say regarding advisory?

2. What does "advocacy" mean? What are its parameters?

3. What does the advisory program mission statement say?

4. What are the basic responsibilities of an advisor?

5. Who in the school will manage and maintain the advisory program?

6. How will advisory groups be formed?

7. When do advisors meet with advisees in groups? When do advisors meet individually with advisees?

Find videos at www.amle.org/TWBinAction

8. How will issues of confidentially be handled?

9. Who will mediate differences of opinion among advisors regarding the resolution of problems with students?

10. What happens when a student wants to switch from one advisory group to another?

11. Should advisory groups contain students who are all at the same grade level, or should more than one grade level be represented?

12. Should the advisor continue with his or her advisees all through middle school, or should students have new advisors each year?

13. Should an advisee participate in an advisor-parent conference?

14. What happens when parents want to meet with a teacher other than the child's advisor?

15. By whom will the advisory program be evaluated?

J. Silverstein, an English and social studies teacher who also served as an advisor for 30 years, understands how advisory made his teaching tasks easier:

> When visitors came to Shoreham-Wading River, they often said that they could not imagine adding the workload of being an advisor to their already overbooked schedules. What they did not realize was that the advisory system made so many aspects of their job easier and that the dividends were well worth the effort. The advisory system, for example, cut down on discipline problems and gave me a natural support system when dealing with students who had poor work habits, troubled home situations, or even those who had behavioral or learning disabilities. Whenever I, as a teacher, had difficulties with a student, an advisor was there to help me find a solution, and often the knowledge that they brought provided the perspective needed to solve any problem. (Personal communication, January 19, 2005)

Ultimately, "an advisory system is a simple method that ensures that no secondary school (middle school, junior high school, or high school) student becomes anonymous" (Goldberg, 1998, p. 1). Anonymity leads to alienation, and, unfortunately, in the minds of some young people, feelings of alienation sanction antisocial behavior. Advocacy for all minimizes the number of students who fall through the cracks. Education has always been a human business, and an advisory program "will appeal to any middle, junior high, or high school that wishes to emphasize personalization" (Goldberg, 1998, p. ix). The more humane and caring the school, the more readily a sense of community will take root and flourish.

Why, then, an adult advocate for every student? Because the roles and responsibilities of today's middle level teachers call for it, and because Marisa and all other middle level students deserve it. As Rubinstein (1994) so eloquently maintained in *Hints for Teaching Success in Middle School*, "The most critical need for any person is to find meaning, purpose, and significance. In order to do this, that person must feel understood, accepted, and affirmed" (p. 26).

Advocacy provides young adolescents with affirmation and acceptance at a critical time in their lives; it is one of the keys to their education. Middle level educators are in a particularly critical position because of the opportunity they have to influence, for better or for worse, not only the students themselves but society at large. Without a doubt, "[t]horoughly preparing all young adolescents to succeed in a demanding and evolving global culture makes the transformation and improvement of middle level education an imperative" (NMSA, 2010, p. 44).

References

Beane, J. A. 1993. *A middle school curriculum: From rhetoric to reality* (2nd ed.). Columbus, OH: National Middle School Association.

Carnegie Council on Adolescent Development. (1989). *Turning points: Preparing American youth for the 21st century*. New York, NY: Carnegie Corporation.

Doda, N. (2003). Relationships in the middle school: Rethinking advisory. *In Transition, 31*(1), 20–24.

DuBois, D. L., Felner, R. D., Meares, H., & Krier, M. (1994). Prospective investigation of the effects of socioeconomic disadvantage, life stress, and social support on early adolescent adjustment. *Journal of Abnormal Psychology, 103*, 511–522.

DuBois, D. L., & Hirsch, B. J. (1990). School and neighborhood friendships of Blacks and Whites in early adolescence. *Child Development, 62*, 524–536.

Felner, R. D., Jackson, A. W., Kasak, D., Mulhall, P., Brand, S., & Flowers, N. (1997). The impact of school reform for the middle years: A longitudinal study of a network engaged in Turning Points-based comprehensive school transformation. *Phi Delta Kappan, 78*, 528–532, 541–550.

Galassi, J. P., Gulledge, S. A., & Cox, N. D. (1998). *Advisory: Definitions, descriptions, decisions, directions*. Columbus, OH: National Middle School Association.

Goldberg, M. F. (1998). *How to design an advisory system for a secondary school*. Alexandria, VA: Association for Supervision and Curriculum Development.

Jackson, A. W., & Davis, G. A. (2000). *Turning points 2000: Educating adolescents in the 21st century*. New York, NY; Westerville, OH: Teachers College Press & National Middle School Association.

James, M., & Spradling, N. (2002). *From advisory to advocacy: Meeting every student's needs.* Westerville, OH: National Middle School Association.

Knowles, T., & Brown, D. F. (2000). *What every middle school teacher should know.* Portsmouth, NH: Heinemann.

Kuntz, S. (2005). *The story of Alpha: A multiage, student-centered team —33 years and counting.* Westerville, OH: National Middle School Association.

Lipsitz, J. (1984). *Successful schools for young adolescents.* East Brunswick, NY: Transaction.

Lounsbury, J. H., & Brazee, E. N. (2004). *Understanding and implementing This We Believe—First steps.* Westerville, OH: National Middle School Association.

MacLaury, S. (2002). *Student advisories in grades 5–12: A facilitator's guide.* Norwood, MA: Christopher-Gordon.

National Board for Professional Teaching Standards (NBPTS). (1994). *Early adolescence/generalist standards for National Board certification.* Washington, DC: Author.

National Middle School Association. (1996). *National Middle School Association 1996 Annual Report.* Columbus, OH: Author.

National Middle School Association. (2010). *This we believe: Keys to educating young adolescents.* Westerville, OH: Author.

Noddings, N. (2005). *Caring in education. The encyclopedia of informal education.* Retrieved from www.infed.org/biblio/noddings_caring_in_education.htm

Rubinstein, R. E. (1994). *Hints for teaching success in middle school.* Englewood, CO: Teacher Ideas Press.

Shoreham-Wading River (SWR) Middle School. (1989). *Advisory activities at Shoreham-Wading River Middle School.* Shoreham, NY: Author.

Shoreham-Wading River (SWR) Middle School. (2004). *Advisory handbook.* Shoreham, NY: Author. Retrieved from http://www.swrcsd.com/schools/pms.asp

Shulkind, S.B. (2007). *Fostering connectedness through middle school advisory programs. Unpublished dissertation.* University of California, Los Angeles.

13

Guidance Services
Comprehensive guidance and support services meet the needs of young adolescents.

Sherrel Bergmann

Spend a day with a middle school counselor, and the guidance needs of young adolescents will be all too obvious. Society and young adolescent culture have changed enough in the past few years to require middle level schools to seriously examine how they are, or are not, meeting the needs of their students. While many schools are attempting to change their climate and focus by providing proactive guidance programs, personnel, and services, others are struggling to maintain the few guidance personnel and services they have. The roles of counselors and social workers have changed significantly as they take on more students who need their help (Paterson, 2004). As societal ills creep into the school or are brought by the students themselves, a typical day for a counselor can include

» One-on-one conferences with students having peer relationship problems,

» A meeting with the sixth grade team about an at-risk student,

» Phone calls from parents or administrators of community agencies,

» Meetings with a probation officer,

» Miscellaneous counseling of students passing in the hall,

» Teaching a seventh grade class about substance abuse,

» Comforting a teacher who is ill and having a bad day,

» Teaching that teacher's class for one period so that the teacher can rest,

» Attending two staff meetings about students recommended for special services,

» Meeting with the seventh grade team during their planning period,

» Welcoming and orienting two new students to the school,

» Meeting with students in the Builders Club who are starting a community service project.

» Administering a standardized test to eighth graders, and

» Meeting with two parents of chronically absent students.

On other days, the same counselor may be asked to do crisis intervention, examine and assess new achievement tests, facilitate a divorce group, and update teachers on drugs found in the community.

With all of the issues that students bring to school with them, the type of services schools provide must be carefully planned and evaluated for their effectiveness. While the particular guidance issues may change from year to year, the need for social and emotional help for young adolescents is ever-present and is not a new need. More than 100 years ago, the social and emotional needs of middle level students were written about and discussed by educators. Brown (1902) stated:

> While the particular guidance issues change every year, the need for social and emotional help at this age is not a new concept.

This is a period of functional acquisition and re-adjustment. Mental change and physical activity appear in intellectual awakening, the storm and stress of doubt, the conversions, the intense emotional life, the fluctuating interests and enthusiasms, the general instability, and, not infrequently, the moral aberrations and perversities. (p. 411)

For many years, the teacher was the one who dealt with all of the social and emotional interactions in the classroom. That is still true today, as many middle grades schools have adopted a cornerstone of the middle school philosophy that recommends every student have an advocate or an advisor in the building. This person gets to know the students as individuals and cares for them. This adult knows the student well enough to know whether or not an individual student requires further guidance services (Alexander, Williams, Compton, & Prescott, 1969; Eichhorn, 1966; Cole, 1981; Galassi, Gulledge, & Cox, 1998; James & Spradling, 2001; National Middle School Association, 2010; Noar, 1961; VanTil, Vars, & Lounsbury, 1967).

An extended, proactive guidance program must be evident in every middle school if our students are to survive their own culture, society's early demands on them, and school as a social system. The model described here is a compilation of the successful steps offered by middle grades schools that have completed the process of establishing a compreshenisve and effective guidance program. All agreed that a school must begin by acquiring a full understanding of young adolescents. This involves knowing the questions that affect the lives of today's 10- to 15-year-olds. Numerous research groups have set out to determine what middle school students really are concerned about. Thousands of middle school students were asked to list the questions they had about the world, our country, themselves, their school, their community, their future, and their peers. Many of the often-repeated questions give insight into the guidance needs of young adolescents in this decade.

> Every school must understand the compelling questions that affect the lives of young adolescents.

> » Why do I feel so uncomfortable around people who are different?
> » Do I have the right friends?
> » Why am I picked on and called names?
> » What do I do about someone who is bullying me?
> » Will I be able to avoid doing drugs?
> » What exactly is safe sex?
> » When is the war going to stop?
> » Why does there have to be war and fighting?
> » Will the world always be so scary?
> » Why are people so violent?
> » Why am I so stressed all the time?

These examples describe what is on the minds of students who are also being asked to assimilate into large groups of peers for the first time; traverse the perils of puberty, transition from elementary to middle grades or middle to high school, and learn everything required in the curriculum.

Oftentimes, the guidance concerns override the curriculum concerns from the student point of view so that the achievement of the student is impaired. Students who are caught up in personal and social issues are unable to give their full attention to the ongoing academic activities making it imperative that schools help students to deal with personal-social issues. In addition, an examination of the culture of the school will reveal the degree to which specific services are needed. For example, is young adolescent alcohol use truly an issue in the community? How many students feel they are bullied at school or on the bus? What do parents see as their role in the school? How many parents are raising their children alone? What are the major health issues of students in our school?

The Process of Developing Multifaceted Guidance and Support Services

Schools that have successfully adopted multifaceted guidance and support services have usually formed a guidance task force of counselors, administrators, teachers, parents, students, and community agency representatives. This task force is the fact finding, needs assessing, program designing, and researching group of the community. Members must be committed to developing services based on the needs of students in their own school. Following is an example of the process used by one task force. It identified five guiding questions to pursue en route to successfully designing guidance and support services.

Guiding question #1: Who are our students and what do they need?

The guidance task force began the process of developing support services in their school began by determining a profile of their students. Many faculty made comments about the changing needs of the students and the "baggage" students brought to school that affects learning. Teachers commented that current students appear to be less respectful, less responsible, and less eager to be involved in school activities than students in previous years. While researching the demographic data of their school community, task force members discovered that there were many extremes within just one grade level. One seventh grade teacher reported that of just his 27 students

» One lived in a house with an indoor pool and bowling alley, while one came from the local homeless shelter.

» Nine lived with single parents, 13 lived with both parents, and five lived with relatives.

» Eight had never been out of the state, three had traveled to Europe, two had recently emigrated from China, and three had come from Mexico a year ago.

» Nine had older siblings, and seven were responsible for younger siblings before and after school.

» Four had been identified as gifted, and seven had learning disabilities.

» Seven distinct cultures were represented.

» Fifteen had a best friend, and five said they had no friends.

» Fourteen rode the bus, and 13 walked to school.

» Ten were involved in after-school activities; 17 were not.

» The range in height was 4' 6" to 6' 1."

All of this information had been relatively easy to gather by reading enrollment data, by making observations, and simply by asking the students. Counselors were able to add other information about students' lives. With the help of social services, students dealt with abusive parents, alcoholic parents, the court system, divorce issues, physical illnesses, and eating disorders. While the caseload of the counselor was increasing for students with serious problems, the time to assist students with the normal day-to-day school concerns was decreasing. There was no time to offer the problem-solving mini-course that had been planned; contacts with parents of students who were having academic difficulties only happened after a crisis was referred.

The focus group is another place where kids can go and express their concerns and maybe have some of their social and academic needs met.
— John Campbell, Math Teacher, Warsaw MS, "Focus Group"

As more and more students were falling through the cracks, teams of teachers discussed those students and tried to provide as much help as they could with classroom issues. As the number of students with problems increased, there was little time for prevention and limited resources for reaction. As school profiles of students were developed, members of the task force were then able to match those profiles with the answers to question #2.

Guiding question # 2: How are guidance and support services currently handled in our school? Who does what, when, and for whom?

The task force identified several programs already in the curriculum that dealt with specific guidance issues. For example,

» DARE (Drug Abuse Resistance Education) was offered to sixth graders, and SNOWFLAKE (a prevention program addressing a broad range of young adolescent concerns) was available to all students who wished to participate. These programs were successful from the students' point of view, but there was no program in place for all eighth graders.

» Guidance issues were a part of the health curriculum, but they were only offered in a nine-week exploratory.

» All teachers and teams had developed time for remedial help for academic concerns, but there was no formal mentoring program for students with reading problems.

» Most of the teams had a problem behavior recognition program, but there was little consistency in the types of recognition being given. Most of the teachers were acknowledging problems in student behavior, attitude, and achievement but were not sure what to do except refer the student to the counselor. Because the role of the counselor was not clear to the teachers, they were passing on many problems that could have been solved by simply talking with a student.

Brainstorming sessions at faculty meetings lead to impressive lists of services and guidance-related lessons provided by teams and individual teachers within the school. These sharing sessions showed who was receiving services and who was being missed. Counselors provided a list of the numbers of students receiving each type of counseling or community service. The services offered by community agencies were explained to the entire staff, and the roles of the counselor, social worker, and other specialists were clarified. With this information gathered, the task force could begin to work on question #3.

Guiding question #3: What are the basic components we must have in our school to meet the multifaceted guidance needs of our students?

Believing in one of the basic tenets of the middle school concept outlined in *This We Believe: Keys to Educating Young Adolescents* (National Middle School Association, 2010), the task force was committed to having every student assigned an advocate. A study group was formed in each school to research how advocacy was implemented in other schools and how it could be implemented in their own. All agreed that one or two counselors could not be advocates for all students but could assist the teachers by offering specific skills such as reflective listening, conflict resolution, and goal setting. The roles of advocates and counselors were clearly defined. Essential activities such as communicating with parents, making referrals, and adding or deleting curriculum content were outlined in the role descriptions.

With input from parents, teachers, students, and the community, the school determined that a drug and alcohol program would become a part of the science and health curriculum in seventh and eighth grade. Use of a well-researched program would provide students with information to make wise decisions, given the pressures found in their community. DARE would continue to be offered in the sixth grade.

Proactive programs such as community service and advisory groups were in place and needed only communication among the grade levels to continue their success. With descriptions of potential programs in place, the task force members were able to move to the question of students with serious problems.

Guiding question #4: What services should be provided for students who are at risk and have serious social and emotional problems?

The guidance task force obtained a realistic overview of the types of problems that counselors and social service agencies were regularly handling. The task force learned the local and state definition of at-risk and defined and discussed trends and current issues in the field. They learned the relation of cultural expectations, media influences, online bullying, gang behavior, use of methamphetamines, and community social activities to middle level students and classroom achievement. Case management for special education and the laws about students with special needs were explained in detail.

The task force found that teachers and parents needed to be educated and updated to broaden the base of support for students. Increased communication among groups already servicing students and extension of that communication to parents and school personnel were needed. After ensuring their school had adequate programs for services governed by law, the task force determined what kinds of further assistance their school needed. The task force found that, as in many schools, dealing with serious guidance issues of 10 percent of the students was requiring 90 percent of specially trained professionals' time. Counselors did not have time to provide proactive guidance for the vast majority of the students. Task force members then tackled question #5.

Guiding question #5: How can we implement proactive guidance and offer essential guidance-related skills to 100% of our students?

No Child Left Behind caused counselors and teachers to prioritize test preparation in core curricular areas, leaving little time for addressing the social and emotional needs of students. Preparation for the testing process, increased data collection, and administrative paperwork were taking the time that guidance personnel formerly spent teaching students how to make decisions, how to study, how to communicate, how to get along with others, how to transition to new schools, how to avoid drugs and alcohol, how to resolve conflicts, and how to develop their talents.

The task force determined what guidance skills their students needed and then developed a purpose statement for each topic and a three-year comprehensive plan. Homeroom, advisory time, block time, interdisciplinary team time, guidance-based units, community presentations, mentoring, parent volunteers, community service, and flexing the schedule were all ways the school extended guidance services. Some guidance "units" lasted only two days, while others were integrated into the content area curriculum, and teachers were trained to teach them. Counselors connected teachers to community agencies that could provide information and experiences for the students. The advocate role was defined, and teachers were trained to use advocacy skills.

The guidance task force's final plan for providing guidance and support services to students included a clear job description of everyone involved, support for training teachers, and a description of the guidance services offered at each grade level. They sought feedback on the plan from a representative group of students. The task force presented their plan to the faculty, parents, and school board for discussion and support. The need for ongoing assessment of guidance issues and services was apparent to all involved. The process allowed all participants to find the most appropriate services for their students and inspired the middle grades school to generate new programs and policies to meet their multifaceted needs.

References

Alexander, W., Williams, E. L., Compton, M., & Prescott, D. (1969). *The emergent middle school* (2nd ed.). New York, NY: Holt, Rinehart, and Winston.

Brown, E. (1902). *The making of our middle schools.* New York, NY: Longmans, Green, and Co.

Cole, C. (1981). *Guidance in the middle school: Everyone's responsibility.* Fairborn, OH: National Middle School Association.

Eichhorn, D. (1966). The middle school. New York, NY: Center of Applied Research in Education.

Galassi, J., Gulledge, S., & Cox, N. (1998). *Advisory: Definitions, descriptions, decisions, directions.* Westerville, Ohio: National Middle School Association.

James, M., & Spradling, N. (2001). *From advisory to advocacy: Meeting every student's needs.* Westerville, Ohio. National Middle School Association.

National Middle School Association (NMSA). (1995). T*his we believe: Developmentally responsive middle schools.* Westerville, OH: Author.

National Middle School Association. (2010). *This we believe: Keys to educating young adolescents.* Westerville, OH: Author.

Noar, G. (1961). *Junior high school: Today and tomorrow.* Englewood Cliffs, NJ: Prentice Hall.

Paterson, J. (2004). *The changing role of school counselors.* Middle Ground, 8(1), 42–43.

VanTil, W., Vars, G., & Lounsbury, J. H. (1967). *Modern education for the junior high school year* (2nd ed.). Indianapolis, IN: The Bobbs-Merrill Co.

14

Health & Wellness

Health and wellness are supported in curricula,
school-wide programs, and related policies.

Jean Schultz

∞∞∞

This We Believe:Keys to Educating Young Adolescents (National Middle School Association,
2010) underscores the importance of health promotion for young adolescents when it
states that in a developmentally responsive middle school "an emphasis on health, wellness,
and safety permeates the entire school, with faculty members sharing responsibility
for maintaining a positive school environment" (p. 38). Schools must systemically and
systematically address the unique opportunities and challenges that young adolescents face
in making choices that will affect their health and academic success. As they experience
biological, cognitive, emotional and social change, they are making significant choices about
their health and developing attitudes and practices that will continue through adulthood.

The health of young adolescents showed significant improvements in the 1980s followed by
an increase in risky behaviors in the 1990s, and young adolescents continue to have high
rates of morbidity and mortality owing to violence, injury, and mental health disorders
(Mertens, 2006). The prevalence of obesity in children six to eleven years old rose from 6.5%
in 1980 to 20% in 2010, and obesity in adolescents 12 to 19 years old rose from 5.0% in
1980 to 18% in 2010 (CDC/National Center for Health Statistics, 2010). As Mertens says
in the 2006 National Middle School Association research summary "Adolescent Health,
Wellness, and Safety:"

The research literature provides overwhelming evidence that the middle level years are "the last best chance" to influence these students' futures. It is during these years that young adolescents begin experimenting with a range of risky behaviors such as alcohol, tobacco, and drug use and unprotected sex. … Resnick et al. (1997) found that parent/family connectedness and perceived school connectedness were protective against every health risk behavior measured, except history of pregnancy. (p.1)

How operational is this health and wellness characteristic in your middle school?

> » Can you map attention to student health across the curriculum, describe student outcomes, or demonstrate the assessment of health-related skills, concepts, attitudes, and behaviors?

> » Are you able to identify those ports of safety within the school building where students may seek shelter from, and assistance with, the frequently rough waters of adolescence?

> » Can you chart the connectedness of school and community services, instructional components, and planned reinforcement that create a coordinated, caring community of learners?

> » Are your health promotion efforts policy-based and clearly articulated?

Responsive middle schools promote health not only among students but also among faculty and staff members through a wide range of school experiences. The support of health-related skills and concepts by all school personnel is, consequently, no longer relegated to accidental reinforcement, concomitant learning, or the occasional teachable moment.

For health and wellness to permeate the entire school, all educators must accept and personalize the inclusion of a health focus in their work at the middle level. Though rarely mentioned in professional preparation programs or even at school sites until recently, all educators have a part to play in promoting healthful behaviors while reducing risky behaviors among young adolescents.

Reasons to Promote Wellness

1. Poor health practices drain resources from education.

In the broadest sense, teachers and educational administrators must be alert to the financial impact poor health practices have on dollars earmarked for education in this country. Consider these points.

Medical care costs continue to rise:

» Poor diet and inadequate physical activity are the second leading cause of death in the United States and together account for at least 300,000 deaths (from Type 2 diabetes, hypertension, heart disease, cancer) and $100 billion in costs annually. (U.S. Department of Health and Human Services, 2006)

» In 2009, the expenditures for Medicaid exceeded the expenditure for Elementary and Secondary Education in 26 states. This trend continues to escalate, making fewer dollars available for education. (National Association of State Budget Officers, 2010, p. 10)

» The financial burden of heart disease and stroke amounts to about $135 billion a year. The annual health care and related costs attributable to alcohol abuse are $184.6 billion. The yearly costs of tobacco use amount to about $193 billion a year. (U.S. Department of Health and Human Services, 2000)

Shortfalls in state and federal health care dollars place education appropriations at risk. Because public education is contingent upon public funds, educators are wise to actively advocate for systemic community and school district action around health promotion. This effort is particularly critical in the middle grades when young adolescents are most receptive to positive health messages and prevention strategies. With systemic support, educators can reinforce and extend community and family efforts to modify risky behaviors and strengthen positive health practices among our youth, thereby increasing our society's quality of life and positively influencing the pool of public funds available for education.

> Heightened academic achievement for all can be realized only when educators and the community invest in school-wide strategies to reduce behaviors that compromise student success.

2. Behavioral, physical, and emotional problems interfere with learning.

Educators' primary job cannot be done unless we address competing needs that students bring through the school doors each day. Those who need dental care; are undernourished; are affected by substance abuse, high mobility, or restricted opportunities; or who do not feel safe cannot focus their attention on learning. "School systems are not responsible for meeting every need of their students. But when the need directly affects learning, the school must meet the challenge" (Center for Mental Health in Schools, 2004, p. 1).

As educators we understand that

> » Among fourth grade students, those having the lowest amount of protein in their diet had the lowest achievement scores. (Parker, 1989)

> » Moderate undernutrition can have lasting effects and compromise cognitive development and school performance. (Center on Hunger, Poverty, and Nutrition Policy, 1995)

> » Participation in a breakfast program improves academic, behavioral, and emotional functioning and leads to higher math grades, lower absenteeism, and improved behavior. (U.S. Department of Health and Human Services, 1996)

Heightened academic achievement for all can be realized only when educators and the community invest in school-wide strategies that will reduce behaviors compromising student success. Our national economy and societal health depend, in part, upon accomplishing this task.

3. Youthful choices affect health.

In the past, health was largely compromised by an array of diseases (rubella, whooping cough, diphtheria, pneumonia, tuberculosis). Today, the quality and quantity of healthy life is primarily determined by what we choose to do. Through a national survey of adolescent behaviors called Youth Risk Behavior Survey (YRBS) (Kolbe, Kann, & Collins, 1993), the Centers for Disease Control and Prevention (CDC) have identified six behaviors that cause premature mortality and morbidity among American youth. From survey results, it is apparent that these widespread behaviors undermine health and the resulting capacity for personal success during adolescence and adulthood. These high-priority risk behaviors, many of which may result in injuries both unintentional and intentional, are

» Tobacco use

» Acohol and other drug use

» Sexual behavior

» Dietary behavior

» Physical inactivity.

The YRBS can provide state by state data on adolescents' behaviors. Schools can use such data to support modifications to curricula and programs. For example, Memphis City Schools used their 2005 middle and high school YRBS results to develop a "Healthy Choice Initiative Tool Kit," which includes information and resources intended to encourage discussion with young adolescents about risk behaviors and their consequences. Teachers, pediatricians, parents, school counselors and nurses, and members of faith- and community-based organizations all use this resource.

In response to their middle school YRBS results, Milwaukee Public Schools decided to use only evidence-based curricula for certain health topics, and Wyoming teachers in grades 6–12 were encouraged to integrate their YRBS data into health instruction (Shanklin, Brener, McManus, Kinchen, & Kann, 2007).

Two days a week during advisory period, all students and faculty participate in physical exercise.

— Video, Warsaw MS, "Morning Exercise.

Risk-laden behaviors are complex; they develop through the interactions of persons and circumstances within and outside the school experience. Therefore, it is important to enlist persons, agencies, and organizations inside and outside the school to challenge these confounding behaviors. Many existing prevention and management services designed to address these problems are funded categorically rather than holistically. There is separate programming for substance abuse, suicide prevention, and tobacco use rather than a collaborative plan for addressing the interrelated and precursor problems of youth at risk.

During this time of shrinking resources and increasing need, the synthesis of new associations between existing and potential student support services is a necessity. New curricular alliances within schools are also needed. Only through holistic organizations that attend to underlying problems can schools and communities address health issues that compromise children's lives.

Each day teachers attempt to engage children whose ability to attend to instruction is diminished in some way. Unfortunately, this occurs as district resources are being reduced, class sizes are increasing, and more youth are being educated than ever before. Health promotion that links school and non-school support systems and services assists teachers by providing an improved safety net for students in need, thus freeing students and teachers to focus on learning tasks. Our current loosely-coupled, differently-funded, and largely unfocused efforts related to health and wellness miss too many children and burden teachers with too many health-related management concerns.

Laying a Foundation for Health Promotion

How does a school incorporate "an emphasis on health, wellness, and safety that permeates the entire school?" The following discussion describes actions that will assist in moving toward an academically successful health-enhancing middle level school.

Community response

Although poor student health negatively affects academic learning, the school need not tackle student health problems alone. Most often, informed community groups successfully spearhead action on behalf of young adolescents. A community-based exploration of local concerns, study of county or city health-related statistics, and an assessment of student needs will reveal that there are many issues a community can choose to address on behalf of its children. Though overworked but under practiced, the African proverb "It takes an entire village to raise a child" is the core of health promotion and disease prevention for young adolescents.

> Though overworked but underused, the African proverb "It takes an entire village to raise a child" is the core of health promotion and disease prevention for young adolescents.

One program stressing that parents and caregivers, elected officials from all levels of government, schools, health care professionals, faith- and community-based organizations, and private sector companies all have roles in reducing childhood obesity is the Let's Move campaign, "America's move to raise a healthier generation of kids" (http://www.letsmove.org). Developed by Michelle Obama to solve the problem of obesity within a generation, the program provides helpful information to parents; fosters environments that support healthy choices; provides healthier foods in our schools; strives to ensure every family has access to healthy, affordable food; and helps children become more physically active. Only by seeking the involvement and support of the community as a whole as in this effort will the "entire village" become part of the health promotion picture.

A school response

In December 2010 the Child Nutrition Act (Healthy, Hunger-Free Kids Act) was reauthorized. In addition to requiring every school receiving federal funds to have a wellness policy, the bill authorized piloting the expansion of farm-to-school programs and organic foods in schools. State Departments of Health and Education have received funds to establish nutrition networks. These entities encourage schools to *establish school health advisory councils* with the broad mission to address topics related to the health of students and staff members.

> The establishment of a school health advisory council is a primary step in a school's effort to raise student achievement scores.

The establishment of a school health advisory council is a sound and early step in a school's effort to raise student achievement scores. As the advisory council focuses on its first charge (physical activity and nutrition issues), school and community-linked members learn of other success-sapping issues, and, over time, the council may expand its focus.

In addition to creating links to the community, a school can identify and weave positive health practices and messages into its formal and informal curriculum (see MacLaury, 2000). A requisite to almost all other health-related initiatives is the establishment of a healthy school environment. Although considerations such as appropriate light and ventilation as well as regular building maintenance contribute to a healthy school environment, the definition is expanded to include the implementation of policies and practices that protect and promote student's emotional, social, and mental health.

How does a school assess its environment?

A coordinated school health program assessment tool, School Health Index (SHI) was developed by the CDC in partnership with school administrators and staff, school health experts, parents, and national nongovernmental health and education agencies to

» Enable schools to identify strengths and weaknesses of health and safety policies and programs.

» Enable schools to develop an action plan for improving student health, which can be incorporated into the School Improvement Plan.

» Engage teachers, parent, students, and the community in promoting health-enhancing behaviors and better health.

SHI modules are based on CDC research-based guidelines for school health programs that identify policies and practices most likely to be effective in improving youth health risk behaviors. The eight components of a coordinated school health program are

1. School Health and Safety Policies and Environment

2. Health Education

3. Physical Education and Other Physical Activity Programs

4. Nutrition Services

5. Health Services

6. Counseling, Psychological, and Social Services

7. Health Promotion for Staff

8. Family and Community Involvement

Teams from schools complete two activities: the eight self-assessment modules and a planning for improvement process. Members from the school community discuss what the school is already doing to promote good health and to identify strengths and weaknesses. Then, the teams prioritize recommendations for actions the school can take to improve its performance in areas that received low scores. The SHI is a self-assessment and planning tool, but not a research or evaluation tool; it is also a community-organizing and educational process (CDC, 1995–2009).

Each member of the school population deserves to feel wellcomed and safe at school. School programs that foster responsibility, respect, and caretaking of emotional as well as physical health enable a school to become that place where everyone is comfortable and "at home." Such is the basis for a high-performance learning environment.

An individual response

Beginning teachers are frequently amazed and appalled at the variety of student concerns that are before them each day. These concerns have little to do with academic content and everything to do with the lives of the children. Students who are in abusive relationships, involved with drugs, neglected, sexually abused, anorexic or bulimic, burdened with adult responsibility, depressed, pregnant, ill, poorly clothed, undernourished, afraid to go home, afraid to walk to school or pass in the halls, painfully shy, or sexually harassed cannot attend fully to academic achievement. Veteran teachers, no longer amazed, work to connect students with resources or provide a supportive environment. What else can an individual teacher do? Actually, quite a lot.

First, inquire regarding the status of efforts already underway to create a comprehensive health program in one's school or school district. Persons in state departments of education or state departments of health may be familiar with the comprehensive and coordinated school health program model (Kolbe & Allensworth, 1987). In addition, various national organizations

A mid-morning nutrition break improves learning and reduces discipline problems.

— Video, William Thomas MS, "Nutrition Break

representing school boards, teachers, principals, superintendents, and other education professionals are working to assist their members in this arena. Consult your state department of education, organization websites, or a web search engine, and search using coordinated school health as keywords. Raising the issue and expressing an interest may get this ball rolling in one's school or district if no serious effort has been initiated. An article by Lyn Fiscus (2008), published in Middle Ground, outlines a year of health activities for young adolescents and provides teachers with useful facts and engaging instructional strategies for helping students in middle grades learn how to avoid becoming "super-sized."

Find videos at www.amle.org/TWBinAction

Second, inquire regarding the health-related skills that are taught in a variety of prevention curricula. In collaboration with the entire staff, choose one for school-wide emphasis. For example, many alcohol and drug prevention curricula include a decision-making strategy. Do all faculty members know this strategy? Is each language arts teacher well-grounded enough to use the strategy while discussing a short-story character? How might it be used by a social studies teacher in discussing a recent event? Does the health educator transfer this strategy to food choices? Does the physical educator use it to assist students in problem solving? Does the science teacher link it to scientific methods?

Note that skill development is not skill inoculation. A skill development lesson in grade six does not transfer to new experiences in grade seven without guidance and practice. Negotiation, coping, decision making, and refusal skills must be revisited, reinforced, and reinterpreted through experience to be useful in the lives of young adolescents. All teachers, if they are familiar with a skill, can use their own academic content to teach and reinforce a skill chosen for school-wide emphasis.

Third, educators can help community members see and understand what educators see and do regarding health-related problems that negatively affect academic achievement. Educators can also advocate for others to bring student health-related problems to the school-community table.

Conclusion

For the students that are before us each day, there is no better time than now to develop a school that is safe and welcoming and that emphasizes wellness and health. The establishment of a school health advisory council and the systematic development of a health-promoting school provides a framework for addressing student health needs and will contribute significantly to NCLB Adequate Yearly Progress expectations. Fashioning a middle level school in which "an emphasis on health, wellness, and safety permeates the entire school" is no less important than the other characteristics of a developmentally responsive middle level school. Although there is much to do, there are also sources of information and guidance. Seek assistance, ask questions, and begin the process on behalf of young adolescents.

References

America's move to raise a healthier generation of kids. (n.d.) Retrieved from www.letsmove.gov

Center for Mental Health in Schools. (2004, Fall). *Mental health in schools: Reflections on the past, present, and future from the perspective of the Center for Mental Health in Schools* (Executive Summary). Los Angeles, CA: Center for Mental Health in Schools, Department of Psychology, University of California at Los Angeles. Retrieved from http://www.smhp.psych.ucla.edu

Center on Hunger, Poverty, and Nutrition Policy. (1995). *Statement on the link between nutrition and cognitive development in children.* Medford, MA: Tufts University School of Nutrition.

Centers for Disease Control and Prevention: National Center for Health Statistics. (2010). Obesity and overweight. Retrieved from http://www.cdc.gov/nchs/fastats/overwt.htm

Centers for Disease Control and Prevention. *School Health Index.* (n.d.). Retrieved from https://apps.nccd.cdc.gov/SHI/Static/Introduction.aspx

Centers for Disease Control and Prevention. (n.d.). *1995–2009 Middle School Youth Risk Behavior Survey data.* Retrieved from http://apps.nccd.cdc.gov/youthonline

Child Nutrition Act: Healthy Schools Campaign. (n.d.). Retrieved from http://healthyschoolscampaign.org/getinvolved/action/childnutrition.php/

Fiscus, L. (2008). A year of health and safety activities. *Middle Ground, 4*(11), 16–19.

Kolbe, L., & Allensworth, D. (1987). The comprehensive school health program: Exploring an expanded concept. *Journal of School Health, 57,* 409–412.

Kolbe, L., Kann, L., & Collins, J. (1993). Overview of the Youth Risk Behavior Surveillance System. Public Health Reports. *Journal of the U.S. Public Health Service, 108* (Suppl.1), 1–2.

MacLaury, S. (2000). Teaching prevention by infusing health education into the advisory program. *Middle School Journal, 31*(5), 51-56.

Mertens, S. B. (2006). Research summary: Adolescent health, wellness, and safety. Retrieved from http://www.nmsa.org/Research/ResearchSummaries/Health/tabid/267/Default.aspx

National Association of State Budget Officers. (2010). *State expenditures report 2009.* Washington, DC: Author. [Electronic Version]. Retrieved from http://www.nasbo.org/LinkClick.aspx?fileticket=w7RqO74llEw%3d&tabid=38

National Middle School Association. (2010). *This we believe: Keys to Educating Young Adolescents.* Westerville, OH: Author.

Parker, L. (1989). *The relationship between nutrition and learning: A school employee's guide to information and action.* Washington, DC: National Education Association.

Shanklin, S. L., Brener, N., McManus, T., Kinchen, S., & Kann, L. (2007). 2005 Middle school youth risk behavior survey. Atlanta, GA: U.S. Department Health and Human Services, Centers for Disease Control and Prevention.

U.S. Department of Health and Human Services. (1996, June 14). Guidelines for school health programs to promote lifelong healthy eating. *Morbidity and Mortality Weekly Report Recommendations and Report, 45*, RR-9.

U S. Department of Health and Human Services. (2000). *Healthy people: 2000 midcourse review and 1995 revisions.* Washington, DC: Public Health Service.

U.S. Department of Health and Human Services. (2001). *The Surgeon General's call to action to prevent and decrease overweight and obesity.* Rockville, MD: Author.

U.S. Department of Health and Human Services. (2006). Fact sheet: Promoting health through physical activity. Retrieved from www.hhs.gov/news/factsheet/physactive.html

15

Family Involvement
The school actively involves families in the education of their children.

Joyce L. Epstein & Darcy J. Hutchins

ᐧᐧ

One of NMSA's expectations is for schools to actively involve families in the education of their children. Most middle grades schools have struggled to implement research-based, comprehensive, and goal-linked partnership programs (Sheldon & Hutchins, 2011). This chapter addresses four questions that will help educators in the middle grades move from strong beliefs about the importance of family and community involvement to action.[1]

(a) What is a research-based, comprehensive, and goal-oriented program of school, family, and community partnerships in the middle grades?

(b) How can teamwork ensure that a school will organize and implement a sustainable program of family and community involvement?

(c) How does family and community involvement link with the other elements of effective middle level schools?

(d) How can schools answer the call for action to develop and sustain productive partnership programs?

For decades studies have shown that families are important for children's learning, development, and school success in all grades. Research is accumulating that shows that a well-organized *program* of partnerships is needed in every school to help all families support their children's education from preschool through high school. Without proactivity from schools, many families reduce their involvement as active partners with the school when their children enter the middle grades. Still, most families want and need good information about

> Studies show that if middle level schools implement comprehensive and inclusive programs of partnership, then many more families respond, including those who would not become involved on their own.

early adolescence, middle level education, special programs available to their children, and other issues and options that affect students in the middle grades (Hutchins, 2011). Studies show that when middle level schools implement comprehensive

and inclusive programs of partnership, many more families respond, including those who most likely would not become involved on their own (Epstein, 2011; Epstein & Lee, 1995; Henderson & Mapp, 2002; Henderson, Mapp, Johnson, & Davies, 2007; Kreider, Caspe, Kennedy, & Weiss, 2007; Kreider & Westmorland, 2011; Sanders & Epstein, 2000; Sanders & Sheldon, 2009; Sanders & Simon, 2002; Sheldon & Epstein, 2005a, 2005b; Sheldon & Van Voorhis, 2004).

A Framework for a Comprehensive Program of Partnerships: Six Types of Involvement

Extensive studies and activities with educators and families led to the development, testing, and confirmation of a framework of six types of involvement that helps schools establish full and productive programs of school, family, and community partnerships (Epstein, 1995; Epstein et al., 2009). This section summarizes these six types of involvement with a few sample practices that are important in the middle grades. Also noted are some of the challenges that must be met to involve all families, and examples of the results that can be expected in the middle grades from each type of involvement if activities are well implemented.

Type 1 – Parenting

Type 1 activities help families understand young adolescent development, parenting skills for the age group, and arranging home conditions to support learning at each grade level. Other Type 1 activities help schools obtain information from families so that educators understand families' backgrounds, cultures, and goals for their children. Type 1 activities reinforce the fact that educators and parents share responsibility for students' learning and development in the middle grades and help develop trust and mutual respect for each other's efforts in guiding student development.

Sample practices. Middle level schools conduct workshops for parents; provide short, clear summaries of parenting issues that arise in early adolescence; and organize opportunities for parents to exchange ideas on topics of young adolescent development including health, nutrition, discipline, guidance, peer pressure, preventing drug abuse and other high-risk behaviors, and planning for their children's futures. For example, at Family Night Teaches Tolerance, Lowndes Middle School in Valdosta, GA, involved parents, students, teachers, community partners, and district leaders. Student presentations, a guest speaker, and dinner helped open a dialogue on diversity and set a base for ongoing activities to increase understanding and tolerance among racial groups at the school (Salinas & Jansorn, 2004, p. 60). Type 1 activities also provide parents with useful information on children's transitions into the middle grades and then into high school, attendance policies, and other topics important for young adolescents' success in school.

Middle grades schools may offer optional parent education classes, family support programs, family computer classes, family literacy programs, parent-to-parent panels, and other services for parents. To ensure family input, at the start of each school year and periodically throughout the year, teachers and counselors may ask parents to share insights about their children's strengths, talents, interests, needs, and goals. For example, Francis Howell Middle School and its feeder elementary schools in St. Charles, Missouri, organized a parent forum (Whose Parents Let Them Do That?) that helped parents meet each other, the principal and the faculty to discuss important topics of young adolescent development (Hutchins, Maushard, Greenfeld, & Thomas, 2010, p. 44).

> If families are part of their children's transitions—elementary to middle and middle to high school—more students should adjust well to their new schools, and more parents should remain involved.

Challenges. One challenge for successful Type 1 activities is getting information to parents who cannot come to meetings and workshops. This may be done with videos, tape recordings, written summaries, newsletters, cable broadcasts, phone calls, computerized messages, school websites, and other print and non-print communications. Another Type 1 challenge is to design procedures and opportunities that enable all families to share information about their children with teachers, counselors, and others.

Expected results. If information flows to and from families about young adolescent development, parents should increase their confidence about parenting through the middle grades, students should be more aware of parents' ongoing guidance, and teachers should better understand their students' families. Studies show that if practices are targeted to help families send their children to school on time, then student attendance should improve (Epstein & Sheldon, 2002; Sheldon, 2007; Sheldon & Epstein, 2004). If families are part of their children's transitions from elementary to middle school and from middle to high school, more students should adjust well to their new schools, and more parents should remain involved across the grades (Elias, Patrikakou, & Weissberg, 2007; Seidman, Lambert, Allen, & Aber, 2003).

Type 2 – Communicating

Type 2 activities keep families informed about school programs and student progress with school-to-home and home-to-school communications such as notices, memos, conferences, report cards, team and school newsletters, phone and computerized messages, e-mails, open houses, and innovative communications. All schools send some information home, but two-way channels of communication are needed in successful partnership programs which will encourage and permit parents to share their ideas, suggestions, questions, and concerns with teachers, counselors, and administrators.

Schools bear responsibility for providing consistent and varied means to maintain communication and build supportive relationships with students' families.

— Video, William Thomas MS, "Student-Led Conferences"; Chapel Hill MS, "Student Agenda Books"; Scuola Vita Nuova, "Community Liaison"

Sample practices. Among many Type 2 activities, middle level schools may provide parents with clear information on each teacher's criteria for report card grades, how to interpret interim report cards, and, as necessary, how to work with students to help them improve their grades. Type 2 activities include conferences for parents with teams of teachers, parent-student-teacher conferences (Tuinstra & Hiatt-Michael, 2004), and the increasingly popular student-led conferences (Maushard, et al., 2007), which all will ensure that students take personal responsibility for learning. Many schools also rely on technology, such as school or teacher websites, e-mail, and the Parent Portal (a system that pulls information from

Find videos at www.amle.org/TWBinAction

the school's SIMS.net management system) to communicate with parents about students' attendance, grades, and other outcomes (Bouffard, 2009; Hutchins, 2011).

Schools may select class parents or block parents, or they may organize telephone trees for more effective communications with parents via designated parent leaders. Some have the equivalent of an educational "welcome wagon" for families who transfer to the school during the school year. Activities may be designed to improve school newsletters to include student work and recognitions, parent columns, important dates, and parent response forms. For example, Lincoln Junior High School in Naperville, Illinois, solicited parent feedback to improve its school newsletter, the *Lancer Ledger* (Hutchins, Maushard, Colosino, Greenfeld, & Thomas, 2009, p. 78). As a result, the newsletter became more colorful, highlighted more student accomplishments, and included more short articles on different departments and student clubs.

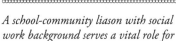

A school-community liason with social work background serves a vital role for teachers, students, and their families.

— Scuola Vita Nuova,
"Community Liason"

Challenges. One challenge for successful Type 2 activities is to make communications clear and understandable for all families, including parents who have less formal education, speak languages other than English at home, or do not read English well. All families must be able to process and respond to the information they receive. A common Type 2 challenge is to develop effective two-way channels of communication so that families can easily contact teachers or counselors, offer ideas and suggestions, and request conferences and information. Middle level schools also must make sure that the students themselves understand their roles in facilitating and participating in all school-family-community partnerships and that they are able to articulate the nature of their ongoing academic activities and deliver home-to-school and school-to-home communications. By the middle grades, students should be central, active agents in all aspects of their lives in school and out, although they still require close and caring supervision from teachers and parents.

Expected results. If information is clear and two-way channels of communication are established, interactions between educators and parents should increase. More families will understand the school's programs and teachers' expectations, follow their children's progress, and attend parent-teacher-student conferences. If computerized phone lines are used to communicate information about homework, more families will know more about their children's daily assignments. If newsletters include respond-and-reply forms, more parents should offer ideas, questions, and comments about school programs and activities. Studies indicate that good communications with families help schools improve student behavior (Domina, 2005; Hill, et al., 2004; Sheldon, 2009; Sheldon & Epstein, 2002) and math achievement (Sheldon & Epstein, 2005b; Van Voorhis, 2009, 2011b).

Type 3 – Volunteering

Type 3 activities improve recruitment and training of parents and others as volunteers and as audiences for various programs and student activities. Type 3 activities may improve the adult-student ratio in a school resulting in closer supervision of students and enabling teachers to provide students with more individualized attention.

Sample practices. Type 3 activities can involve collecting information on family members' talents, occupations, interests, and availability to serve as volunteers and enrich students' subject classes; improve career explorations; serve as foreign language translators; conduct attendance monitoring; work on "parent safety patrols" for safety; and organize and improve activities such as clothing and uniform exchanges, school stores, and fairs.

> If tasks, schedules, locations, and training for volunteers are varied, more parents, family members, and others in the community will support the school and students' activities.

Schools may also create opportunities for mentors, coaches, tutors, and leaders to serve in after-school programs. For example, Roosevelt Middle School, in Blaine, Minnesota, developed the Student Organizational Help Program in which volunteers helped students organize their lockers, notebooks, homework planners, desks, and folders so that clear thinking and good work could follow (Hutchins, Maushard, Greenfeld, & Thomas, 2010, p. 47).

Challenges. Challenges for successful Type 3 activities are to recruit widely so that many parents become actively involved as volunteers; create flexible volunteering schedules for parents who work during the school day; and provide training so that volunteers contribute productively in the school, classroom, after-school, and other programs or projects (Hutchins, 2011). It helps if one or two volunteers serve as coordinators to match volunteers' times and skills with the needs of teachers, administrators, and students.

Schools may meet this challenge by changing the definition of "volunteer" to mean anyone who supports the school and students' activities at any time and in any place. This opens options for schools to recognize parents as "volunteers" if they come as audience members to support school concerts, assemblies, sports activities, and other events. A related challenge is to help students in the middle grades understand how volunteers help their school, and to encourage students to volunteer, themselves, to help their school, family, and community.

Expected results. If tasks, schedules, locations, and training for volunteers are varied and purposeful, more parents, family members, and others in the community will support the school and students' activities. A directory detailing volunteers' time, talents, and resources will assist teachers in calling upon parents and other volunteers to assist in school programs and activities. More parents might attend student performances and other events as members of the audience if they know that their presence is viewed as "volunteering."

In summary, volunteers can have measurable results for students.

» When volunteers serve as attendance monitors, more families are alerted which helps students improve attendance (Sanders, 1999).

» When volunteers conduct a "hall patrol" or are active in other locations, school safety increases and student behavior problems decrease due to a better student-adult ratio and more supervision.

» When volunteers discuss careers, students become aware of more options for their futures.

» When volunteers serve as tutors in various classes, student tutees improve their skills and achievement in those subjects.

One study found that when parent volunteers shared artwork linked to social studies units, students in the middle grades gained art appreciation experiences and knowledge about art and artists that they did not have before (Epstein & Dauber, 1995). Thus, volunteers can assist teachers in improving the school climate and student learning in specific subjects if the volunteers have appropriate training for working with students in the middle grades.

Type 4 – Learning at Home

Type 4 activities involve families with their children in academic learning activities at home. This includes interactive homework, goal setting for improved achievement, curriculum-linked activities, and participating in decisions about academic courses and school programs. Type 4 activities link teaches with students and parents on curricular issues.

Sample practices. Among many Type 4 activities, middle level schools may provide information to students about the demands of each course and about each teacher's homework policy. Schools also may implement activities that help families encourage, praise, guide, and monitor their children's work using interactive homework, student-teacher-family contracts, long-term projects, summer home-learning packets, student-led conferences about their writing, goal setting activities, homework hotlines of daily assignments, or other interactive strategies that keep students and parents talking about schoolwork at home. For example, the Teachers Involve Parents in Schoolwork (TIPS) process enables teachers to design homework for students to share and discuss their work and ideas with a family partner. In this way, parents can see how and what students are learning in math, science, and language arts in the middle grades without thinking that they must teach middle grades subjects (Epstein, Salinas, & Van Voorhis, 2001; Epstein & Van Voorhis, 2001; Van Voorhis, 2009, 2011a, 2011b, 2011c; Van Voorhis & Epstein, 2002). As another example, Ellen Ochoa Middle School in Pasco, Washington, involved parents in Reading at Home Awareness by sending home monthly magnets with ideas for parents to encourage students' reading for pleasure for about 40 minutes a night and to talk about books with their young adolescents (Hutchins, Maushard, Greenfeld, & Thomas, 2010, p. 12). Still another interesting Type 4 example is Dessert under the Stars at William Hubbard Middle School in Forsyth, Georgia, which actively engaged students and their families in student- and family-led experiments in astronomy, earth science, physical science, and life science (Hutchins, Maushard, Greenfeld, & Thomas, 2010, p. 21).

Challenges. One challenge for successful Type 4 activities is to implement a regular schedule of interactive homework that requires students to take responsibility for discussing with family members important things they are learning, interviewing family members, recording reactions, and sharing their work and ideas in other ways at home. Another Type 4 challenge is to create procedures and activities that involve families regularly and systematically with students on short-term and long-term goal setting for good or better report card grades, behavior, attendance, development of personal talents, and plans for high school and postsecondary education.

Expected results. When Type 4 activities are well-designed and well-implemented, students should improve their homework completion, report card grades, and test scores in specific subjects (Sheldon, 2003). More families will know what their children are learning in class and how to monitor, support, and discuss homework. There will be more positive conversations between students and parents or other family members about their school work and academic ideas. Both students and teachers will be more aware of family interest in students' work. Several studies show that interactive homework in the middle grades increased parental involvement with students about their homework, improved homework completion, report card grades in language arts and science (Balli, Demo, & Wedman, 1998; Epstein, Simon, & Salinas, 1997; Van Voorhis, 2003; Van Voorhis, 2009, 2011a, 2011b, 2011c).

Type 5—Decision Making

Type 5 activities call for families being involved in developing a school's vision and mission statements, and in designing, reviewing, and improving school policies and in other school decisions. Family members become active participants on school improvement teams, committees, and district councils and in the Action Team for Partnerships, and PTA/PTO or other parent organizations. Parents also may be part of independent advocacy groups and task forces for school improvement.

Sample practices. Type 5 activities include parent representatives on all committees for school improvement, including curriculum, safety, supplies and equipment, partnerships, and career development committees. Schools may support the organization of an active parent association and offer parents and teachers training in leadership, decision making, and collaboration. Type 5 activities may be designed to distribute information for families about school policies, course offerings for students, programs and services, and tests and assessments.

Middle level schools may use a variety of technologies including low-tech summaries and high-tech e-mail lists to share information with *all* parents and gather parents' ideas and reactions to policy questions and school procedures—not only the parent leaders on committees. We have learned that parents, other family members, teachers, administrators, students, and community partners all must be represented on an Action Team for Partnerships (ATP), which plans and monitors the development of the school's program of family and community involvement (see next section). Parents may lead the implementation of some school-wide activities. For example, Park Middle School, located in Kennewick, Washington, invited parents of English language learners, who had shied away from involvement, to plan and conduct the Cinco de Mayo Fiesta (Hutchins, Maushard, Colosino, Greenfeld, & Thomas, 2009, p. 55). The result was an exciting and successful event that increased participation and strengthened the involvement of many more parents.

Challenges. One challenge for successful Type 5 activities is to ensure that there are active parent representatives on school committees from all of the racial and ethnic groups, socioeconomic groups, and geographic communities that are present in the school. A related challenge is to build capacity in parent leaders to serve as true representatives who obtain information from and provide information to other parents about questions, options, and decisions. An ongoing challenge is to help parents and teachers on committees to trust, respect, and listen to each other as they work toward common goals for school improvement.

> One challenge is to ensure that there are parent representatives on school committees from all of the racial and ethnic groups, socioeconomic groups, and geographic communities present in the school.

Expected results. If Type 5 activities are well-implemented, more parents will have input into decisions that affect the quality of their children's education; students will be aware that families have a say in school policies; and teachers will increase their understanding of family perspectives on policies and programs for improving the school.

Type 6—Collaborating with the Community

Type 6 activities coordinate the work and resources of community businesses; agencies; cultural, civic, and religious organizations; colleges and universities; senior citizens and other groups and individuals in the community to strengthen school programs, family practices, and student learning and development. Other Type 6 activities enable students, staff, and families to contribute their services to the community.

Sample practices. Among many Type 6 activities, middle level schools may inform students and families about programs and resources in their community that support learning and development, such as after-school recreation, tutorial programs, health services, cultural events, service opportunities, and summer programs. Schools may arrange "gold card" discounts with local merchants to recognize students who improve attendance and report card grades or who demonstrate other accomplishments.

Collaborations with community businesses, groups, and agencies also may strengthen all other types of involvement. For example, parent education workshops or meetings for families may be conducted at community or business locations (Type 1); local radio and TV (including foreign language stations), places of worship, clinics, supermarkets, and laundromats may help schools communicate information to parents on school events (Type 2); people from businesses and the community may serve as school volunteers (Type 3); artists, scientists, writers, mathematicians, and others in the community may enrich student learning in specific subjects (Type 4); and community members may serve on school and district decision making councils and committees (Type 5).

A partnership with Youth Guidance, a community group that provides arts activities for special education students, has had a positive impact on students' academics and self-confidence.

— Video, Thurgood Marshall MS, "Art-Based Partnerships"

Students may also participate in initiatives that give back to the community. For example, students at Spooner Middle School in Spooner, Wisconsin, conducted the Souper Bowl of Caring—a food drive and "chili feed" (Hutchins, Maushard, Colosino, Greenfeld, & Thomas, 2009, p. 84). This community service project pressed students to study local and world hunger and raised funds and items for the local food pantry.

Challenges. One challenge for successful Type 6 activities is to help all students and families "know" their community and to increase the equity of access for diverse students and families to community resources and programs. Another challenge is to solve "turf" problems, such as who will lead and who will fund school-community collaborations. Still another Type 6 challenge is to link students' valuable learning experiences in the community to the school curriculum, including lessons that build on non-school skills and talents, such as students' work as volunteers and as members of student clubs and groups. It also is challenging to inform and involve the family in community-related activities that affect their children so that families are aware of how others care for and assist their children.

Expected results. Well-implemented Type 6 activities help families, students, and educators know which resources and programs in their community will help students attain important school and personal goals. By increasing equal access to community programs, more and different students and families will participate and benefit from various programs. Coordinated community services could also help more students and their families solve problems that arise in early adolescence before they become too serious. Type 6 activities also should support and measurably enrich school curricula and extracurricular programs (Sanders, 2006; and see Chapter 16 on the structures, content, and benefits of collaborating with the community in programs of school, family, and community partnerships).

In summary these six types of involvement create a comprehensive program of partnerships, but the implementation challenges for each type must be met to reach and engage all families. The expected results are directly linked to the quality of the design and goal-oriented content of the activities.

Not every practice to involve families will result in students' higher achievement test scores. Rather, practices for each type of involvement can be selected to help students, families, and teachers reach specific school improvement goals and results. The discussions included a few examples from hundreds of possible activities that may help middle level schools improve their partnership programs. For more examples, visit the website of the National Network of Partnership Schools at www.partnershipschools.org and follow the paths to middle grades schools' success stories.

A Team Approach for a Comprehensive Partnership Program

The framework of six types of involvement identifies activities that help parents become involved in their children's education in different ways, but, the types of involvement are just one part of a partnership program. Research and field work show that, along with clear policies and strong support from district leaders and from the school principal, an Action Team for Partnerships (ATP) is an essential structure in each school. At the middle level, schools improve the quality of their plans and practices, outreach to families, and results for students when they have a dedicated committee—an Action Team for Partnerships—of teachers, administrators, parents, and community partners (Epstein et al., 2009, Chapter 6; Galindo & Sheldon, 2011).

Responsibilities

The ATP is an official, permanent committee of the School Improvement Team or Council. This makes the organization of the school's program, plans, and practices of partnerships an integral and sustainable component of school organization (Epstein & Sheldon, 2006).

The ATP has responsibility for organizing family and community programs, writing an action plan with selected activities representing the six types of involvement that are linked to specific goals for student success. For example, middle level schools may have clear goals to improve students' reading skills and attitudes, increase attendance, reduce peer pressure or bullying, develop students' talents, or they might have other academic or behavioral goals and targets for student success. The school's Action Team for Partnerships will schedule and develop the activities for family and community involvement linked to these very goals so that students, teachers, parents, and the community are working together to help more students reach their full potential and succeed in school.

The ATP also has responsibility for identifying present family and community involvement practices, identifying needed partnerships, and implementing some activities and delegating others. That is, although the members of the ATP lead some involvement activities, they may be assisted by other teachers, parents or parent groups, students, administrators, and community members who can take leadership or support roles for planned partnerships.

The ATP checks to see that the six types of involvement are represented so that parents are involved in different locations and in different ways. That way, many more parents can be involved than if all activities were conducted at the school building. The ATP evaluates the overall quality of implemented activities and the progress of the school's partnership program. The team also identifies next steps to continue to improve the program of family and community involvement as a standard, expected aspect of school organization.

Members Are Partners in Education

The ATP team should include at least two or three teachers from each grade level, department, or specialty; at least two or three parents from different neighborhoods or cultural groups with children in different grade levels; and at least one administrator. Teams may also include one or more members of the community. Others who are central to the school's work with families also may be included as team members, such as a school counselor, social worker, nurse, school psychologist, cafeteria worker, secretary, or custodian. The diverse members ensure that the team will plan activities that take into account the various needs, interests, and talents of all who share an interest in student success.

The chair or co-chairs of the ATP should be good communicators with all partners in children's education and have the respect of the other team members. At least one member of the ATP should also serve as the linking member to the School Improvement Team or Council.

The work of the ATP improves on past practices that assigned one person (e.g., the principal or parent liaison or active parent) to take responsibility for parental involvement. By contrast the ATP is an official school committee; includes representatives of all partners in students' education; and ensures, by writing an annual plan for goal-linked family and community involvement, that the school's partnership program will continue even if some ATP members move or change schools. For more information on planning, evaluating, improving, and funding the ATP and the program of family and community involvement, see Epstein et al., 2009.

Linking Partnerships to Other NMSA Middle Level Characteristics

NMSA's sixteen characteristics of responsive middle level schools all are important. Taken together, their three foci—curriculum and instruction, leadership and organization, and culture and community—make clear that successful middle grades schools aim to have compassionate, high- quality teachers and staff; challenging curricula; engaging, motivating, and empowering instruction; meaningful assessments of student progress; and excellent and equitable family and community involvement (NMSA, 2010). The recommended elements combine to promote all student learning in the middle grades in schools that are inviting, stimulating, and joyful. The intent, clearly, is for district leaders, principals, teachers, parents, community partners, and students to work together in ways that promote successful middle level schools *and* successful students.

Although all of the sixteen characteristics are very much interrelated, family and community involvement often has been overlooked. On careful examination it becomes clear that family and community involvement is directly relevant to and interacts with each and every one of the other characteristics. For example, one essential element of an excellent middle level school is that "Educators value young adolescents and are prepared to teach them." To do this, teachers, principals, and counselors must know their students' families and implement partnership programs and practices that engage parents in ways that support early adolescents' learning and development (Epstein & Van Voorhis, 2010; Van Voorhis & Sheldon, 2004). As another example, NMSA expects middle level schools to ensure that "Curriculum is challenging, exploratory, integrative, and relevant." Studies show that more students will be motivated to learn and will increase their skills if educators design class work and homework that enable students to draw from their families' "fund of knowledge" to understand the real-world applications of school skills (Epstein & Van Voorhis, 2001; Hill, Tyson, & Bromwell, 2009; Moll, Amanti, Neff, & Gonzalez, 1992).

School, family, and community partnerships have important connections with all other elements of effective middle level schools. A comprehensive program of family and community involvement not only ensures that families remain important, positive influences in their young adolescents' education, but also that all partners at home, at school, and in the community focus their attention on the quality of education in schools for young adolescents.[2]

Notes

[1] This chapter updates and extends earlier versions of this information in Epstein, 2005 and Chapter 6 in Epstein, et al., 2009.

[2] The National Network of Partnership Schools (NNPS) at John Hopkins University provides ongoing guidance on developing and evaluating research-based programs of school, family, and community partnerships. For information about NNPS, visit http://www.partnershipschoools.org

References

Balli, S. J., Demo, D. H., & Wedman, J. F. (1998). Family involvement with children's homework: An intervention in the middle grades. *Family Relations, 47*, 149–157.

Bouffard, S. M. (2009). Tapping into technology: Using the Internet to promote family-school communication. In N. E. Hill & R. K. Chao (Eds.), *Families, schools, and the adolescent: Connecting research, policy, and practice* (147–161). New York, NY: Teachers College Press.

Domina, T. (2005). Leveling the home advantage: Assessing the effectiveness of parental involvement in elementary school. *Sociology of Education, 78*, 233–249.

Elias, M. J., Patrikakou, E. N., & Weissberg, R. P. (2007). A competence-based framework for parent school community partnerships in secondary schools. *School Psychology International, 28*, 540–554.

Epstein, J. L. (1995). School/family/community partnerships: Caring for the children we share. *Phi Delta Kappan, 76*, 701–712.

Epstein, J. L. (2005). School-initiated family and community partnerships. In T. O. Erb (Ed.), *This We Believe in Action: Implementing successful middle level schools* (pp. 77–96). Westerville, OH: National Middle School Association.

Epstein, J. L. (2011). *School, family, community partnerships: Preparing educators and improving schools* (2nd ed.). Boulder, CO: Westview Press.

Epstein, J. L., et al. (2009). *School, family, and community partnerships: Your handbook for action* (3rd ed.). Thousand Oaks, CA: Corwin Press.

Epstein, J. L., & Dauber, S. L. (1995). Effects on students of an interdisciplinary program linking social studies, art, and family volunteers in the middle grades. *Journal of Early Adolescence, 15*, 114–144.

Epstein, J. L., Galindo, C., & Sheldon, S. B. (2011). Levels of leadership: Effects of district and school leaders on the quality of school programs of family and community involvement. *Educational Administration Quarterly, 47*, 462–495.

Epstein, J. L., Salinas, K. C., Van Voorhis, F. L. (2001). *Teachers Involve Parents in Schoolwork (TIPS) manuals and prototype activities for the elementary and middle grades.* Baltimore, MD: Center on School, Family, and Community Partnerships, Johns Hopkins University.

Epstein, J. L., & Sheldon, S. B. (2002). Present and accounted for: Improving student attendance through family and community involvement. *Journal of Educational Research, 95*, 308–318.

Epstein, J. L., Simon, B. S., & Salinas, K. C. (1997). Effects of Teachers Involve Parents in Schoolwork (TIPS) language arts interactive homework in the middle grades. *Research Bulletin, 18*, (September). Bloomington, IN: Phi Delta Kappa, CEDR.

Epstein, J. L., & Van Voorhis, F. L. (2010). School counselors' roles in developing partnerships with families and communities for student success. *Professional School Counseling, 16*, 1-14.

Henderson, A. T., & Mapp, K. L. (2002). *A new wave of evidence: The impact of school, family, and community connections on student achievement.* Austin, TX: Southwest Educational Development Laboratory.

Henderson, A. T., Mapp, K. L., Johnson, V. R., & Davies, D. (2007). *Beyond the bake sale.* New York, NY: New Press.

Hill, N. E., Castellino, D. R., Lansford, J. E., Nowlin, P., Dodge, K. A., Bates, J. E., & Pettit, G. S. (2004). Parent academic involvement as related to school behavior, achievement, and aspirations: Demographic variations across adolescence. *Child Development, 75*, 1491–1509.

Hill, N. E., Tyson, D. F., & Bromell, L. (2009). Parental involvement during middle school: Developmentally appropriate strategies across ethnicity and socioeconomic status. In N. E. Hill & R. K. Chao (Eds.), *Families, schools, and the adolescent: Connecting research, policy, and practice* (pp. 53–72). New York, NY: Teachers College Press.

Hutchins, D. J. (2011). *Parent involvement in middle school: Cultivating comprehensive and inclusive programs of partnership*. Unpublished doctoral dissertation, University of Maryland, College Park, College Park, MD.

Hutchins, D. J., Maushard, M., Colosino, J., Greenfeld, M. D., & Thomas, B. G. (2009). *Promising partnership practices*. Baltimore, MD: National Network of Partnership Schools.

Hutchins, D. J., Maushard, M. Greenfeld, M. D., & Thomas, B. G. (2010). *Promising partnership practices*. Baltimore, MD: National Network of Partnership Schools.

Kreider, H., Caspe, M., Kennedy, S., & Weiss, H. (2007). Family involvement in middle and high school students' education. *Research Brief, #3*. Cambridge, MA: Harvard Family Research Project.

Kreider, H., & Westmoreland, H. (Eds.). (2011). *Promising practices for family engagement in out-of-school time*, (pp. 71–84). Charlotte, NC: Information Age.

Maushard, M., Martin, C. S., Hutchins, D. J., Greenfeld, M. D., Thomas, B. G., et al. (2007). *Promising partnership practices*. Baltimore, MD: National Network of Partnership Schools.

Moll, L. C., Amati, C., Neff, D., & Gonzalez, N. (1992). Funds of knowledge for teaching: Using a qualitative approach to connect homes and classrooms. *Theory Into Practice, 31*(2), 132–141.

National Middle School Association. (2010). *This we believe: Keys to educating young adolescents*. Westerville, OH: Author.

Salinas, K. C., & Jansorn, N. R. (2004). *Promising partnership practices 2004*. Baltimore, MD: Johns Hopkins University Center on School, Family, and Community Partnerships.

Sanders, M. G. (1999). Improving school, family, and community partnerships in urban schools. *Middle School Journal, 31*(2), 35–41.

Sanders, M. G. (2006). *Building school-community partnerships: Collaboration for student success*. Thousand Oaks, CA: Corwin Press.

Sanders, M. G., & Epstein, J. L. (2000). Building school, family and community partnerships in secondary schools. In M. G. Sanders (Ed.), *Schooling students placed at risk: Research, policy and practice in the education of poor and minority adolescents*. Mahwah, NJ: Erlbaum.

Sanders, M. G., & Sheldon, S. B. (2009). *Principals matter: A guide to school, family, and community partnerships*. Thousand Oaks, CA: Corwin Press.

Sanders, M. G., & Simon, B. S. (2002). A comparison of program development at elementary, middle, and high schools in the National Network of Partnership Schools. *The School Community Journal, 12*(1), 7–27.

Seidman, E., Lambert, L. E., Allen, L.,& Aber, J. L. (2003). Urban adolescents' transition to junior high school and protective family transactions. *Journal of Early Adolescence, 23*, 166–193.

Sheldon, S. B. (2003). Linking school-family-community partnerships in urban elementary schools to student achievement on state tests. *Urban Review, 35*, 149–165.

Sheldon, S. B. (2007). Improving student attendance with school, family, and community partnerships. *Journal of Educational Research, 100*, 267–275.

Sheldon, S. B. (2009). Improving student outcomes with school, family, and community partnerships. In J. Epstein, et al., *School, family and community partnerships: Your handbook for action* (3rd ed., pp. 40–56). Thousand Oaks, CA: Corwin.

Sheldon, S. B., & Epstein, J. L. (2002). Improving student behavior and discipline with family and community involvement. *Education in Urban Society, 35*, 4–26.

Sheldon, S. B., & Epstein, J. L. (2004). Getting students to school: Using family and community involvement to reduce chronic absenteeism. *School Community Journal, 4*(2), 39–56.

Sheldon, S. B., & Epstein, J. L. (2005a). School programs of family and community involvement to support children's reading and literacy development across the grades. In J. Flood & P. Anders (Eds.), *Literacy development of students in urban schools: Research and policy* (pp. 107–138). Newark, DE: International Reading Association.

Sheldon, S. B., & Epstein, J. L. (2005b). Involvement counts: Family and community partnerships and math achievement. *Journal of Educational Research, 98*, 196–206.

Sheldon, S. B., & Hutchins, D. J. (2011). *Summary 2010 update data from schools in NNPS*. Baltimore, MD: Johns Hopkins University.

Sheldon, S. B., & Van Voorhis, F. L. (2004). Partnership programs in U.S. schools: Their development and relationship to family involvement outcomes. *School Effectiveness and School Improvement, 15*, 125–148.

Tuinstra, C., & Hiatt-Michael, D. (2004). Student-led parent conferences in middle schools. *The School Community Journal, 14*(1), 59–80.

Van Voorhis, F. L. (2003). Interactive homework in middle school: Effects on family involvement and students' science achievement. *Journal of Educational Research, 96*, 323–339.

Van Voorhis, F. L. (2009). Does family involvement in homework make a difference? Investigating the longitudinal effects of math and language arts interventions. In R. Deslandes (Ed.), *International perspectives on student outcomes and homework: Family-school-community partnerships* (pp. 141–156). London, England: Taylor and Francis.

Van Voorhis, F. L. (2011a). Adding families to the homework equation: A longitudinal study of family involvement and mathematics achievement. *Education and Urban Society, 43*, 313–338.

Van Voorhis, F. L. (2011b). Costs and benefits of family involvement in homework. *Journal of Advanced Academics, 22*, 220–249.

Van Voorhis, F. L. (2011c). Engaging families in student homework: Action steps for educators. In H. Kreider & H. Westmoreland (Eds.), *Promising practices for family engagement in out-of-school time* (pp. 71–84). Charlotte, NC: Information Age.

Van Voorhis, F. L., & Epstein, J. L. (2002). *Teachers Involve Parents in Schoolwork (TIPS): Interactive homework CD for the elementary and middle grades*. Baltimore, MD: Center on School, Family, and Community Partnerships at Johns Hopkins University.

Van Voorhis, F. L., & Sheldon, S. B. (2004). Principals' roles in the development of U.S. programs of school, family, and community partnerships. *International Journal of Educational Research, 41*, 55–70.

16

Community & Business Partners

The school includes community and business partners.

Mavis G. Sanders

∞∞

Community partnerships can help middle level schools become learning environments in which young adolescents thrive. Defined as connections between schools and individuals, organizations, and businesses, these partnerships can expand, deepen, and extend middle grades students' learning opportunities. They can make resources and supports available to the families of middle school students, provide middle grades educators with professional development, and achieve other goals linked to middle grades students' success. Community, within this definition of school-community partnerships, refers to the social interactions and relationships that "can occur within or transcend local boundaries" (Nettles, 1991, p. 380; Sanders, 2001, 2003).

This chapter seeks to promote deeper understanding of the role of community partnerships in structuring more effective middle level schools. It first discusses rationales for school-community partnerships and then describes their different forms. Next outcomes of school-community partnerships are identified, followed by a description of four factors that facilitate their effective implementation. Lastly, five questions are presented that middle level schools should consider when preparing for community partnerships that support young adolescents' success in school and beyond.

Rationales for School-Community Partnerships

Families and schools traditionally have been viewed as the two institutions with the greatest effect on the development of children. Communities, however, have received increasing attention for their role in socializing youth and ensuring students' success in a variety of societal domains. Epstein's (1987, 1995, 2011) theory of overlapping spheres of influence, for example, identifies schools, families, and communities as major institutions that socialize and educate children. A central principle of the theory is that certain goals, such as student academic success, are of interest to each of these institutions and are best achieved through their cooperative action and support.

Proponents of community involvement in schools have emphasized its importance for youths' development and academic success, contending that schools and families alone cannot provide sufficient resources to ensure that all children receive the experiences and supports needed to succeed in the larger society (Heath & McLaughlin, 1987, 1994; Merz & Furman, 1997; Dryfoos, 1998; Dryfoos & Maguire, 2002; Waddock, 1995). While much of their research and writings have focused on youth in urban communities, Bauch (2001) described school-community partnerships as a strategy to achieve rural school renewal as well. She argued that rural schools are set in a "community context that values a sense of place and offers a unique set of conditions for building the social capital important for helping students succeed in school" (pp. 204–205).

> Schools and families alone cannot provide sufficient resources to ensure that all children receive the experiences and supports needed to succeed in the larger society.

Similarly, when describing the importance of community involvement in educational reform, Shore (1994) focused on the mounting responsibilities placed on schools by a nation whose student population is increasingly placed at risk. She contended that schools need additional resources to successfully educate all students, and that these resources, both human and material, are housed in students' communities. Others have also emphasized the importance of schools, families, *and* communities in school reform, arguing that through collaborations, schools can become more responsive and innovative learning environments for today's youth (Decker, Decker, & Brown, 2007; Fullan, 2000; Sanders, 2006; Shirley, 1997; Toffler & Toffler, 1995).

Other proponents have suggested that school-community partnerships can also facilitate community development and neighborhood revitalization (Benson, 1997; Davies, 2002; Mediratta, Shah, & McAlister, 2009; Warren, 2005). Schools as community organizations are seen as sites for local activism that links education reform to broader community development goals. Through such partnerships, community, family, and school leaders work collaboratively to address often interrelated concerns about education, health, employment, and safety.

> Through such partnerships, community, family, and school leaders work collaboratively to address often interrelated concerns about education, health, employment, and safety.

Forms of School-Community Partnerships

School-community partnerships can range from simple (e.g., student incentive program) to complex (e.g., after-school tutoring program). Simple partnerships require very little coordination, planning, or time. Thus, they are relatively easy to implement, especially for schools that may lack the experience and resources needed for more complex partnerships. When well implemented, the impact of partnerships is likely to be positive, albeit limited. As school-community partnerships increase in complexity, activities are longer term and characterized by bidirectional or multidirectional exchange, high levels of interaction, and extensive planning and coordination.

School-community partnerships can also take a variety of forms. The most common linkages are partnerships with businesses, which can differ significantly in focus, scope, and content. Other school-community linkages involve universities and educational institutions, health care organizations, government and military agencies, national service and volunteer organizations, faith-based organizations, senior citizen organizations, cultural and recreational institutions, media organizations, sports franchises and associations, social services agencies, charitable organizations, and other community-based organizations and community volunteers that can provide resources and social support to youth and schools (see Table 1).

Partnership activities may also have multiple foci (also see Table 1). Activities may be student-centered, family-centered, school-centered, or community-centered. Student-centered activities include those that provide direct services or goods to students, such as mentoring and tutoring programs, contextual learning and job-shadowing opportunities, as well as the provision of awards, incentives, and scholarships to students. Walton Middle School in Compton, California, for example, partnered with a faith-based organization to identify and train interested adults to work with students as tutors, mentors, and role models. Conducted throughout the year, the varied activities, including field trips and career nights, helped to increase students' confidence, self-esteem, and achievement (Maushard et al., 2007).

A partnership with a local music store enables students to take piano lessons at school at no charge to the family.

— Video, William Thomas MS, "Piano Lab"

Family-centered activities are those that identify parents or entire families as their primary focus. This category includes parenting workshops, GED and other adult education classes, parent/family incentives and awards, family counseling, and family fun and learning nights. For example, recognizing the middle grades as a critical transition for parents as well as students, C. Alton Lindsay Middle School and C. Vernon Spratley Middle School in Hampton, Virginia, partnered with their local YMCA to hold a parent retreat. Using funds from a GEAR UP grant, the schools organized the parent retreat to provide parents with information on how to support their young adolescents' work and progress toward college and career readiness (Hutchins, Maushard, Greenfeld, & Thomas, 2010).

School-centered activities are those that benefit the school as a whole, such as beautification projects or the donation of school equipment and materials, or activities that benefit the faculty, such as staff development and classroom assistance. For example, Madison Junior High School in Naperville, Illinois, partnered with the school district grounds department, a local artist, a garden landscape company, a local nursery, and a team of volunteers to create a new school entrance way. This landscaping project addressed a flooding problem and created a more welcoming front entrance for the school (Jansorn, Salinas, & Gerne, 2002).

The community and its citizens are the primary focus of community-centered activities such as charitable outreach, art and science exhibits, and community revitalization and beautification projects. These types of partnerships can be linked to the curriculum to provide middle grades students with project-based learning opportunities that are positively associated with their

Find videos at www.amle.org/TWBinAction

Table 1. **Community Partners And Foci Of Partnership Activities**

Activity Focus (Examples)	**Community Partners** (Examples)
Student-Centered (awards, student incentives, scholarships, trips, tutors, mentors, job shadowing, and other services and students)	**Businesses/Corporations** (local businesses, national corporations and franchises)
	Health Care Organizations (hospitals, health care centers, mental health facilities, health departments, health foundations and associations)
	Government and Military Agencies (fire departments, police departments, chambers of commerce, city councils, other local and state government agencies and departments)
Family-Centered (parent workshops, family fun-nights, GED and other adult education classes, parent incentives and rewards, counseling and other forms of assistance)	**National Service and Volunteer Organizations** (Rotary Club, Lions Club, Kiwanis Club, VISTA, Concerned Black Men, Inc., Shriners, Boy and Girl Scouts, YWCA, YMCA, United Way, Americorp, Urban League)
	Faith-Based Organizations (churches, mosques, synagogues, other religious organizations, charities)
	Senior Citizens Organizations (nursing homes, senior volunteer and service organizations)
School-Centered (equipment and materials, beautification and repair, teacher incentives and awards, funds for school events and programs, office and classroom assistance)	**Cultural and Recreational Institutions** (zoos, museums, libraries, recreational centers)
	Media Organizations (local newspapers, radio stations, cable networks)
	Sports Franchises and Associations (minor and major league sports teams, NBA, NCAA)
	Social Services Agencies (children and family services, aid programs, adult services)
Community-Centered (community beautification, student exhibits and performances, charity and other outreach)	**Charitable Organizations** (local and national food banks, local shelters, wildlife foundations)
	Other Community Organizations (fraternities, sororities, neighborhood and alumni associations)
	Community Individuals (individual volunteers from the surrounding school community)

academic learning and engagement (Krajcik, Blumenfeld, Marx, & Soloway, 1994). At Spooner Middle School in Spooner, Wisconsin, for example, students, families, and school staff partnered with three area non-profit organizations that worked to alleviate hunger and poverty. Students conducted research on hunger and poverty in their community and in the world. They then led several activities including a silent auction and food-drive to raise money and collect food items for the local charities (Hutchins, Maushard, Colosino, Greenfeld, & Thomas, 2009).

Outcomes of School-Community Partnerships

School-community partnership activities can lead to measurable outcomes for students and schools (Sanders & Campbell, 2007). Mentoring programs have been found to have significant and positive effects on students' grades, school attendance, and exposure to career opportunities (McPartland & Nettles, 1991; Yonezawa, Thornton, & Stringfield, 1998). After-school programs have had measurable effects on students' achievement (Blank, Melaville, & Shah, 2003; Fashola & Cooper, 1999; Gardner et al., 2001). School-community collaborations focused on academic subjects have been shown to enhance students' attitudes toward these subjects as well as the attitudes of teachers and parents (Beyerbach, Weber, Swift, & Gooding, 1996). Documented benefits of school-linked service integration initiatives include both behavioral and academic gains for students who receive intensive services (McMahon, Ward, Pruett, Davidson, & Griffith, 2000; Newman, 1995). Research also has shown improved immunization rates and student attendance and conduct at schools providing coordinated services (Amato, 1996). Finally, partnerships with businesses and other community organizations have provided schools with needed equipment, materials, and technical assistance for student instruction (Longoria, 1998; Mickelson, 1999; Sanders & Harvey, 2002). School-community partnerships, then, can be vital elements in schools' programs of improvement and reform and an important part of a comprehensive program of school, family, and community partnerships.

What Schools Can Do
to Promote Community Involvement

Case study research has identified four factors that support a school's ability to develop and maintain meaningful community partnerships (Sanders & Harvey, 2002; Sanders & Lewis, 2005). These factors are:

a) a high commitment to learning,

b) principal support for community involvement,

c) a welcoming school climate, and

d) two-way communication with potential community partners about their level and kind of involvement.

High commitment to learning

Interviews with community partners representing faith-based organizations, non-profit foundations, health care organizations, businesses, educational institutions, and senior citizens organizations revealed a common desire to support students' academic achievement. Community partners wanted to be a part of an effective school that was visibly focused on students' learning and to engage in activities that had demonstrable effects on student outcomes. Not surprisingly, community partners identified schools that were well-organized, student-centered, family-friendly, and academically rigorous as the most desirable partners for collaboration.

Principal support for community involvement

Community partners also stated that a principal's support for community involvement was critical for a successful collaboration program. Their view was that in order for effective collaboration to occur, the principal needs to not only allow for such collaboration but be an active participant and supporter. Indeed, principal support largely explained the community partners' continued engagement in one case school. In another case, a community partner stated, "I don't want to pinpoint any schools, but I've gone into some and have been totally turned off by the administration. If I'm turned off, what's the interest in helping you . . .?"

> For effective collaboration to occur, the principal needs to not only allow for it but be an active participant and supporter.

A welcoming school climate

Similarly, community partners expressed the importance of a school that is receptive to and appreciative of community involvement. Community partners stated that being greeted warmly at the school by staff, faculty, and students strengthened their commitment to the partnership and increased the enjoyment of their involvement. Although most community partners in the study agreed that formal acknowledgment was not necessary, they valued the school's expressions of gratitude, which came in the form of student thank you letters and notes, verbal expressions from parents and students when passing on the streets, and acknowledgements by intercom broadcasts, in the school newsletter, and by certificates at awards ceremonies.

Two-way communication

Community partners and school administrators interviewed for the case study also emphasized the importance of honest, two-way communication between schools and potential partners. One school principal stated that honest, initial conversations prevented both parties from "wasting each other's time." The principal used a single criterion to determine if a community partnership was right for the school; her measure was simply whether the partnership would be positive for students.

The four factors delineated above that promote community partnerships were linked to the principal's actions as school leader. By maintaining a school environment in which teachers and parents focus on students' academic success, by modeling for faculty and staff a genuine openness to and appreciation for community partnerships, and by actively networking with individuals in the community to identify possible areas for collaboration, the principal created fertile ground in which school-community partnerships flourished.

Preparing for School-Community Partnerships

School leaders can prepare for partnerships by considering the following five questions. Answers to these questions will help schools assess their levels of readiness for community collaboration, the forms and foci of partnerships that are most suitable, and the levels of partnership complexity for which they are prepared.

1. ***What is your school's vision?*** What is it that you want your school known for? What represents your core value? What do you feel is the prime goal? There is an old adage, "If you don't know where you are going, you probably won't get there or you will end up someplace else." School leaders, with faculty members, parents, students, and community leaders need to collaborate in constructing a commonly shared vision of excellence for their school long before trying to launch community partnerships.

2. ***What is the goal this partnership will help to achieve?*** Community partnerships should be developed to achieve important school goals. Whether school-, student-, family-, or community-focused, school-community partnerships should be implemented to move a school closer to its vision of excellence. Many schools may be tempted to enter a partnership without clear purpose, solely to meet external requirements, expectations, or guidelines. Despite such pressures, school leaders

should maintain a measured, purposeful approach to community partnership development. Furthermore, to measure the success of a partnership, it is important to have not only a clear goal but some measurable indicators of success.

3. ***What school resources, including time, space, and personnel, will the partnership require?*** School-community partnerships, whether simple or complex, require some effort ranging from writing thank-you letters to conducting training for community volunteers with many and varied tasks in between. Before entering a partnership then, a school should realistically assess its capacity to exert the needed effort. Such an assessment will help school leaders decide on the appropriateness of an alliance or, perhaps, determine needed modifications that need to take place. School leaders should communicate openly with potential community partners to ensure that they, too, understand and can commit to the required resource exchange.

4. ***Is the community partnership project in compliance with school, district, and state guidelines?*** No two states, districts, or schools are exactly alike. Some districts have very strict rules regarding school-community partnerships and the types and value of resources being exchanged. Other districts have few or no restrictions, leaving the final say with school principals. Likewise, some districts encourage individual schools, and some schools encourage individual teachers, to engage in community partnerships. Others require that a central authority arrange such partnerships. Before beginning community partnerships, then, to avoid later misunderstandings, schools should take the time to investigate building and district policies.

5. ***Who in the school will be responsible for overseeing partnership planning, implementation, and evaluation?*** A team approach helps schools to successfully plan and implement school-wide partnerships without overtaxing one individual. School leadership or site-based management teams, for example, can be organized into committees, one of which could be responsible for working with others in the school and local community to incorporate family and community involvement in school improvement plans and activities. Several variations of this approach are encouraged and indeed required by the National Network of Partnership Schools that was described in Chapter 15.

A team or committee focused on partnerships should assign members to planning, implementation, and evaluation tasks that are required for partnership program development, such as developing and monitoring budgets, maintaining records, and corresponding with partners. The team leader, therefore, must be amenable to distributed or shared leadership. A successful team leader might be an assistant principal; an experienced teacher, counselor, or social worker; or a home-school coordinator with well-honed collaborative skills. It is also important that the team leader be committed to the role and can give the time necessary to honor the commitment. Because time is so critical and always in short supply, many teams establish a co-chair arrangement.

Conclusion

Research to date indicates that to ensure young adolescents' success, middle schools must be restructured to promote more positive student-adult relationships and offer more responsive and student-centered instruction (Eccles, Lord, & Midgley, 1991; NMSA, 2010). These changes are critical for students' social, emotional, and academic growth and overall well-being. School-community partnerships are a key strategy in achieving these goals for youth. However, to develop school-community partnerships that have this transformative capacity, middle level educators must take an intentional approach, as outlined in this chapter. Community partnerships, especially as they increase in complexity, require forethought and planning on the part of school leaders. With such planning, middle level schools can become learning environments in which young adolescents are empowered to address the challenges and meet the demands of the 21st century.

References

Amato, C. (1996). Freedom elementary school and its community: An approach to school-linked service integration. *Remedial and Special Education, 17*(5), 303–309.

Bauch, P. (2001). School-community partnerships in rural schools: Leadership, renewal, and a sense of place. *Peabody Journal of Education, 76*(2), 204–221.

Benson, P. (1997). *All kids are our kids: What communities must do to raise caring and responsible children and adolescents.* San Francisco, CA: Jossey-Bass.

Beyerbach, B. A., Weber, S., Swift, J. N., & Gooding, C. T. (1996). A school/business/university partnership for professional development. *School Community Journal, 6*(1), 101–112.

Blank, M., Melaville, A., & Shah, B. (2003). *Making the difference: Research and practice in community schools.* Washington, DC: Coalition for Community Schools, Institute for Educational Leadership.

Davies, D. (2002). The 10th School revisited: Are school/family/community partnerships on the reform agenda now? *Phi Delta Kappan, 83*(5), 388–392.

Decker, L., Decker, V., & Brown, P. (2007). *Diverse partnerships for student success: Strategies and tools to help school leaders.* Lanham, MD: Rowman & Littlefield.

Dryfoos, J. (1998). The rise of the full-service community school. *High School Magazine, 6*(2), 38–42.

Dryfoos, J., & Maguire, S. (2002). *Inside full-service community schools.* Thousand Oaks, CA: Corwin.

Eccles, J., Lord, S., & Midgley, C. (1991). What are we doing to early adolescents? The impact of educational contexts on early adolescents. *American Journal of Education, 99*(4), 521–542.

Epstein, J. L. (1987). Toward a theory of family-school connections: Teacher practices and parent involvement. In K. Hurrelmann, F. Kaufmann, F. Losel (Eds.), *Social intervention: Potential and constraints* (pp. 121–136). New York, NY: DeGruyter.

Epstein, J. L. (1995). School/family/community partnerships: Caring for the children we share. *Phi Delta Kappan, 76*(9), 701–712.

Epstein, J. L. (2011). *School, family, and community partnerships: Preparing educators and improving schools,* (2nd ed.). Boulder, CO: Westview Press.

Fashola, O., & Cooper, R. (1999). Developing the academic talents of African-American students during the non-school hours: Four exemplary programs. *The Journal of Negro Education, 68*(2), 130–137.

Fullan, M. (2000). The three stories of education reform. *Phi Delta Kappan, 81*(8), 581-584.

Gardner, III, R., Cartledge, G., Seidl, B., Woolsey, M., Schley, G., & Utley, C. (2001). Mt. Olivet After-School Program: Peer-mediated interventions for at-risk students. *Remedial and Special Education, 22*(1), 22–23.

Heath, S. B., & McLaughlin, M. W. (1987). A child resource policy: Moving beyond dependence on school and family. *Phi Delta Kappan, 68*, 576–580.

Heath, S., & McLaughlin, M. (1994). The best of both worlds: Connecting schools and community youth organizations for all-day, all-year learning. *Educational Administration Quarterly, 30*(3), 278–300.

Hutchins, D., Maushard, M., Greenfeld, M., & Thomas, B. (2010). *Promising partnership practices.* Retrieved from http://www.csos.jhu.edu/p2000/ppp/index.htm.

Hutchins, D., Maushard, M., Colosino, J., Greenfeld, M., & Thomas, B. (2009). *Promising partnership practices.* Retrieved from http://www.csos.jhu.edu/p2000/ppp/index.htm.

Jansorn, N., Salinas, K., & Gerne, K. (2002). *Promising partnership practices.* Retrieved from http://www.csos.jhu.edu/p2000/ppp/index.htm.

Krajcik, J., Blumenfeld, P., Marx, R., & Soloway, E. (1994). A collaborative model for helping middle grade science teachers learn project-based instruction. *The Elementary School Journal, 94*(5), 483–497.

Longoria, Jr., T. (1998). *School politics in Houston: The impact of business involvement.* In C. Stone (Ed.) Changing Urban Education, (pp.184–198). Lawrence, KS: University Press of Kansas.

Maushard, M., & Associates (2007). *Promising partnership practices.* Retrieved from http://www.csos.jhu.edu/p2000/ppp/index.htm.

McMahon, T., Ward, N., Pruett, M., Davidson, L., & Griffith, E. (2000). Building full-service schools: Lessons learned in the development of interagency collaboratives. *Journal of Educational & Psychological Consultation, 11*(1), 65–92.

McPartland, J. M., & Nettles, S. M. (1991). Using community adults as advocates or mentors for at-risk middle school students: A two-year evaluation of project RAISE. *American Journal of Education, 99*, 568–586.

Mediratta, K., Shah, S., & McAlister, S. (2009). *Community organizing for stronger schools: Strategies and successes.* Cambridge, MA: Harvard University Press.

Merz, C., & Furman, G. (1997). *Community and schools: Promise and paradox.* New York, NY: Teachers College Press.

Mickelson, T. (1999). International business machinations: A case study of corporate involvement in local educational reform. *Teachers College Record, 100*(3), 476–512.

National Middle School Association. (2010). *This we believe: Keys to educating young adolescents.* Westerville,OH: Author.

Nettles, S. M. (1991). Community involvement and disadvantaged students: A review. *Review of Educational Research, 61*(3), 379–406.

Newman, L. (1995, April). *School-agency-community partnerships: What is the early impact on students' school performance?* Paper presented at the annual meeting of the American Educational Research Association, San Franciso, CA.

Sanders, M. G. (2001). A study of the role of "community" in comprehensive school, family, and community partnership programs. *The Elementary School Journal, 102*(1), 19–34.

Sanders, M. (2003). Community involvement in schools: From concept to practice. *Education and Urban Society, 35*(2), 161–181.

Sanders, M. G. (2006). *Building school-community partnerships: Collaboration for student success.* Thousand Oaks, CA: Corwin Press.

Sanders, M., & Campbell, T. (2007). Securing the ties that bind: Community involvement and the educational success of African American children and youth. In J. Jackson (Ed.), *Strengthening the African American educational pipeline* (pp. 141–164). Albany, NY: State University of New York Press.

Sanders, M. G., & Harvey, A. (2002). Beyond the school walls: A case study of principal leadership for school-community collaboration. *Teachers College Record, 104*(7), 1345–1368.

Sanders, M.G., & Lewis, K. (2005). Building bridges toward excellence: Community involvement in high schools. *High School Journal, 88*(3), 1–9.

Shirley, D. (1997). *Community organizing for urban school reform.* Austin, TX: University of Texas Press.

Shore, R. (1994). *Moving the ladder: Toward a new community vision.* Aspen, CO: Aspen Institute.

Toffler, A., & Toffler, H. (1995). Getting set for the coming millennium. *The Futurist, 29*(2), 10–15.

Waddock, S. A. (1995). *Not by schools alone: Sharing responsibility for America's education reform.* Westport, CT: Praeger.

Warren, M. (2005). Communities and schools: A new view of urban education reform. *Harvard Educational Review, 75*(2), 133–175.

Yonezawa, S., Thornton, T., & Stringfield, S. (1998). *Dunbar-Hopkins Health Partnership Phase II Evaluation: Preliminary Report-Year One.* Baltimore, MD: Center for Social Organization of Schools.

17

Lessons Learned:
Keys to Future Growth

Edward N. Brazee & John H. Lounsbury

∞∞

The Way It Is

Sally Diaz looked up as she entered the building, and the Grover Middle School sign caught her eye. She wondered how the school would be different from when she was a student at this same school 36 years ago. She thought of those days fondly, remembering the ninth grade prom, playing on the basketball and volleyball teams, writing for the yearbook, and singing in the choir. Grover Junior High School had been good for her, but since she became an educator, she often wondered if it had been a good place for all students? Now in her role as educational consultant, she would be able to see what the school with its different name was like. Having had only a few minutes on the phone with the new principal, Gary Evans, to get a quick rundown on the school, she was anxious to see it firsthand. Gary had received the school board's approval to bring in Sally to help his faculty assess the school. Was it meeting all its stated goals? Was the community satisfied with the quality of education the school provided? Were teachers preparing their students well for life after Grover Middle? Was the school offering the best possible educational experiences for all the young adolescents enrolled?

Six weeks later, having spent considerable time during several visits, Sally knew Grover Middle School inside and out. Like so many other schools since the 1970s, it was clear Grover had taken the name middle school, but little else had changed. Or to be fair, Grover had made some positive strides in the first years after becoming a middle school. Four-teacher interdisciplinary teams with common planning time had been instituted. Also, an advisory program, liked by most students and a few teachers, had been established to help meet the personal-social needs of students. These were heady changes in their time, and faculty members felt they were making changes needed, ones supported by the majority of their colleagues—at the time. But people moved on, and the institutional memory of what and why they were changing—the essentials of the middle school concept—faded, leaving some of the original innovations and their rationales behind.

Sally recognized she had a great deal of work to do, helping this entrenched faculty improve their practices across much of the school; she knew that the contentious part would occur when she asked them—including a few of her former teachers—to reconsider the middle school practices they had kicked around and discarded years ago, never having fully adopted them. How would she help these teachers adopt practices that have been proven to improve student learning, practices such as integrated curriculum, authentic assessment, and small group learning? How could they organize the school to achieve maximum benefit for students? How could Grover's faculty utilize fully the opportunities that teaming provides? Could they move to institute several smaller partner teams wherein students and teachers together plan learning activities?

One thing was clear; every teacher and administrator needed to study, reflect on, and in some cases, rediscover the basic concepts of middle level education. This faculty needed to explore in depth the philosophical questions that undergird the middle school concept. And Ms. Diaz knew that visits to excellent middle level schools should be arranged. The heavily tracked, subject-centered, teacher-directed school she saw in Grover, while supported by a small, but vocal group of teachers and some community members, was sadly out of touch with current research and the full range of the educational and growth needs of its diverse young adolescents.

And while no one had asked students what they thought of the school, the numbers of discipline referrals, suspensions, and absences told their own story. Another fact of life at Grover was that very few teachers, parents, or community members were really happy or satisfied with the school in its present form as a retro-junior high school. In fact, the opposite was true. "Keeping the lid on" was an apt descriptor for life at Grover as students, faculty, and administration struggled daily, almost as adversaries. As Mr. Evans said to Ms. Diaz after the first round of the assessment, "There is nowhere to go but up.

The chapter authors in this book, all accomplished veterans, knowledgeable scholars, and strong teachers, have been among that still-growing host who have advocated for young adolescents and middle level education beginning in the 1960s—but not for the limited cosmetic changes made at Grover Middle School. These educators, as we, are convinced that the middle school concept, *more than ever*, holds the answer to fully educating 10- to 15-year-olds in a manner that helps them develop as high-achieving learners, and responsible, capable, and productive citizens. To achieve these goals, schools and faculties with the active support of parents and communities must commit to improving middle level schools in long-lasting and educationally sound ways. This task will require that everyone with direct responsibility for the education of young adolescents use what research and cumulative experience make evident as we develop schools that put into practice the vision of *This We Believe: Keys to Educating Young Adolescents* (National Middle School Association, 2010). The now well-established research base that supports the validity of the middle school concept is substantial and clear (Backes, Ralston, & Ingwalson, 1999; Felner, Jackson, Kasak, Mulhall, Brand, & Flowers, 1997; Flowers, Mertens, & Mulhall, 2003; Lee & Smith, 1993; Mertens, Flowers, & Mulhall, 1998; Mertens & Flowers, 2003; Picucci, Brownson, Kahlert & Sobel, 2004: Wilcox & Angelis, 2007; Roney, Anfara, & Brown, 2008: Balfanz, 2009; NMSA, 2010; McEwin & Greene, 2011). The research-based generalization that evolved, simply stated, is: *Schools that implement substantially the tenets of* This We Believe *over time report clear improvements in students' learning in academic achievement and in their personal development as they become healthy, productive, and ethical adults.*

Although we know that implementing sound middle school philosophy and practices does make a positive difference for young adolescents whether enrolled in a 6-8, 5-8, or K-8 building, too few schools have implemented the middle school concept consistently, thoughtfully, and yes, aggressively. Middle schools have been in existence for more than 40 years, and there are many excellent examples of highly successful, fully functioning middle schools in every state—schools willing to take risks, to buck the common tide of mediocrity, willing to stick to their beliefs and build academically and personally responsive schools for young adolescents. But regrettably, there are not nearly enough models. Why? Is the concept faulty?

Some critics have claimed the "middle school" has failed. Not so. The middle school concept has not been practiced and found wanting; rather it has been found difficult to implement fully and practiced then only partially. Because putting the whole concept into operation calls for a number of changes that run counter to long-standing, traditional school practices,

> The middle school concept has not been practiced and found wanting; rather, it has been found difficult to implement fully and then practiced only partially.

ones that lie outside the experiences of all but a handful of educators, the full concept has had difficulty gaining an adequate foothold in most schools. The marked success in achieving the organizational aspects of the middle school, however, has led many to the false conclusion

that the middle school concept itself was in force; therefore, lack of improvement in student performance was incorrectly attributed to the concept itself.

Jackson and Davis (2000), authors of the widely acclaimed *Turning Points 2000*, refuted the notion of the failure of the middle school while recognizing that "gains in student achievement and other positive outcomes for students require comprehensive implementation of reforms over an extended period of time" (p. 16); they optimistically claimed, "Far from having failed, middle grades education is ripe for a great leap forward" (p. 17). Dickinson (2001), in his definitive book *Reinventing the Middle School* stated emphatically, "There is nothing wrong with the middle school concept. . . . The concept is as valid today as it was in either of its previous iterations at the turn of the 20th century or in the early 1960s." The problem, he says, is that the middle school itself is suffering from "arrested development" (pp. 3-4)—a point well taken.

What Have We Learned in 38 Years of Advocacy?

What lessons have emerged? What problems plague us? What barriers stand in our way? What successes have been recorded? Following are a number of sound generalizations that emerged as we put the development of middle level education in perspective. These can be keys indicating specific actions that will bring about the improvements needed.

"The real difficulty in changing the course of any enterprise lies not in developing new ideas but in escaping from old ones."

This statement by noted economist John Maynard Keynes is particularly applicable to educational reform. Consider that 85 years ago, prominent educator Harold Rugg (1926) made these rather sobering observations, ones that would still be valid if voiced today:

> Not once in a century and a half of national history has the curriculum of
> the school caught up with the dynamic content of American life. . . . Partial,
> superficial, and timorous "revision" rather than general, fundamental, and
> courageous reconstruction characterizes curriculum making in the public
> schools . . . the existing program is always taken as a point of departure. . . .
> Thus curriculum making becomes a process of accretion and elimination. There
> is little, indeed almost no movement under way in public schools to initiate
> curriculum-making from the starting point either of child learning or of the
> institutions and problems of American life. For over fifty years, tinkering has
> characterized the attack on the curriculum. (p. 3)

And so the sound, new ideas advanced by the progressive education movement, for the most
part, have lain dormant. In recent decades the middle school movement has revived many
of these ideas, moved beyond tinkering, and, indeed, initiated curriculum-making "from the
starting point of child learning or of the institutions and problems of American life." But those
of us who are passionate middle school champions are, like Rugg, frustrated by not being able
to put more of our advocacy into practice.

Why has it been so difficult to understand that fundamental changes, not merely surface
level changes, must be made—and then tackle them? An overreliance on those commonly
criticized but still entrenched textbooks, teacher-dominated classrooms, and that all-too-
prevalent practice of "sorting and selecting"—
rather than educating all students to their
maximum—are among inappropriate practices
that still dominate too many of our schools.
Educators and their communities shouldn't
"tinker toward utopia" as Cuban and Tyack

> Why has it been so difficult to understand
> that fundamental changes, not merely
> surface level changes, must be made—
> and then tackle them?

(1995) said. We have the grand vision of This We Believe to guide us in changing the culture
of schools, a process that entails exposing the outdated and seldom examined assumptions
that underlie traditional practices.

It boggles our minds when we realize what a hold on people's thinking the terms *subjects,
periods, classes,* and *tests* have. The general public and even educators have trouble envisioning
or articulating how formal education might be conducted except by using these containers
or terms, and so cannot escape "from old ones." The Alpha team at Shelburne Community
School, Vermont, is an excellent example, however, of what can happen when educators

break out of these barriers (Kuntz, 2005). Eschewing the routine and the regular, members of that multiage team, which has been in operation for 33 years, tested nearly every "regularity" of school—from periods, to curriculum, to assessment, to what it means to be educated. These pioneer educators realized that the common routines and practices of school did not help young adolescents become real independent learners, whereas alternate ways of organizing for learning would. The Watershed and Soundings Programs (Springer, 1994, 2006) in Radnor, Pennsylvania, are among highly successful programs that demonstate what is possible when educators and students are freed from the restrictions of classes, periods, and subjects. In such situations, the role of the teacher undergoes a basic shift from being an instructor to becoming a facilitator or coach of learning. Reformers need to develop a sense of how effective middle level education can be when, as the popular cliché puts it, we "think outside the box." Today's reform and accountability efforts, however, continue to work in and on schools as they are currently organized, when what is needed are serious efforts to make schools different, to bring them more in harmony with what we know about learning and human development.

> Today's reform and accountability efforts, however, continue to work in and on schools as they are *currently* organized, when what is needed are serious efforts to make schools *different*.

There is little doubt that the focus in the first decade of the 21st century on student achievement as determined by standardized tests has had a deadening effect on middle level education. However, instead of abandoning efforts to implement the middle school concept because it is difficult and not politically correct, we must stay the course. Ironically, just as we are fighting regression, middle school ideas such as teaming and advisory are now being adopted by high schools, elementary schools, and even universities, indications of their inherent validity. Schools enrolling the middle grades must continue to serve, without apology, the broad responsibilities that fall on middle level education. Ultimately, the public should come to recognize that success both in future schooling and in life itself will depend not so much on what content has been covered, but rather on what skills, dispositions, and habits of mind have been developed. When the widely accepted goal of academic excellence is examined thoughtfully, it really comes down to being as much a matter of skills and attitudes as it is the possession of certain portions of knowledge. And the overemphasis on improving test scores works against developing the very attributes needed to succeed in today's world—initiative, teamwork, and the ability to solve problems, organize information, and articulate ideas—all parts of what are now called 21st century skills.

"The whole is greater than the sum of its parts."

This adage, attributed to Aristotle, has become part of our common wisdom. It expresses a truth about the middle school concept, for that educational advocacy encompasses a spirit and a philosophy that adds a dimension making it bigger than all its organizational and instructional practices put together. Those who seek to create a true middle school must be cognizant of this reality. The middle school concept cannot be implemented by initiating a series of separate elements in a nonsupportive culture. Early advocates often chose selected middle school elements or characteristics but

> The heart and soul of the middle school concept must be played out in curriculum, instruction, and assessment.

did little more. Hundreds of middle schools organized interdisciplinary teams and declared victory. Others implemented advisory programs, exploratory experiences, and activity programs, which, while responsive to the needs of young adolescents, were by themselves incomplete. Far too many schools stopped here, leaving the majority of each school day little changed. In school after school the heart and soul of the middle school concept that has to be played out in curriculum, instruction, and assessment has not been made operational. Nancy Doda (Doda & Thompson, 2002) has described well this incomplete implementation:

> Professional development initiatives have far too often been about enticing teachers to use models, means, and methods without inviting them into an examination of the critical philosophical beliefs and assumptions that give those practices educational leverage and value. As a result, some middle schools have remained merely junior high schools with flair. (p. 349)

The 16 *This We Believe* characteristics must not be seen as a checklist of items to be implemented one at a time. They are interdependent and constitute a web of beliefs about education, ones that have to be held by the faculty and staff in successful middle level schools.

"Good is the enemy of great."

This concept (Collins, 2001) can be applied to those many schools that put into practice some middle school characteristics, but stopped short of full and thoughtful implementation; they are good schools, better than they were before carrying out some middle school practices but still not all they could and should be.

If middle schools are to become great, they must move beyond the easy-to-achieve structural and organizational aspects. While such changes may be typical in a good middle level school, great middle level schools recognize that such aspects are means, not ends, first steps only in building a school culture that is responsive to every student and engages each one in learning that is high-level, profound, and meaningful. Great middle level schools employ teaming and other ways of collaborating—keys to making long-lasting changes, but they do not stop there. Traditional four- or five-teacher teams may be replaced by two- or three-teacher teams that reduce significantly the number of different students teachers work with, while increasing the time that these teachers spend with that smaller number of students. The result is teachers more able to know their students and effectively guide their learning and growing. Curriculum integration occurs more frequently in smaller teams, many of which may stay together for two or three years in a looping arrangement.

> If middle schools are to become great, they must move beyond the easy-to-achieve structural and organizational aspects.

In great middle level schools, professional development is ongoing, embedded, and meaningful. Heartened by Margaret Mead's observation: "The most extraordinary thing about a really good teacher is that he or she transcends accepted educational methods," teachers, administrators, and students are encouraged to take risks, make mistakes, and be as creative and innovative as possible.

The ultimate goal is always improved student learning. Such learning extends far beyond a narrow test-determined goal of academic achievement and includes preparing young adolescents for a rich and fulfilling life. The major goals of middle level education set forth in *This We Believe* make clear the broad responsibilities that middle level education must seek to fulfill. The vision of a staff committed to such a mission is ever-present in great schools and very evident in their practice and policies—a yardstick used by everyone, every day.

Middle schools too often counter Mother Nature.

The almost universally employed organizational practices of grouping by chronological age, having periods of 45 to 50 minutes, and class sizes of approximately 25 to 30 students, are bereft of any research to justify their continued existence. Educators and policy makers need to stop and consider that reality rather than continue to assume such practices are valid and mandatory. And, especially at the middle level, these practices increasingly run counter to the nature of young adolescents who are rapidly changing and maturing physically, socially, emotionally, morally, and intellectually. Continuing to organize and operate as if 10- to 15-year-olds were still children, school practices regularly conflict with human development. Curricula are planned for groups rather than individuals; yet young adolescents are distinguished by the degree they differ, making one lesson for all seldom appropriate. While it may be justifiable at the elementary level to have largely teacher-directed classrooms in which a prescribed curriculum is covered, continuing such practices with middle grades youth further institutionalizes passive learning and hinders teachers in meeting young adolescents' *intellectual* needs.

Mother Nature provides, at this key transition time of life, a golden opportunity to take learning to a higher level, to move beyond rote learning, to challenge students intellectually, and to engage them actively in the teaching-learning enterprise. They are ripe at this age for being drawn into their education in new and more meaningful ways. Young adolescents are capable of learning and achieving at levels seldom realized. Although individuals differ in exactly when they gain this new mental maturity, we know that sometime during the middle level years almost all students begin to demonstrate the ability to analyze, question, hypothesize, and think about thinking. To bring this new mental prowess into bloom, teachers need to prod, entice, and even cajole students, not simply "cover" content. As Ted Sizer has reminded us, "School isn't about old folks donating ideas to young folks. It is about young folks learning on their own and being provoked by old folks."

> Mother Nature provides a golden opportunity to take learning to a higher level, to move beyond rote learning, to challenge students intellectually, and to engage them actively.

In addition, young adolescents seek increased independence and responsibilities, desirable traits the school should foster, not thwart. Schools, however, continue to approach education as something done to students—when the innate, intrinsic desire to learn and students' heightened curiosity could readily be tapped. The chance to exploit the possibilities for reflective thinking and engaged learning is not only ignored, it is directly countered when schools underestimate the potential of young adolescents and follow tightly prescribed curricula.

"We learn what we live, and we learn it to the degree that we live it."

This maxim enunciated long ago by the famous progressive teacher and philosopher William Heard Kilpatrick is most appropriate for middle level education. In these days of politically initiated educational reform that focuses on prescribing a curriculum that will, presumably, yield higher test scores, we often overlook the fact that the school itself is a powerful teacher, presenting its lessons silently but surely. The middle school is not and cannot be just a physical place where teachers conduct classes; it is an

> The middle school is not a teaching factory, but a laboratory of living, not just a learning place, but a growing place.

environment in which youth come of age, acting out new roles as maturing social beings. The middle school is not a teaching factory, but a laboratory of living, not just a learning place, but a growing place.

Many of the accepted objectives of education, in fact, the ones most likely to be in play in one's daily life in the years ahead, cannot be taught by direct instruction; they have to grow incrementally from multiple experiences. And, more often than not, those lessons that last a lifetime are by-products of a positive relationship between teacher and student. There is, then, real danger if we let the mission of the middle school become too small, too narrow. The middle school must not marginalize the development of those traits and dispositions required for a meaningful and productive life. While the academic achievement mission is central, the effective middle school has to be bigger than that. Its mission also calls for a school that deals openly and directly with character education, ethics, values, and self-concepts. It is particularly harmful if middle schools become too narrow in focus, because young adolescents are going through that period of life when they are deciding for themselves what they believe in, what they might aspire to be, and they are forming attitudes and dispositions that will guide their behavior as adults. All of these are facets of education that students will encounter and make decisions about during the middle level years—with or without the help of schools and teachers.

Character is neither inherited nor learned in the usual sense of the word; rather, it is acquired gradually by the cumulative effect of many thoughts, actions, and experiences. Middle level teachers, next to parents, are often the significant others whose modeling makes the biggest difference. Somehow we must help the public grasp a bigger and better vision of what constitutes an "education" and recognize the importance of the teacher as a person and as a model. Conventional wisdom about young adolescents and the critical lifelong influence of the educational experiences they encounter still lag.

Our nation's problems, when one thinks about it, are, with rare exceptions, the result of consciously chosen behaviors of individuals. And, ultimately, all education is directed toward changing behavior. Middle schools must exert the influence on behavior that, by the nature of young adolescents, they are uniquely suited to yield. Inescapably, middle school teaching is a moral enterprise, and an education in its fullest sense has to involve heart as well as head, attitude as well as information, spirit as well as scholarship, and conscience as well as competence.

> An education in its fullest sense has to involve heart as well as head, attitude as well as information, spirit as well as scholarship, and conscience as well as competence.

If middle schools do not fulfill their rightful role in developing ethical, responsible, self-motivated, thinking individuals, they will have failed fulfilling their most important responsibility. Middle schools simply must be concerned about what students are becoming, not just about what test scores they are making. We should all consider carefully the serious point made by Mark Twain when he joked, "I never let my schooling interfere with my education"; for it appears schools are so emphasizing the limited informational aspects of an education that they are neglecting the critical behavioral ones.

We need middle schools with missions big enough to help youngsters decide what to read as well as simply how to read. Big enough to ensure that their mastery of mathematics will not be applied in an embezzlement scheme. Big enough to recognize their history lessons apply to their futures as well as to the past. John Ruskin put it thus: "Education does not mean teaching people to know what they do not know. It means teaching them to behave as they do not behave." And Teddy Roosevelt warned: "To educate a person in mind and not in morals is to educate a menace to society."

Looking Ahead

In 1982, the original *This We Believe* set forth a vision of middle level education that became the foundation for the ideas expressed in later editions and in this volume. The successful practices you see in the accompanying videos are outgrowths of that vision. In 1989, the

Carnegie Corporation's influential report *Turning Points: Preparing American Youth for the 21st Century* called middle level education "the last best chance" for young adolescents and recommended changes that were very much in line with the vision of *This We Believe*. Guided by such visions, we have made marked progress in the intervening years, but we still have a very long way to go before common practices reflect this vision of how young adolescents can be well served during these challenging middle years of schooling.

Not long after we have moved beyond the current narrow definition of educational excellence, and the related testing mania has abated, we will look back with disbelief and wonder why we continued practices so out-of-line with what we know about young adolescents and the principles of learning. We are confident that the middle school concept will be the standard as schools strive to provide the full and meaningful education every 10- to 15-year-old deserves. We believe the middle school concept is, indeed, the conscience of American education and will prevail.

As you read, re-read, reflect on, and discuss with colleagues the chapters in *This We Believe in Action* and see examples of successful middle schools, you should be able to visualize how your school would look if you took the initiative to implement such a vision. Imagine what your school would be like

» If each student were held to high expectations and passionately engaged in learning.

» If each student had opportunities to pose and answer in-depth questions about world and personal issues.

» If each student had an active adult advocate who knew that student well and guided that individual's educational program.

» If various digital tools were effectively used by both teachers and students to bring about new ways to learn and new worlds to study.

» If all parents felt supported, and they, in turn, actively provided support in the work of the school.

» If students evaluated their own work, and there were no competitive grades.

» If what students studied was intellectually stimulating and viewed by students as worth learning.

» If democracy were not just studied but practiced.

» If learning activities were focused on the skills and dispositions needed for a productive life as much as on content.

» If the school were truly responsive to the educational and developmental needs of each and every student.

We are convinced that as the middle school concept becomes more widely known and accepted in the hearts and minds of untold numbers of educators, its implementation will spread. The good sense and the research-based validity of the vision set forth in *This We Believe* can't remain a well kept secret. As the limitations and negative effects of educational reform by tests and sanctions becomes ever more apparent, and as the marked success of middle level schools that pursue vigorously this vision become known, the middle level movement will experience dramatic new acceptance.

The Way It Could Be

Maria hoisted her backpack as she walked up the steps of Worthington Middle School. The new 8:45 a.m. start was a great relief and she now actually came to school feeling rested on most days. Last year in sixth grade, her school day started at 7:35 a.m., and she began every day feeling tired.

Today she was 15 minutes early because she and two of her classmates, Jessica and Manuel, needed one last tryout of a presentation they were to make later in the morning. They had worked for over a month on a feasibility study for a new senior citizens' center by collecting information about its economic, environmental, and cultural impact on their small town.

As a part of this rigorous service learning project which drew on all the major subject areas as well as the arts and humanities, they met with two builders, the town manager, town council, and many citizens of various ages. Much of their work was done on laptops on which they took notes all day, wrote their initial and subsequent drafts of position papers, and logged into several databases to track the data they collected. Using the Internet to find other towns that had built similar senior citizens' centers in Arizona, Florida, and Ohio, was invaluable. In each of those states, middle school students collected and sent to Maria and her research group essential project information later incorporated into the final report.

Mentally clicking down the list of key points for the presentation, Maria was excited but became nervous when she discovered that the review board hearing their presentation would include the town manager from a neighboring town, the director of the gerontology program at the university, a contractor for the project, and a vice-president of the local bank. Yet, proud of the work her group had done, she was anxious to hear the board's response.

Jessica and Manuel were waiting for Maria. Several other students were also in the room working quietly, reading, or logging into their laptops to check e-mail or to join one of several continuing discussions about various school projects. This large, open room had been the home for the team and its two teachers for the last two years. It was carpeted, comfortable, warm, and inviting, with tables and chairs, a couch and several lounge chairs, books everywhere, and student work prominently displayed. Collecting information for their own projects, two students were talking on cell phones.

In fact, it was difficult for someone new to this school to recognize the official beginning of the school day. The late start gave all teachers common planning time early every day when they met to talk about current projects, conduct parent conferences, or work with individuals or small groups of students. A recent visitor to the school noted that the atmosphere of every room in the building was purposeful, unhurried, focused, and intent. It looked and sounded like a well-run laboratory with highly qualified people enjoying both their work and each other.

As their final task, the three students checked their well-worn copies of the Common Core State Standards to make sure they had included the English-language arts performance indicators on "stylistic and rhetorical aspects of reading and writing" in their handouts. Their report would present a detailed plan for creating a senior citizens' center with specific timelines and areas of responsibility. This report would clearly illustrate how they had used a variety of skills by drawing content from various academic areas—all of which built a positive attitude about what they had learned doing this project. Pleased with their work and plan, but still anxious about the upcoming public presentation, they placed their laptops, notebooks, and papers on their own desks and moved to the center of the room where they joined their 38 classmates and two teachers for opening ceremonies.

Another day of good learning and growing begins at Worthington Middle School.

References

Backes, J., Ralston, A., & Ingwalson, G. (1999). Middle level reform: The impact on student achievement. *Research in Middle Level Education Quarterly, 22*(3), 43–57.

Balfanz, R. (2009). *Putting middle grades students on the graduation path: A policy and practice brief.* Westerville. OH: National Middle School Association.

Carnegie Council on Adolescent Development. (1989). *Turning points: Preparing American youth for the 21st century.* New York: Carnegie Corporation.

Collins, J. (2001). *Good to great.* New York: Harper Collins.

Cuban, L., & Tyack, D. (1995). *Tinkering toward utopia.* Cambridge, MA: Howard University.

Dickinson, T. (2001). *Reinventing the middle school.* New York, NY: RoutledgeFalmer.

Doda, N., & Thompson, S. (Eds.). (2002). *Transforming ourselves, transforming schools: Middle school change.* Westerville, OH: National Middle School Association.

Felner, R., Jackson, A., Kasak, D., Mulhall, P., Brand, S., & Flowers, N. (1997). The impact of school reform for the middle grades. In R. Takanishi & D. A. Hamburg (Eds.), *Preparing adolescents for the twenty-first century: Challenges facing Europe and the United States* (pp. 38–69). Cambridge, UK: Cambridge University.

Flowers, N., Mertens, S., & Mulhall, P. (2003). Lessons learned from more than a decade of middle grades research. *Middle School Journal, 35*(2), 55–59.

Jackson, A., & Davis, G. (2000). *Turning points 2000: Educating adolescents for the 21st century.* New York, NY & Westerville, OH: Teachers College & National Middle School Association.

Kuntz, S. (2005). *The story of Alpha: A multiage, student-centered team— 33 years and counting.* Westerville, OH: National Middle School Association.

Lee, V. E., & Smith, J. B. (1993). Effects of school restructuring on the achievement and engagement of middle-grade students. *Sociology of Education, 66*(3), 164–187.

McEwin, C.K., & Greene, M.W. (2011). The status of programs and practices in America's middle schools: Results from two national studies. Westerville, OH: National Middle School Association.

Mertens, S. B., & Flowers, N. (2003). Middle school practices improve student achievement in high poverty schools. *Middle School Journal, 35*(1), 33–43.

Mertens, S. B., Flowers, N., & Mulhall, P. (1998). *The middle start initiative, phase I: A longitudinal analysis of Michigan middle-level schools.* (A report to the W. K. Kellogg Foundation). Urbana, IL: University of Illinois. Retrieved from http://222.cprd.uiuc.edu

National Middle School Association, (2010). *This we believe: Keys to educating young adolescents.* Westerville, OH: Author.

National Middle School Association, (2010). *Research and Resources in Support of This We Believe.* Westerville, OH: Author.

Picucci, A. C., Brownson, A., Kahlert, R., & Sober, A. (2004). Middle school concept helps high-poverty schools become high-performing schools. *Middle School Journal, 36*(1), 4–11.

Roney, K., Anfara, V., & Brown, K. (2008). *Creating organizationally healthy and effective middle schools: Research that supports the middle school concept and student achievement.* Westerville, OH: National Middle School Association.

Rugg, H. (1926). *Curriculum-making: Past and present, twenty-sixth yearbook of N.S.S.E.* Chicago, IL: National Society for the Study of Education.

Springer, M. (1994). *Watershed: A successful voyage into integrative learning.* Columbus, OH: National Middle School Association.

Springer, M. (2006). *Soundings: A democratic student-centered education.* Westerville,, OH: National Middle School Association.

Wilcox, K., & Angelis, J. (2007). *What makes middle schools work – A report on best practices in New York State middle schools.* Albany, NY: State University of New York.

Authors

by order of appearance in this publication

∞∞

C. Kenneth McEwin, a past president of NMSA, is professor of education at Appalachian State University, Boone, North Carolina.

Thomas S. Dickinson, former editor of *Middle School Journal,* is professor of education studies at DePauw University, Greencastle, Indiana.

Gert Nesin is an eighth grade teacher on an integrated partner team at Leonard Middle School in Old Town, Maine.

Chris Stevenson is professor emeritus of education at the University of Vermont and now resides in Pinehurst, North Carolina.

Penny A. Bishop is a professor of education and director of the Tarrant Institute for Innovative Education at the University of Vermont, Burlington.

Barbara L. Brodhagen is a school reform coach for the University of Wisconsin, Madison.

Susan Gorud is a teacher at Sherman Middle School, Madison, Wisconsin.

Sue C. Thompson, a former middle school principal and district director of middle grades education, is associate professor of urban leadership and policy studies at the University of Missouri, Kansas City.

Dan French is executive director of the Center for Collaborative Education, Boston, Massachusetts.

Sue Swaim, a past president of NMSA, served as Executive Director of National Middle School Association from 1993–2007.

Candy Beal is associate professor of education at North Carolina State University, Raleigh.

John Arnold is professor emeritus of education at North Carolina State University and now resides in Pinehurst, North Carolina.

Patti Kinney, former principal of Talent Middle School (Oregon) and a past president of National Middle School Association, is the associate director of middle level services for National Association of School Superintendents and Principals in Reston, VA.

Linda Robinson, an educational consultant, is a retired principal from Alvin, Texas, and a past president of National Middle School Association.

Deborah Kasak is executive director of the National Forum to Accelerate Middle-Grades Reform and resides in Champaign, Illinois.

Ericka Uskali is a professional development consultant at ROE SchoolWorks in Rantoul, Illinois.

Marion Johnson Payne, a past president of National Middle School Association, is an educational consultant residing in Hilton Head Island, South Carolina.

Ross M. Burkhardt, a former teacher at Shoreham-Wading River Middle School (New York) and a past president of National Middle School Association, is an educational consultant in Las Cruces, New Mexico.

J. Thomas Kane, an educational consultant, is a past president of both the New York State Middle School Association and the New Jersey Middle School Association and a retired principal of Holdrum Middle School in River Vale, New Jersey.

Sherrel Bergmann, who retired from National Louis University, is an educational consultant residing in Charlevoix, Michigan.

Jean Schultz is regional lead at Alliance for a Healthier Generation in Sacramento, California.

Joyce L. Epstein is the director of the Center on School, Family, and Community Partnerships and the National Network of Partnership Schools and a research professor of sociology at Johns Hopkins University, Baltimore, Maryland.

Darcy J. Hutchins is a senior program facilitator for the National Network of Partnership Schools at Johns Hopkins University.

Mavis G. Sanders is a professor of education at Johns Hopkins University, where she directs the Graduate Certificate Program in Leadeship for School, Family, and Community Collaboration. She also serves as senior advisor to the National Network of Partnership Schools.

Edward N. Brazee, a former publications editor for National Middle School Association and professor of education emeritus at the University of Maine, now serves as a consultant in educational technology.

John H. Lounsbury, a former editor of *Middle School Journal* and dean of education emeritus at Georgia College, Milledgeville, continues as a consulting editor for the Association for Middle Level Education.